WIZOO Pro Guide

The Perfect Music Pc

Rainer Hain

The Perfect Music Pc

Imprint

Publisher   Peter Gorges

Author   Rainer Hain

© Copyright 2000 by Wizoo GmbH
Bremen, Bundesrepublik Deutschland
Printed in Germany
ISBN 3-934903-26-6

Translation   Tom Green
Editing, proofreading   Len Sasso
Layout and typesetting   Uwe Senkler, Hamburg
Cover design   design-box, Ravensburg
Printed by   Druckhaus E A Quensen GmbH

Welcome to the Machine...

In this book, we'll pursue our goal—to make you the lordly master rather than the lowly slave of your Pc—with missionary zeal. You may have had years of experience with music and computers or you may be entirely new to this brave and foolish game, either way, one thing is certain: the hard- and software headaches that threaten at times to drive us to dementia are the same for pros and novices alike.

If you're a newbie, it may have just dawned on you that those Charles Atlas-like claims printed on the manufacturer's pretty packaging—just ten minutes to a chart-topping worldwide hit—are, to put it bluntly, lies. Although well-meaning, journalists crowing about audio software in magazine articles fail to mention all the obstacles the computer can throw your way. The cold, hard truth is that it might take ten minutes and five tries just to get the program launched—that global hit is a long, long way off yet.

If you're a professional who's just turning to the Pc, you've presumably noticed that standard computer savvy won't get you far in the digital audio world.

This is what this book is here for. It'll help you understand the Pc and acquire the skills required to troubleshoot problems. If you're already familiar with computers, all the better. You'll find out a few tricks you haven't come across before. In any case, it will help you put aside those understandable fears inspired by all that ridiculous computer jargon and get down to the business of making music.

To this end, we'll look at all the different categories of software step by step and discuss what these programs' hardware requirements are. Then we'll take a closer look at the actual hardware and the technology behind it. Once you've the basics down pat, we'll look at how to go about troubleshooting problems. You'll soon discover that Windows is no great mystery and that installing a new audio card is in fact easier and certainly less painful than, say, attempting to iron your shirt while wearing it.

To give you a little guidance when you're ready to go shopping, in each chapter I'll share some tips on the best hardware. This information will help you get what you want and need, not what has been gathering dust in the dealer's storeroom.

Our ultimate goal is to create the perfect music Pc for your purposes. And once we do, here's hoping that making music on a computer makes you as stupidly happy as it, at times, does me.

Rainer Hain

Table of Contents

Table of Contents

1 Getting Started

Although the Pc has been around for as long as the Apple computer and even longer than the Atari, its tale as a musical tool is a short story.

It wasn't until the early 1990s that popular Atari and Macintosh programs were ported to the Pc, making them an attractive option to the average musician on the street.

The reason that vendors started to focus on the Pc was that it had the potential to deliver heaps more performance than the Atari and it was much cheaper than a comparable Macintosh. Today the difference in price is no longer as dramatic, but the popularity of the Pc in other areas seems to have made an indelible mark on the minds of manufacturers and musicians alike.

The fact that the Atari and Macintosh have long been used for musical applications puts Pc users at a disadvantage:

People who can help you with general Pc-related problems are a dime a dozen. However, if your audio software or sequencer is giving you trouble, you're on your own. Most Pc dealers and computer nerds don't know the first thing about the quirks and eccentricities of a music computer. Musical instrument dealers and studio pros may be able to explain an application in great detail, but they can't tell you why a Pc refuses to run. And well-meaning advice to the tune of ›should have bought a Mac‹ will probably just lead to violence and mayhem after you've laid down a stack of bills for your brand-new Pc.

But fear not, despite first appearances you'll be able to turn your Pc into a reliable, stable music computer.

Music Begs for Real-time

I'd like to be up-front with you: The notion that you can buy a stock Pc, switch it on, and immediately use it as a professional tool is as unlikely a scenario as my getting a date with Christy Turlington. In fact, this will only be the case (the ready-to-run Pc, not the rendezvous) if you seek out a specialized dealer who sells pre installed Pcs fine-tuned specifically for making music.

Perhaps you already own a Pc and want to use it for audio and Midi applications for the first time. You're in the same boat as someone who is shopping for a new Pc because back when you bought it you probably weren't thinking about turning it into a musical instrument.

Even if some software, books and magazines promise that in just 10 minutes time you'll be able to produce a worldwide hit on a run-of-the-mill Pc, take these claims with a large grain of salt, for this just isn't so. Talk is cheap, and even well-meaning journalists let their enthusiasm get out of hand. Perhaps you've discovered as much on your own and that is why you bought this book in the first place.

The vast majority of Pcs are used for word processing and spreadsheet programs—80 percent of the time is the figure that is routinely bandied about. The rest they spend trying to cope with ever larger and more sophisticated Internet browsers. For these applications, just about any Pc made some time in the past four years will suffice. Indeed, over this time I've beefed up my home computer a half a dozen times, tripling its nominal performance with each upgrade.

However, the word processor that I am using to write this is not perceptibly faster than it was before I turbo-charged my Pc. The difference is of course measurable, but as long as the online spell-checker has done its job before I write the next word, the computer is fast enough for my purposes. In other words, 90 percent of the time the computer is faster than the user. It spends most of its life bored to distraction, waiting for your next keyboard input. For this type of application, this is real-time—indeed, it doesn't get any more real than this.

Unfortunately, audio and MIDI are areas where real-time becomes a real problem. When you hook up a microphone to your soundcard and sing a little heartfelt ditty to your significant other, you're generating quantities of data that an entire battery of skilled secretaries in the typing pool would be hard-pressed to match.

Now say you want multi-track vocals (somehow the Mormon Tabernacle Choir is never around when you need it). You record several tracks, one after the other and with each pass, play back the stuff that's already in the can. You can bet that your computer will be groaning under this heavy load.

Let's take this scenario a step further: Say a voice you've recorded isn't showcased properly in the dusty sonic environment of a ›dry‹ track and you decide to slap on cavernous reverb to disguise some of its shortcomings. Now you're getting into performance requirements that a computer with two-digit MHz specifications simply can't satisfy.

Although it may be annoying, it's not a huge problem if a word processor takes five rather than two seconds to format text. However, in audio and MIDI applications, we're talking about data streams (which means that a lot of numbers are being shipped to an fro). If these are interrupted for just a fraction of a second, the track is history—believe me, unless you've a Jones for very experimental music, this type of glitch is not something worth hearing.

This is why a compromise won't cut it—it's either full steam ahead or never leave the port. The human ear—apart perhaps from those attached to heads that routinely ›enjoy‹ hearing music over sound systems cranked to the pain threshold—is able to perceive differences between two signals and rhythmic discrepancies so minor that they're measured in milliseconds. The notion of real-time takes on an entirely new meaning here.

Then there's the fact that when you're recording and playing back audio and MIDI, you're putting the entire system through its paces. Data must be shuttled continuously from the hard drive to the memory. The processor labors hard to execute computations and write the results back to the memory. From this ›warehouse,‹ data is rushed back to the soundcard so that you can hear what's going on.

At the same time, data is being trucked in from the other direction. The soundcard is shoveling oodles of information into memory. Presumably you didn't invest in this rig to simply capture the sound of you worrying the frets of your guitar or hammering your keyboard, you probably want the world to hear the warble of your golden throat as well. This data also has to be shipped to the hard drive.

It would be nice to see what you're doing, so at the same time, payloads of data have to be hauled to the monitor—not seeing the Record button makes it rather difficult to click on it. After all my ranting, you can probably appreciate that we're dealing with a fairly complex system. All of the gears must mesh and the Pc's components must work together in the spirit of brotherly love so that it lives up to our expectations of a music computer. This may be the case with a new computer, but there's certainly no guarantee.

Generally, Pcs ship with a pre installed operating system, in the vast majority of cases this will be the latest version of Windows. At the time that this book went to press, Windows 98 ruled the world (although the Us judiciary was rallying all its not inconsiderable might to crush Microsoft's monopoly). In any case, what pre installed actually means is that the computer will launch when you power it up. You'll see an image on your monitor, but its resolution will probably be extremely coarse and your screen will flicker. If your Pc is equipped with a soundcard that Windows fails to recognize on its own, you probably won't hear a thing.

Windows Quickstart

If your Pc suffers these symptoms, this doesn't mean that it's totally unfit for working with audio and MIDI software. Chances are good that you'll be able to swiftly set your computer up to serve our purposes.

You're probably champing at the bit and raring to go. Fair enough I'll begin with some information that should get you off to a good start. The first thing you'll have to do is tune the Windows installation. And you'll need to now how to identify and fix problems that commonly crop up.

Even if you're in a huge hurry, it behooves you to follow the next few steps precisely. You'll come across the Windows Device Manager often enough in this book and if you stick with music and computers, you'll install many more drivers in your lifetime then anyone in their right mind would want to.

This rudimentary course will give you a sound underpinning when you go to fine-tune your system later on. Once you have a handle on these rudimentary steps, you'll know how to deal with the most interesting Windows configuration options (doubters who contend that there is no such animal hold your peace).

Launching the Device Manager

First we'll take a look at Windows' Device Manager. This is your most important tool for configuring hardware.

You can access the Device Manager via the Start menu.

1 Click on Start, then on Settings, and finally on Control Panel.

2 Double-click the System icon.

3 Click on the tab labeled Device Manager.

The following window will appear:

The Device Manager, Windows' command center.

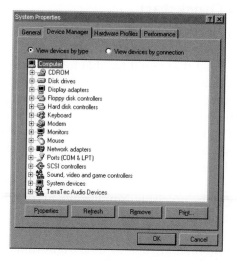

▶ You can take a look at this fascinating process in a short video called Tutor_1.avi, which is located in a folder called Tutorial on the CD that we've included with the book. Simply double-click on this file and you'll enjoy the cinematic pleasure of watching yours truly call up the Device Manager on my system.

As you can see, the Device Manager lists all of the hardware components of your Pc under the Computer icon. Windows is unable to recognize anything that is not listed here with one exception—dated drivers written for Windows 3.11. These do not show up in the Device Manage, however you *can* use them. The section ›Windows‹ on page 145 discusses where these fossils may be found and how to handle them once you've unearthed them.

If your Device Manager looks exactly like the one pictured above—it indicates hardware components with plus signs in front them that let you access lower branches of the tree— then you can be fairly sure that at least the essentials were installed properly on your computer.

In this case, you can skip the rest of this chapter and not look back until the time comes when you want to install a new driver. Of course you may first find it helpful to know what a driver actually is. Fear not, enlightenment will be yours once you have read the chapter on Windows.

However, if one of the branches in the Device Manager is open and you're looking at a component graced by the dubious distinction of a yellow exclamation mark, then you have a problem that definitely needs solving. You're most likely to encounter problems with your display adapter and audio card for the simple reason that many computer discounters can't be bothered to install the right drivers, not to mention up-to-date versions.

We're going to fix this right now, and while we're at it, you'll find out how to install drivers. We'll assume that the soundcard and display adapter of your brand new computer were installed by Bellowing Bob, the reigning hog calling champion of Kissing Cousins County.

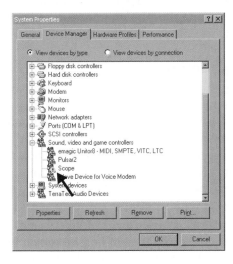

The Device Manager: This is what it should not look like. The exclamation marks indicate bad things about the display adapter and soundcard.

Installing Drivers

I don't want to burden you with too many details on drivers—we'll take a closer look in the chapter ›The Operating System‹ starting on page 143.

For now, all you need to know is that a driver is a little interpreter that helps Windows talk to your hardware. The driver is actually a translator for the Babylonian confusion of languages spoken by myriad devices—a file with parameters and data that assure communication between the installed hardware and the operating system. You'll need a driver for every soundcard, every printer, every network card, and just about anything else that can conceivably be connected to a computer, except perhaps your boot or a couple of rounds from a .357 Magnum.

Basically, you have two options for installing drivers under Windows. For hardware drivers, the option that you'll use depends on the mood of the manufacturer of the card on the day he decided to implement the installation routine.

Installing via Setup

♦ Generally, the installation program for the add-on card is located on a diskette or CD-ROM that ships with the card. In most cases, it will be called something imaginative like `install.exe` or `setup.exe`. All it takes to install the program is a double-click on the program symbol. Let's assume that the incorrectly installed display adapter comes with a driver designed to be installed to the system by this method. This makes things extremely simple.

All you have to do is insert the given medium into your CD-ROM or disk drive (depending on which of the two the dealer packed into the box) and launch it with My Computer. On the disk, you'll find a one of the aforementioned files. Start it.

Some driver diskettes and CD-ROMs will feature entire families of drivers, often for several different operating systems. If this is the case, you'll probably have to step through a few subdirectories before you find the setup routine that your computer craves.

You'll find that these folders generally have unambiguous names. For example, the installation program for Windows 95 will be in a folder called WIN95 rather than say ›X-Files or Why Can't Aliens Abduct My Sister?‹.

Virtually all driver diskettes and CD-ROMs feature a file called Readme.txt. Rarely read by anyone other than its author, it should tell you everything you need to know about installing drivers and also point out the bugs that the program is known to have.

◆ If the driver is on a CD-ROM, the installation sequence or a selection menu will launch automatically as soon as you insert the CD-ROM into the drive.

Installing via Inf File

This is the mechanism that Microsoft originally intended for use with Windows. In our hypothetical case—the incorrectly pre installed computer—the procedure would be as follows:

1 In the Device Manager, simply click on the symbol twice that, by displaying the yellow ›!‹, is indicating that it wants your help.

2 A window will appear. In it, click on the tab labeled DRIVER. The following window will appear:

This window invites you to install and update drivers.

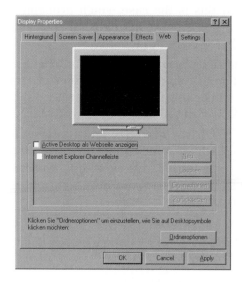

3 At the bottom right, you will find a button called Update Driver. Not surprisingly, you are meant to click on it.

Now you will meet the Update Device Driver Wizard. Although a mouthful to utter, it is a friendly little companion that will guide you through the installation routine. Incidentally, the following instructions refer to Windows 98. In Windows 95, this assistant looks slightly different. The principle, however, is the same and the majority of windows that follow will look much like those depicted here.

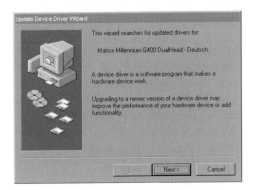

The assistant for device driver updates.

1   For your first step, you must tell Windows if you want it to search for a driver or if you already know which driver you want to install.

2   Let's assume that you want Windows to search for a driver. Click on the button called Next in this dialog.

3   Now you can tell Windows where you want it to start searching. You of course know if the driver is on CD or diskette, so click on the appropriate option and then click Next.

If at this point Windows fails to find a driver, then in all probability it is located in a subdirectory. In this case, you must select the folder manually.

4   For this purpose, click on Browse.

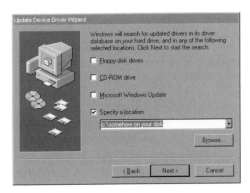

Select the folder in which the driver files are located in this window.

You'll know you've found the right folder when a file appears at the upper right of the window with the extension INF.

5 Click on OK, and Windows will kindly reveal its complete name.

In some instances, you'll find several entries here. This means that the installation information (the data contained in an *.inf file) pertains to several versions of a card. Should this be the case, select your card from the list.

When in doubt, simply take a look at the card's packaging or the documentation that the dealer included. He did include it didn't he? If not, you'll have to give him a call—try to refrain from threatening bodily harm. If you install the wrong driver now, then your hardware will not work any better than it did before we started this little song and dance.

For the purpose of our little exercise, let's assume that Windows found just one driver or that you know exactly what the name of your driver is. Don't get over-excited now, but you're just one click on the Next button away from a proper installation. Once you've done that, Windows will copy the files.

▶ Surprise, surprise: Some versions of Windows 95 are plagued with a bug in this system. What happens is that Windows will ask you to point out the location of files even though you found the folder in the previous step and told Windows as much. This your cue to throw a tizzy fit and write an abusive letter to the company. Once you've finished, you'll have to step through the directories again to indicate the location before Windows will continue installing the driver. This problem has been remedied in later versions of Windows 95 as well as in Windows 98.

Once the installation procedure is complete, you'll probably be asked to re-launch the system. Do so, then take a look at the Device Manager. The exclamation mark should have vanished into the digital ether.

Congratulations, you've just earned your driver installation badge. Wear it proudly.

Installing Drivers in Windows 95

Let me take you down memory lane—back to the beginning of the procedure. You recall meeting the Assistant for Device Driver Updates. You probably recall that there was a second option available to you, namely to select a driver from a specific folder. Under Windows 95, you have just this one option and I'll take you on a quick tour of it now.

In the next step, Windows will show you all the drivers that it has in its System folder. This is no great help because if any of these were the one that you needed, you wouldn't have a problem with the Device Manager. By the way, these are not drivers written by the maker of your hardware, they are drivers written and included on the Windows installation CD by Microsoft.

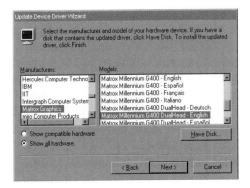

For this driver installation option, you can select from the list of factory-included drivers.

In the window you are looking at now, you'll see a button at the bottom right called Have Disk. When you click this button, the same windows and dialogs that I described earlier will appear.

Don't let the term Have Disk confuse you—the driver files may also reside in a folder on your hard drive. This will most likely be the case if you downloaded the files from the Internet, so even if you don't have disk, you can still travel.

You must click on the Have Disk button to install a driver from a CD-ROM or diskette.

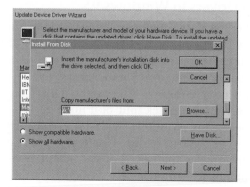

The rest of the procedure is the same as the one I just described. Once installation is complete, you'll be asked to relaunch the system. Again, the exclamation mark in the Device Manager should have headed for the hills. If this is not the case, you've probably done everything right but you've come across what's called a resource conflict.

Though less violent than other conflicts, this is a polite term for a whole lot of trouble. Before you savage your box, be aware that you'll find out what causes this problem and how to take care of it in the chapter ›The Mainboard,‹ specifically in the sections ›IRQs‹ on page 70 and ›Hardware Installation‹ on page 98.

In any case, your Device Manager should now list all the usual suspects—the different classes of devices—one after the other. The exclamation marks should also have made a quick getaway. This doesn't mean you've solved all the ills that may beset your box, but at least you can begin installing the software with which you intend to make music.

2 Music Software

In this chapter, we'll take a closer look at the main categories software that you'll be dealing with. I'm not going to give you a detailed list or any recommendations just yet. Why then are we looking at software categories now? Because different types of software place different types of demands on your computer and it would seem prudent to give software some consideration before taking an in-depth look at hardware or discussing how to optimize the operating system

Recording Software

By far the most common music software application is MIDI and/or audio recording—programs that do this are called sequencers. Nowadays, some kind of sequencer ships with every soundcard. These little software add-ons are merely scaled-down versions of the big professional programs and their operating principals are the same—they work like a virtual tape machine for playing and recording MIDI and audio data.

The term ›sequencer‹ was coined for the first analog devices that could only be programmed and played back in steps. These served as the inspiration for contemporary programs, which were made possible by MIDI and digital audio technology.

MIDI Recording

Since 1983, MIDI has been the established standard for communication and reciprocal control of music instruments and peripheral devices. Originally, MIDI was designed to enable the keyboard of one synthesizer to address and control the sound generator of another.

Intrepid programmers soon discovered that these command signals could be recorded to a computer, where they could be edited or played back. Notably, the actual sound of an instrument isn't shuttled back and forth. Instead, MIDI data serves as remote control messages that are generated when you press a key, turn a wheel, or release a foot pedal. This information isn't converted into, say, a piano sound until your synthesizer receives MIDI data and you have told the device to play back the signals it is receiving using a piano sound

Today's sequencers can record all manner of MIDI data on a virtually infinite number of tracks and play back everything simultaneously. Although MIDI data doesn't have a huge appetite for computer performance, you can make your computer work up a digital sweat when you opt to play back and process dozens of tracks. Also since MIDI is a relatively slow serial protocol, transferring large amounts of MIDI data can result in serious latency problems.

From MIDI to Audio

Back in the dark days of digital audio, MIDI sequencers were only able to handle MIDI data. Audio signals were recorded to tape machines just like Grandpa used to do. Once hard drives and, particularly, decent audio converters became affordable for the rank and file, this task could be carried out in the digital domain, resulting in what we now call hard disk recording.

Instead of capturing audio signals on magnetic tape, digital audio data is stored to hard disks. Initially, stand-alone devices called HD recorders were used for this purpose. These operated autonomously and weren't integrated with MIDI sequencers. As hardware and technology advanced, MIDI and audio sequencing was combined.

Audio Recording

Most contemporary sequencers can process both MIDI and audio. When you connect a signal source to your soundcard, it converts the analog audio signal into digital data. This data can be saved, edited and played back. In marked contrast to tape machines, you can mangle individual tracks as you please. You can cut them, splice them back together and copy them as often as you like because unlike analog, digital replication is loss-free.

For novices, the difference between audio and MIDI is often confusing, particularly because soundcards support both. Every soundcard has a sound generator on board that is addressed via MIDI. In terms of functionality, it's no different than an external synthesizer, except that since it's inside your computer, you can't mash buttons and fondle faders. Of course, the soundcard is also able to play audio back and record signals you send to its audio input.

Soundcard Primer

The majority of soundcards also feature what is called an external MIDI port. This is usually addressed by the joystick connector on the rear panel; sometimes it's also implemented as a real MIDI port on a 5.25-inch plug-in. Not surprisingly, these connectors are designed to take the cables of external MIDI devices.

Don't confuse these three components of the soundcard with one another. They are completely different functional units that just happen to be soldered to the same board.

One of the first questions that the astute newbie asks is, ›How are MIDI tracks transformed into audio tracks?‹ Bear in mind that a MIDI signal doesn't become audible until a sound generator has received the signal and does what it was designed to do—generate a sound. So the only way that MIDI tracks can be translated into audio tracks is also the simplest—play back the MIDI and record the sound generator's output on an audio track.

This means that if you're using external devices, you must somehow connect the audio outputs of your sound generators to the soundcard. The same holds true for a synthesizer integrated into a soundcard (usually called a Wavetable synthesizer). Although you don't have to connect any cords manually because signal routing takes place entirely in the digital domain, it is still a recording process.

There are programs called MIDI renderers—a software synthesizer by any other name—that can take standard MIDI files and compute audio files from them. The results, however, will only be good as the quality of sounds that these programs deliver (i. e. always pitiful).

Back to Audio Sequencers

The fact that sequencers offer MIDI is taken for granted, which is why a sequencer with audio functions is called on audio sequencer even though it can handle both.

The latest versions of these sequencers—generally distinguished from simple MIDI versions by an extension such as ›Audio,‹ ›VST‹ or ›Studio‹—not only offer basic audio and MIDI recording and playback, but also feature powerful real-time audio processing. The range of available virtual gadgetry is staggering—everything from mixing consoles to Fx devices, all available in the form of plug-ins.

More recently, crafty manufacturers have created software synthesizers and samplers, also available as plug-ins, which gave rise to the notion of virtual studios—›virtual‹ because you don't have towering racks of peripheral devices standing next to a hardware mixing console. Instead, all this stuff is housed in the computer leaving your significant other with a lot less cubic feet of gear to gripe about.

The most popular audio sequencers are ›Cubase VST‹ by Steinberg, ›Logic Audio‹ by Emagic, and ›Cakewalk‹ by Twelve Tone Systems. These three programs pretty much rule the global market.

All audio sequencers are now available in real 32-bit versions. If you're wondering what that bit of information means, you'll have to wonder a little longer—we'll go over it in detail in later chapters of this book. Although early versions of these programs were often one-way tickets to the psycho-ward, today most of the kinks and sound quality problems have been ironed out.

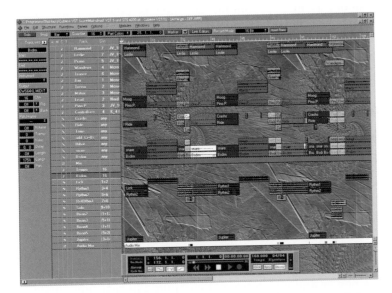

Cubase Vst—a popular audio sequencer

In the digital Stone Age, the structure and operation of these three sequencing programs had about as much in common as say Hank Williams and Neil Armstrong. If your system was set up to run flawlessly with one program, it would perform ineptly with either of the other two. This is all ancient history and the tuning tips I'll share with you here will work equally well for them all.

An audio sequencer is a performance hog and your computer will have to work overtime to feed it. The hard disk has to hustle when you're playing back audio tracks, and the many tracks and plug-ins put your processor to the test when you're editing and mixing. When you want to send audio tracks to numerous physical outputs of a multi-channel card, the architecture of the driver and the performance of your mainboard also become critical factors.

Memory is like money—no matter how much you have, it's never quite enough. Even for something as mundane as a buffer for numerous samples for your virtual drum machine,

memory is at a premium. The fact is that your audio sequencer can give the *coup de grâce* to even a modern, high-
performance computer by simply activating enough tracks
and effects.

Audio and Sample Editors

Audio sequencers are optimized for the arranging songs.
Generally, these won't offer many options for editing audio
files (nowhere near as many as a real sample editor). If you
want to process the sounds of an external sampler or soundcard, master stereo recordings and perhaps burn them to
Cd, the sequencer is not to the right tool for the job. These
chores are better left to audio editors.

Audio editors also support plug-ins. In most cases we're
talking about unusual effects that demand heaps of computing power and which are not computed in real-time. Instead,
the computer calculates these effects offline. Offline plug-ins
will work with a less powerful computer, they'll just longer to
compute.

There's a trio of dominant market leaders: ›Wavelab‹ by
Steinberg, ›Soundforge‹ by Sonic Foundry and ›Cool Edit
Pro‹ by Syntrillium.Wavelab 3.0 and Cool Edit Pro feature
multitrack functionality, but no Midi. Wavelab and Soundforge offer tools that let you burn several stereo files to an
audio Cd and these programs support virtually all standard
burners.

Audio editors are fairly obliging when it comes to computing performance requirements. Most of the time, you'll be
working with stereo files (i. e. only two tracks) and the hard
disk doesn't have to be particularly fast. The amount of main
memory is not a decisive factor either. Whereas with a sequencer, the speed of the processor plays a pivotal role, processing power isn't as important to the performance of an
audio editor. With the sequencer, everything has to take

place in real-time, otherwise you simply can't get the job done. With an audio editor, a sluggish computer will do just fine—you'll just have a lot of long coffee breaks.

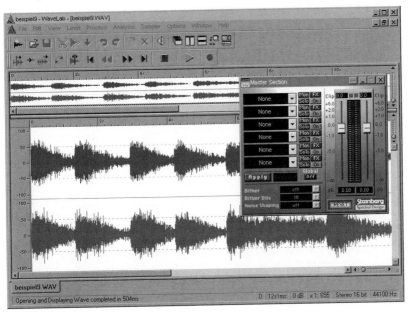

↑ One of the preeminent audio editors: Wavelab

Software Synthesizers and Samplers

This breed of music software has garnered a great deal of attention lately. For years, hardware synthesizers—from gargantuan keyboards to tiny boxes in 19-inch format—have consisted of nothing more than a few chips and the appropriate software. Since these were fully digital instruments it seemed like a good idea to get rid of the unwieldy housings and pack the plumbing into the Pc. This saves on Ac power packs, processors, chassis, and control features, which spells more money in your pocket. Besides, it's great for stealth spending—a hammond organ with a Leslie cabinet standing in your den are a bit hard to overlook, whereas with software toys your significant other can't see where your allowance is going.

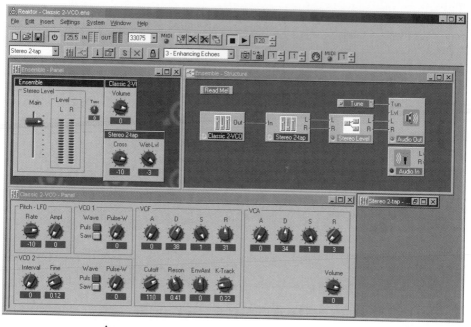

⬆ A high-performance software synthesizer: Reaktor

The software synthesizer accesses the Pc's processor to compute sounds, which is why you'll often hear the terms ›host Cpu‹ and ›native processing.‹ Audio signals are simply to the outside world by the soundcard or written to the hard disk digitally. If a given software synthesizer doesn't offer this functionality, you'll need a soundcard that lets you mix tracks down digitally. More on this in the chapter ›The Soundcard‹ starting on page 221.

›Rebirth‹ by Propellerheads, ›Reaktor‹ by Native Instruments and ›Reality‹ by Seer Systems are pure software synthesizers. These are just a few examples, there are scores more virtual drum machines and synthesizers available—many in the form of shareware.

To learn more on this topic, be sure to check out the WIZOO Guide, ›Top 30 Windows Music Shareware.‹

A software synthesizer is a glutton—it always wants as much computing power as you can give it. How many voices it is able to generate depends almost exclusively on the Pc's processor: the faster it is, the more voices you'll have to play with. Memory size and the type of hard disk play subordinate roles, too. Some factors that are very important to other applications, for example the quality of the mainboard, aren't all that relevant, provided of course that it's good enough to allow the program to run at all.

Software samplers are the kissing cousins of software synthesizers. Just like software synthesizers, they simulate the hardware that they emulate—playing samples stored in the main memory of the computer. Typically their operation and functionality is very similar that of a software synth. Among the more popular software samplers are ›Gigasampler,‹ ›Unity‹ by Bitheadz and ›Reaktor‹ by Native Instruments.

Software samplers usually don't place a huge load on the computer, depending on how sophisticated a sound generator they sport—when they play back samples all they're actually doing is reading data from the memory while a soft synth typically has to compute the actual sounds. However as technology is making strides, their roles are overlapping. For example, Reality, Reactor and Unity are all hybrids that mix sample-based sound generation with computed algorithms. For these hybrids, the Pc's processor plays a more prominent role.

Main memory is what every type of sampler wants. A good sound bank can be enormous, so that if you've less than a megabyte RAM at your disposal, ›fun‹ won't be a word you'll use to describe the time you spend fiddling with a software sampler. Bear in mind that vast amounts of data have to be transported from the memory to the card, so the stability of the mainboard and the Pci bus is very important. More on this later.

Gigasampler also likes a fast hard drive. The reason for this is that the program can load samples of any size from the hard disk and play them back simultaneously. This means that when you play a 10-voice Rachmaninoff chord with a grand piano sample, we're talking about the equivalent of approximately 10 tracks on a hard disk recorder. If you have a Jones for this program, don't skimp on the hard drive.

Pure Midi Applications

Programs that process, receive and send Midi data exclusively are elusive beasts rarely found in the virtual forest. Generally, these are highly specialized—often serving just a single purpose (e. g. to control external synthesizers with your computer).

Editors such as ›SoundDiver‹ by Emagic enable you to program and administer sounds for a vast number of external devices. The editor of the ›Nord Modular‹ synthesizer by Clavia also belongs to this category of software.

System exclusive data, abbreviated SysEx, is used for this purpose. As its name implies, SysEx is exclusive to each manufacturer—it is not standardized in the Midi protocol and varies wildly from device to device. Note that unlike other Midi data, SysEx messages can be arbitrarily long.

For this type of software, your choice of processor, memory and hard disk isn't decisive. Often the only truly decisive factor is the Midi interface and the quality of its driver.

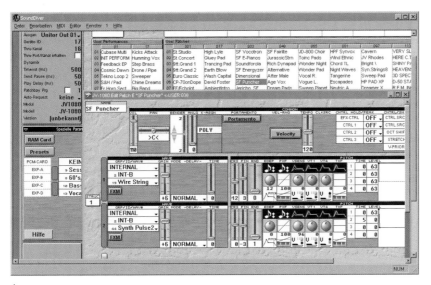

⬆ A pure MIDI application: SoundDiver

While a sequencer's MIDI output through late-model sound-cards works fairly well, SysEx messages sent through the same output can be riddled with errors or so slow that the season may have changed by the time you get outdoors again. The reason for this is that SysEx data is often too much for the driver of your MIDI interface to handle. If you should run into this problem, check out chapter ›The MIDI Interface‹ starting on page 239.

3 The Processor

The processor, also called the Cpu (Central Processing Unit), is the engine room of every computer. This is why when you're thumbing through the pages of a computer catalog processor performance specs are always highlighted. The processor is, however, not the only important factor. For example, it plays no role whatsoever in determining how stable a computer runs. And as you learned in the previous chapter, depending on the application there are legion other factors germane to performance. But the processor is a good place to kick off our tour of the computer's hardware.

When you select a Cpu, you're pretty much determining the performance class of your computer. The reason for this is that a processor requires a suitable environment—it needs a comfy pad to deliver good performance.

A high-performance Cpu requires high-performance components, some to assure that the processor works at all, others that won't slow it down. This is exactly where all-in-one packages can lead to tearful recriminations and physical injury to sales reps. If you didn't plan wisely, you may soon run into problems when you use one of these Pcs as your recording workhorse. In this chapter, we'll take it from the top and look at how to go about selecting the right processor.

What Does a Cpu Do?

Ever since man first beat plowshares into computer housings, the Cpu's job has been to do the math. It works with the four basic mathematical operations and with whole numbers only. It loads both data and a part of the program that is currently active in small memory compartments called registers. It then applies the rules of computation that the program dictates to it, computes the data, and loads the results back to the main memory. Although over-simplified, this pretty much explains how the process works.

About Bits and Bytes

Before we get into differences between individual processors and start throwing about mysterious terms such as ›bit‹ and ›byte,‹ you'll need a quick introduction to binary numbers.

A digital unit always represents precisely two states, zero and one. That's all there is to a bit. In electronics, this is expressed by means of switching status, either ›current off‹ or ›current on.‹ This basic rule holds true even for a complex unit such as a Pentium processor.

If your computer used just one bit, it could only represent two numbers, namely ›0‹ and ›1‹. This would be fine if it were a light switch, but, obviously, it won't do for much else. Even in a computer, life is not black and white, there are many shades in between.

So if you want to use more numbers, the system has to be expanded by using more bits. Each bit is assigned a different value and these are added up. Sounds complicated, but it's not. To understand how this works, take a look at the following table:

128	64	32	16	8	4	2	1
Bit 8	Bit 7	Bit 6	Bit 5	Bit 4	Bit 3	Bit 2	Bit 1
0	1	0	0	1	1	1	0

The binary number in the bottom line is equivalent to the decimal number 78. Now how did I arrive at this number?

Each bit represents the power of 2 indicated in the top row of the illustration. The bottom row tells whether each bit is ›set‹ or ›cleared.‹ The result is determined by adding those numbers in the top row (powers of two) whose bit is set. In the example, this means adding $64 + 8 + 4 + 2 = 78$. Another way of looking at it is that you first multiply each number in the top row by the corresponding number in the bottom row then add up all the results: 128×0 + 64×1 + 32×0 + 16×0 + 8×1 + 4×1 + 2×1 + 1×0 = 78.

It's no coincidence that this table is comprised of eight bits. Way back in the dark days of computing, someone decided that eight bits would make up a ›byte.‹ This means that one byte can represent the 256 numbers 0 through 255—please feel free to do the math.

As you can well imagine, 256 steps is not an overwhelming number, particularly in terms of audio data. If you sample an analog audio signal using just 256 values, the resolution will be too coarse to reproduce acceptable sound quality—let alone sound of CD quality. (Vintage samplers used 256-bit resolution which is why they deliver that typically gnarly LoFi sound.)

To remedy this situation, 16 bits (i. e. two bytes) became the standard. 65,536 numbers could now be represented which for a time was sufficient. Whenever larger numbers were necessary for text processing and spreadsheet calculations, wily programmers simply added up several 16-bit numbers—this was good enough for these bread-and-butter applications.

When people began dreaming of treating images and audio on a computer, 16-bit resolution no longer made the grade and successively processing multiple 16-bit fragments was simply too slow. This is where the development of today's state-of-the-art processors began. Now we use 32-bit systems that can process computer words of this length at one go.

The Coprocessor

We're still talking whole numbers here, which, in computerese, are called integers. Hard on the heels of the Stone Age, humans began using decimal numbers—and now the time had arrived for the processor to get with the program.

Most of us can multiply two times three in our heads with some facility. Now imagine you're asked to multiply 2.35289946 times 3.55739876. Your head hurts, right?

Just as you would whip out your trusty calculator, back then engineers gave Cpus such as the 80286 or 80386 a little helping hand in the form of co-processors.

These were independent chips called Fpus (Floating Point Unit). For these, the computing functions were hard-wired into silicon, which is why they could compute these equations up to five times the speed of fixed decimal point processors.

Back in those pioneering days, a company called Cyrix set the standards—their co-processors were significantly faster than those of the competition. Eventually, starting with the Intel 486 processor, the Fpu has been integrated into the Cpu. But it wasn't until the Pentium Intel processor arrived that our little hearts began to flutter. The Pentium was so fast that the competition was left choking in the dust. Recently, the Amd Athlon processor has started to give Intel's star sprinter a run for its money.

Many programs don't use the floating point unit at all. Word processors for instance, work just fine with whole numbers. You've probably already surmised which breed of software makes liberal use of the floating point unit—that's right, audio applications.

The most common internal format for audio data is 32-bit floating point. The reason for this is that the rounding errors that occur when many of these processing steps are executed successively are held to a minimum (and thus hopefully remain inaudible).

Without the services of a good Fpu, the virtual studio would've remained some computer nerd's wet dream. Incidentally, a Power Macintosh is equipped with an extremely fast Fpu, which set the stage for and inspired Cubase Vst. (This is why Vst didn't run on the Pc until Intel rolled out the Pentium.)

Clock Speed

Every processor marches to the beat of a different drummer, a specific clock speed. Put simply, this is the pace at which a processor carries out commands, although this explanation is somewhat misleading because the processor doesn't necessarily carry out a complete command with every clock cycle.

For the majority of commands (meaning Cpu commands a. k. a. ›assembler‹), even a state-of-the-art processor requires several clock cycles. Until the Intel 80386 processor reared its little head, the processor clock speed also dictated the pace for the rest of the system. The processor communicates with the memory, its chip set and the hard drives at the clock frequency of its Cpu.

When the 80486, the predecessor of the Pentium, saw the light of day, its clock speed was so high that external components couldn't keep up. The cost of upgrading peripheral devices so that they could perform at these speeds was prohibitive. Moreover, at the time it wasn't possible to make boards that didn't develop a personality crisis at these frequencies—anything over 66MHz and they thought they were shortwave radios.

This is why the frequencies were de-coupled. Internally, the processor used its own clock speed, also called core clock. An external clock was used for external communication, primarily with the chipset and memory. Today, this data channel is called a ›Front Side Bus‹ (Fsb)—different name, same principle.

Then there are the circuits by which peripherals are addressed. As described in the chapter ›The Mainboard‹ starting on page 61 these are generally Pci buses with a clock speed of 30 or 33MHz. The Agp bus for the display adapter is usually clocked at 66MHz.

All of these clock speeds are derived from the main clock, which is the Fsb clock. The Cpu clock is derived by multiplication, those of the Pci and Agp buses by division.

There are a few mainboards available on the market that are able to run the Pci and Agp buses asynchronously. All that this means is that their clock remains 33 or 66MHz, respectively, even when the Fsb is clocked at a higher rate.

When computer dealers tout their offerings, often the only specification that receives mention is the clock speed of the processor. Yes, it's the most impressive spec. No, it's not the only spec that counts.

The fact is that a computer equipped with a 600MHz processor is in the best-case scenario 80% faster than a comparable box with a 300MHz processor.

The big processor could only compute at twice the speed of its little brother when data is shoveled into its maw at twice the rate and it is able to spew it back just as quickly. As soon as it comes time to send data to peripheral gear—and you will always want to do this for audio/Midi applications—the chipset and the processor's interface to its environment make all the difference in the world.

Obviously, if you own a multi-I/O card with eight inputs and outputs, you will want to patch signals through these circuits. The whole object of hard disk recording is to do fun stuff like shuttle recorded data from the hard drive, feed it your trusty plug-in, and slap enough reverb on it to make your guitar sound like the feathery wing-beat of angels rather than the hardscrabble scratchiness of a manic chicken.

The problem is that as the speed of Cpu increases, the rest of the computer drudges have trouble keeping up. This is precisely why Intel has upped the clock speed of the Fsb to 100MHz and now to 133MHz.

The bottom line is that no matter how high the performance power of a processor, its environment has to be able to put it to good use before it will do you any good. Speed is important, but it's not everything. For example, if you're into hard disk recording, you'll soon learn to cherish good memory performance because you're constantly shifting a vast amount of data to and from. If, on the other hand, your gig is working with a software synth that delivers as many voices as possible, pure processor performance will be at a premium.

More on this in the section ›Memory‹ on page 66.

Mmx and Isse Extensions

Multimedia extensions (Mmx for short) has been around for while now. This is a command set that is chopped up into little tidbits (instead of being served up in one huge bite) so that the little registers of the processor can deal with them in one step.

The problem is that often these registers offer just 16 bits. So, although in principle this is a pretty speedy approach to computing, the operative term here is ›16 bits,‹ which is exactly why audio software vendors do not use these commands.

There's another complication: In Intel Cpus, Mmx and Fpu are an either/or proposition—they can only be used successively, not simultaneously. Also, some preparation is necessary to switch modes. For example, the memory content of the processor's registers has to be stored first because it would be lost when another mode is activated. So now we've come full circle to the original problem—it takes too long. In practice, Mmx doesn't even get a bit part in professional audio software—the classic Fpu, however, plays a starring role.

(I'm aware of just one professional audio application that actually uses Mmx commands: the interface of Creamware's ›Pulsar/Scope‹ platform.)

With the Pentium III (PIII for short), Intel introduced an enhanced version of this command set called Isse. In addition to containing a bunch of additional commands, the key registers now have a size of 32 bits, which is the standard format for audio sequencers. This is why some audio software vendors have opted for this innovation: both Cubase Vst and Samplitude support these new multimedia extensions. However, support is still rudimentary. Floating point unit performance remains the decisive factor, and this is what you should focus on when you're selecting a processor.

Cache

Another issue that we need to focus on is the cache. This is an extremely fast buffer that the system is able to access very quickly—much quicker than normal DRAM (Dynamic Random Access Memory). One of the reasons that it's so accessible is that it doesn't have to be constantly refreshed like its counterparts on the mainboard, the display adapter, and sampler. This is why the memory for cache is called SRAM (Static Random Access Memory).

Since the arrival of the 486, computers have offered something called › 1st or First Level Cache,‹ which is a buffer integrated right into the processor. It is generally very small, on current CPUs we're talking 16KB for data and commands each—sometimes slightly more.

Incidentally, this type of cache runs at the processor's full internal clock speed. Back then, this was sufficient because typical PC code was largely local. In other words, the computer is dealing the tiny fragments that are repeatedly applied to process data.

As processors began to pick up speed, cache became so much faster than memory that a second level of buffers was created, the aptly named ›Second Level Cache‹ (or L2 cache). Today the typical L2 cache is sized at 256 or 512KB. Depending on the type of CPU, it resides on the mainboard or holds hands with the processor on a carrier board.

For audio applications, cache is one of those components where size and speed counts—the bigger and faster, the better. The reason for this is that audio processing is usually carried out by relatively compact algorithms that are applied repeatedly to each sample in your song. These algorithms largely remain in the processors cache so they don't have to be retrieved from the relatively sluggish main memory.

However, don't go overboard: You're better off investing the ducats you would shell out for a Xeon processor with a 2-Mb cache in other components of your system.

Processors were once soldered directly onto the boards, but for decades now they have been plugged into sockets. This makes it easy to swap them (at least in theory). Unfortunately, virtually every new Cpu ships with a new version of these sockets. In a prime example of creeping capitalism, state-of-the-art computers are equipped with slots designed to take a board onto which a processor is soldered.

In terms of performance, all of this is meaningless. If, however, you're planning on upgrading your system at some point in the future, you'll need to take this into consideration. For this reason, we'll take a closer look at the socket versus slot issue at the end of the chapter where we focus on upgrading options.

State-of-the-Art Processors and Performance

Pentium

This make of processor has demonstrated the greatest staying power, which is why so many versions of the Pentium are available.

In the dubious articulations of computerese, a ›Pentium Classic‹ is any Cpu without the now standard Mmx unit. Consider anything lower than 166MHz useless for musical applications.

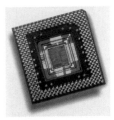

The standard Pentium Classic in its old version for Socket 7

The fastest classic Pentium is the P200. Although you won't be setting any new performance records with this type of Cpu, you will be able to record a couple of tracks and even use a TrueVerb (a popular plug-in noted [or perhaps feared] for its voracious appetite for Cpu performance).

For its first level cache, this Cpu is equipped with 8Kb each for data and commands. Its second level cache resides on the mainboard and runs ›only‹ at the external clock speed, i. e. at

50, 60 or 66MHz. If you own this type of computer, you should find out if it has any cache at all. Many bargain-basement computers ship without cache altogether to cut costs. Many problems, particularly in connection with Cubase and Logic, can be attributed to a lack of cache because these programs use it extensively.

Macintosh users will also be familiar with this ›phenomenon.‹ Some older Macintoshes shipped without second level cache, which is why this issue is blabbed about perhaps more than any other in the FAQs of the Macintosh audio community.

Pentium MMX

This model features the enhanced command set MMX that we looked at earlier. It is also equipped with a larger first level cache (16KB each for data and commands), which is primarily responsible for its improved performance. The fastest Pentium MMX runs at 233MHz, and much the same can be said of it as for its little brothers of the Classic series. As mentioned earlier, MMX is immaterial to audio applications, but at least it won't get in your way.

The Pentium and Pentium MMX are similar in one more respect—they're both mounted to Socket 7 on the board.

Pentium Pro

The Pentium Pro

This model was the designated heir of the Pentium. It is equipped with what was then a newly developed core and a 256-KB second level cache—sometimes more—integrated into the chip. This cache runs at the full processor clock speed and was one of the drivers of the PPro's good performance. The most common version of this chip is the 200MHz model. The original versions of Cubase VST and Wavelab were developed on machines equipped with this chip.

When Intel developed the Pentium Pro, the company evidently assumed that by the time it was introduced to the market, 32-bit software would rule the world. The Pentium

Pro was fine-tuned to deliver optimum performance with this breed of software, which is why its 16-bit performance is less than stellar.

Moreover, the integrated second level cache posed some problems. Back then, very few modules could keep pace with this high speed. If this expensive add-on component sold by third party vendors didn't make the grade, the equally expensive processor was rendered instant junk.

For this reason the Pentium Pro was always too expensive for mass-market appeal. If, however, you are offered this type of CPU, possibly secondhand, at a good price, you may want to consider it, but only if the mainboard is included in the price.

The Pentium Pro lives in Socket 8, a place where no other processor before or since has resided. Although longevity is not a term commonly associated with processors, this should nonetheless tell you that this breed of CPU is even less future-proof than most.

PII (Klamath)

We are making headway on our slow approach to the current processor generation and oddly enough, gaining a lesson in geography—specifically Oregon's rivers. Intel has habitually assigned code names derived from U.S. geography to new CPUs. These nicknames tend to stick, which is why they'll often pop up when computer freaks shoot the breeze.

The first version of the PII in a housing

The PII, originally known under its code name Klamath, is basically a PPro with an MMX unit. Intel also evicted the cache from the processor's core. Now it is located next to the CPU on a board, although both have been encased in a plastic housing. Beyond that, this cache runs at just half the processor clock speed, making it cheaper to produce and easier to obtain.

The first two models (233 and 266MHz) were not a vast improvement over the Pentium Pro, especially not in terms of audio applications. Here the halved cache speed certainly had an impact. Major strides weren't made until the PII 300 saw the light of day. This Cpu is still fairly up-to-date. Since its arrival, plug-in users have enjoyed simultaneous services of two or three sophisticated reverb units. When you're shopping for processors, don't let anyone talk you into a PII with less than 300MHz. If you're looking for a bargain, there are cheaper alternatives.

Along with the PII, Intel introduced Slot 1, which supplanted the socket. This Cpu shipped in a high-end housing made of aluminum and plastic called Secc. The company later rolled out a version featuring a housing named, with dazzling originality, Secc2. It lacked the aluminum rear panel, undoubtedly to cut costs. This has no impact on performance, but it does require different cooling fans and processor mounts. If you want to upgrade your computer with a new Slot 1 Cpu, regardless of which model you're considering, ask your dealer to provide the appropriate cooling fan and processor mount.

PII (Deschutes)

The highest possible speed at which the ›old‹ PII could be clocked was 300MHz. To come up with a faster processor, Intel had to roll out a new processor core, which answers to the name of another river, ›Deschutes.‹ These PII Cpus are known for their higher clock speeds, both for the actual processor as well as the external clock used for the memory. It is now clocked at 100MHz (PE 2350 and higher). However, due to the fast L2 cache, this didn't have quite as great an impact as with the boards in processors of the pre-PII era. When you're looking for a fast Cpu that will serve you well for audio applications, the Deschutes models (300, 333, 350, 400, 450) are a good option.

Again resorting to TrueVerb as a benchmark, a 400MHz chip has been known to deliver eight audio tracks with five TrueVerbs. Although this is pretty much the end of the line as far as performance goes, bear in mind that we're talking about five plug-ins that, as TDM versions, will even make the Pro Tools standard system beg for mercy. Indeed, a system offering this level of performance merits the moniker ›audio workstation.‹

Celeron

This processor was designed for the low-cost market. Although it features a Deschutes core, it ships sans L2 cache and housing. It's available in 266- and 300-MHz versions. To put it bluntly, if you're interested in experiencing anything other than abject frustration, hands off for audio applications. Although the FPU is decent, there's no L2 cache and therefore not sufficient speed for creating great reverb effects.

The Celeron

Also, beware of marketing trickery. If you see an ad for a computer featuring ›PII technology,‹ this is what they're talking about. Much to Intel's credit, it has always called this processor by its rightful name, Celeron.

Celeron (Mendocino)

Since the original Celeron failed to set the world on fire, Intel opted to develop a new processor core, the ›Mendocino.‹ As you would expect, it contains an internal L2 cache. Although at just 128KB it is relatively small, it runs—like its great-granddaddy the Pentium Pro—at full processor speed.

This CPU is available under the name of ›Celeron 300A‹ (the ›A‹ is decisive because it distinguishes this processor from the aforementioned lemon) and there are versions running at 333, 400, 433, 466 and 500MHz. The latter do not carry the ›A‹ extension simply because there are no Celerons without cache available that deliver this kind of speed.

All Celerons run at an external clock of 66MHz. Data transfer from and to the memory is perceptively slower than with the PII Deschutes. This of course is significant in hard disk recording because you're carting heaps of data back and forth. Although the fast cache does compensate somewhat, any PII/PIII clocked at more than 400MHz is superior. In other words, if you have your heart set purely on working with plug-ins and software synthesizers, a Celeron ›A‹ will keep you satisfied. If, however, you want to work on larger projects with loads of tracks, go for a PII/III.

If you're strapped for cash, Celerons definitely deliver the biggest bang for your buck. Intel offers new Celerons featuring PPGA (Plastic Pin Grid Array) design. This is a fancy name for a back-to-the-roots approach to production. The processor looks like an old Pentium Classic and requires a socket (Model 370) instead of a slot, which is why a special mainboard is used for this processor type. The downside is that you can only plug PPGA versions of the Celeron into it. Faster processors that fit this socket won't be made in the future, but there is an alternative. With the benefit of an adapter, the PPGA Celeron will fit into a Slot 1 mainboard, and you can upgrade it later with a PII/III Coppermine processor. This is the more sensible alternative.

PIII (Katmai)

The latest generation of computers is equipped with this processor, named for a volcano in Alaska. Other than added multimedia functionality (ISSE), this chip is identical to its predecessor PII. But it does come in racier packages featuring clock speeds of 450, 500, 533, 550 and 600MHz.

PIIIE (Coppermine)

A current Celeron featuring a PPGA design for a socket

When AMD presented the Athlon to the world, in the process leaving the competition choking in its dust, Intel scurried to develop a new processor. The code name ›Coppermine‹—this time taking the river theme up to the frozen north of Canada—was used for this new processor. Unwisely, the marketing department chose to name it PIII with an ›E‹ tacked on. Even more confusingly, this extension is only used for 600-MHz models.

A 700MHz version is also available, although here the ›E‹ extension is missing because, following Intel's unique logic, the company doesn't offer a Katmai PIII3. Next to these models, which feature an external clock of 100MHz, there are also models sporting a ›B‹ extension designed for 133MHz Fsb. These have clock speeds of 667, 700, and 733MHz.

The latest Intel processor: PIIIE Coppermine

Like the Celeron, the Coppermine features a down-sized 256-Kb L2 cache that runs at full clock speed. The architecture of the processor core was also re-engineered, undoubtedly to give the rival Amd a run for its money. However, at the time that this book went to press, a high-performance chipset for this processor was unavailable. Moreover, this Cpu is one hot tamale and requires big-time cooling. Initial benchmarks point to the fact that this processor is on par with the Athlon by Amd. The latter nonetheless seems the wiser choice for applications such as audio that require good Fpu performance.

Amd K6

Yes, the undisputed market leader does have a rival. Originally, Amd's K6 was pitted against the first PII (Klamath). It was great at computing integers. Unfortunately, Amd did a less stellar job with the floating point unit. Depending on the application, this takes its toll in the form of some 20 to 30 percent poorer performance.

Although this processor can handle Mmx—Amd has a license exchange agreement with Intel—this doesn't mean squat for our purposes. The K6 is a unquestionably a good processor for office applications, but it's not worth further consideration for audio applications.

Amd K6 II

This chip's best feature is an extension sporting the rather breathless moniker ›3DNow!‹. Beyond that it can, just like the PII Deschutes, run at external clock speeds up to

100MHz. ›3DNow!‹ was designed to compensate for the K6's shortcomings in the Fpu department.

Alas, as its name would indicate, this expanded command set primarily benefits graphics applications. Out of the box, it is useless for audio applications, for it requires a special software adaptation. Although DirectX 6 features this type of upgrade, it serves merely to boost the performance of Direct-Draw graphics. Plug-in audio programs don't benefit. The reason for this is that the actual Fpu performance hasn't improved. I can't recommend the K6II for audio applications.

Amd K6III

This is the fastest of the processors that support Socket 7. It is available in clock speeds of up to 450MHz. Although Amd enthusiastically tweaked some of the details, its Fpu performance is still not what you'd call impressive. Go for this processor only if you're dead set against swapping mainboards.

Athlon

The Athlon is Amd's flagship—at the time of its release, it was the fastest processor in the Pc world. It is equipped with a 512-Kb L2 cache that runs on half the processor's clock speed. It is versed in the Mmx command set as well as 3DNow!, but not Intel's Isse extension.

AMD's heavyweight contender: Athlon

On the upside, it does feature a relatively large L1 cache and up to 19 parallel computing units, including a superior floating point unit. To belabor the point, the latter is critical to audio applications. Hence, the Athlon comes highly recommended—in fact, other than the PIII-E (Coppermine), it puts all other Cpus to shame. Beyond that, its architecture is innovative and geared toward supporting future clock speeds of well over 1GHz.

The Athlon also plugs into a slot and is encased in a housing. Called Slot A, it looks suspiciously like Intel's Slot 1. Looks, however, can be deceiving: you can't plug the Intel processor into an Athlon mainboard or vice versa.

The Athlon also runs at an external clock of 100MHz, but it can transport data on both flanks of the signal. This is why you might hear talk about ›100MHz times two‹—the effective clock rate is actually 200MHz. This is the speed at which it communicates with its chipset (see the chapter ›The Mainboard‹ on page 61) significantly enhancing overall performance. It also means that the Athlon requires Pc100 Dimms for its memory.

Upgrading your system with this Cpu can cost a pretty penny. If we're talking about an older Intel system, you'll probably need new memory components in addition to a new mainboard. If however, you're thinking about buying a new computer, the Athlon (next to a Coppermine computer) should be at the top of your shopping list.

Cyrix MII 300

Cyrix/Ibm has also produced a processor designed to play in the big leagues. Unfortunately, the Fpu of this processor is an even more pitiful specimen than that of the Amd K6, so the thrill factor for serious audio applications is negligible. Akin to playing baseball with a toothpick, this Fpu just doesn't give you the firepower you need—we're talking some 40% poorer performance depending on the application.

The future of Cyrix is iffy, so I wouldn't recommend buying this processor for a new computer or even for an upgrade. If you use a computer equipped with this Cpu, I implore you to ditch the processor and, while you're at it, the mainboard.

▶ There's been an ugly rumor circulating on the Internet that certain audio software will not run with Cyrix or Amd processors. This is patently untrue. This hearsay was born of an illegal copy of an early Cubase Vst beta version. True, the software refused to run, but since it was a pirated copy of an unapproved version, no one should have been trying to get it to run in the first place. The official versions of all known audio programs will run on Amd and Cyrix processors, although, other than with the Athlon, not at blinding speeds.

A Brief Discourse on the Subject of Over-clocking

To nip a flurry of FAQs in the bud, I'd like to expound a bit about the popular subject of ›over-clocking:‹

This is a tuning option that intrepid do-it-yourselfers like to use to eke out a tad more performance. Admittedly, I'm guilty of it myself, but, as a proponent of safe tweaking, I've always been cautious about it.

If you're dealing with contemporary Pentium II CPUs, discretion is definitely the better part of valor. Depending on the clock speed, Intel uses different cache components. These have different access speeds. And as you now know, PIIs may have different cores even if when their nominal clock speed is identical.

For example, crank a Klamath up to 350MHz, and you'll end up with an instant crispy fritter. If you unwisely attempt to do this, you probably wouldn't get any further than the start screen because some models of this series feature integrated over-clocking protection. There are Deschutes out there that have been down-sized to 266 and 300MHz, and therefore could handle some tweaking. However the cache components can't, at least not for long.

The Celeron models 300A and 333 are also quite often the object of home tuning experiments. Due to these chips' fixed multiplier (this is the factor by which the external clock speed is derived from the processor clock), we're talking about huge increments here. For example, the next step up from a 300A is a 450MHz processor (100×4.5). When you bear in mind that the Celeron A carries in its core an L2 cache unit that runs at full speed, my experience with the Pentium Pro leads me to believe that you'd be asking for trouble here.

Some brave souls have risked it, but the tales they tell vary wildly. This is where prudence pays: If you like or depend on your computer, don't try this trick at home.

Counterfeit Chips

While we're on the subject, of late, there've been a rash of counterfeit chips flooding the marketplace. Indeed, there are even professional sweat shops in which the resistors on the CPU boards are re-soldered to trick the processor ID functionality of the BIOS processor. Even upstanding vendors have been duped by these counterfeit chips.

If your computer routinely crashes without any apparent reason, take a look at the housing of your Pentium II to see if it looks like it has been tampered with. These CPUs are of course running at faster speeds than they were designed for and particularly the cache modules can give you a great deal of grief. As I pointed out earlier, Cubase and Logic are fickle about the kind of cache they will work with—they tend to crash when it's unreliable.

Unfortunately, counterfeiters have become so sophisticated that they will even fake serial numbers. Even a conscientious check by your local dealer can't guarantee that you end up with an original chip.

The kindly folks of the magazine *c't* have come up with a tool that can be of help. You can download it at http://www.heise.de/ct/p2info/. The downside is that this is highly technical information that won't be of much use to you unless you're a specialist because you have to compare the data that you've researched with the information in Intel documents, which you'll find at http://developer.intel.com/design/PentiumII/specupdt/243337.htm.

Maybe your computer dealer is of a rare breed and willing to help you out. Give him these two Web addresses and ask him to see if he can't find out if your chip is a fake. However, don't blame the dealer—in most cases he's just as much a victim as you are.

Which Cpu Is Best for Which Application?

Pure Midi Applications

For this purpose, a 486 processor and an elderly version of Cubase or Cakewalk will do just fine. Your big brother's computer gathering dust in the basement could do the trick.

Midi and Audio

Here you'll need to set your sights little higher. If you stick with Cubase up to version 3.0, Cakewalk up to 5.0 and Logic Audio up to 3.0, you can even work with a Pentium 90. If you want to play with more tracks, you should opt for at least a Pentium 133.

Midi, Audio, and Plug-in Effects

Nothing lower than a Pentium 166 will do, but even then, it's unlikely that you will be able to get more than one high-end plug-in to run—two at the same time is wishful thinking. In this game comfort doesn't come a cut-rate price—you'll have to invest in a PII 300 or higher.

A Fully-loaded Virtual Studio

Assuming that we're talking about a truly comprehensive solution here—say a macho rig that can run at least three high-end reverb plug-ins simultaneously, compressors for at least 10 channels, a three-band equalizer, delay and chorus—you'll need at least a PII with 400MHz, the faster the better. You'll get the biggest bang for your buck when you go for models that were state-of-the-art six months ago. By this time, prices have generally dropped so that they've become affordable for mere mortals, but you're still going to enjoy close to the best performance available.

At this time, this narrows down your options to the AMD Athlon and the PIII-E (Coppermine) with clock speeds of 500 or 600MHz. All other processors, even the ›normal‹ PIII, don't measure up when the going gets rough.

For clock speeds of 500 and 550MHz, I'd recommend the Athlon at this time. This Cpu is cheaper than a PIII system. The mainboards are still a little more expensive, but they deliver better performance for audio applications.

Let's look at that old standby, the TrueVerb test: The Athlon gives you one TrueVerb entity more than the Intel chip. However, at speeds of 600MHz and higher, the PII-E rivals the Athlon. It features an L2 cache with full clock speed, which means that its performance for audio applications has been improved.

Your choice will, on the one hand, hinge on the market price on any given day and, on the other, whether or not your software supports the Isse extensions, which only the PIII can offer. At the time this book went to press, these were limited to select modules of Cubase and Samplitude. Most parts of these programs still rely on the floating point unit, so in terms of speed Amd and Intel are running pretty much neck-to-neck.

Upgrading Options

Now that you've learned a few facts on which to base your decision when you're buying a new computer, you might be thinking something along the lines of, ›Why not upgrade my old box?‹

The following is a brief survey of the many available upgrading options. Depending on your current system, an upgrade may be worth your while if you don't have to swap the mainboard and any major components. Unfortunately, the this is not often the case, particularly with computers that are older than the tender of age of two. In this short a time, everything from memory to the shape of the housing has changed. In this case, upgrading is only a feasible if you're a gifted do-it-yourselfer or and enjoy tinkering.

Pentium 90 to 233

The only sensible option here is to swap the processor. If your computer isn't equipped with cache, then you could opt to install this buffer—in many cases, this will work wonders. For every other option, you'll have to replace the mainboard and memory. These computers feature the outdated AT design, which means you'll have to buy a new housing as well. In a nutshell, we're talking ›money pit‹ here.

If you own a Pentium 200/233, replacing the processor is also akin to buying a new computer.

Upgrading your box with an AMD K6 processor will only boost performance if the clock speed of your old Pentium is 166MHz or lower. If it's higher, in view of its poor performance for audio applications, the K6 won't do you any good. Also, with older boards you'll run into problems with the power supply, so this option is not the way to go.

Pentium 233 to 300

Here to, you can swap the processor for a faster Celeron. Externally, it runs at 66MHz, which your mainboard will support. For later model PPGA Celerons, you will require an adapter for Slot 1, which is what your old PII uses. If your board is equipped with an AGP slot, you should replace the current PCI graphics card with an AGP card. Upgrading memory is less worthwhile because this generation of computers works with PS/2 EDO-RAM. When you finally retire your old computer, you won't be able to salvage this memory and install it in your new computer. In other words, if at some point you buy a later generation PC, kiss the money goodbye that you invest now in memory.

Pentium II 350 to 500

Again, you can drop in a new Cpu to upgrade your box. But don't expect a boost in performance commensurate with the increase in clock speed. This type of upgrade is feasible if you need a tad better performance for your software synthesizer and plug-ins. However, in all likelihood, it won't fix poor timing or remedy sync problems.

If you use software samplers or hardware that accesses main memory (›Soundblaster Live,‹ ›Creamware Pulsar‹), it will be worth your while to install more memory. This generation of Pc runs on an external clock of 100MHz, so investing in 100MHz Dimm modules makes sense. Even though the future of the format is still hazy, these Dimms won't be obsolete for at least another generation of computers.

If your box is equipped with a Pci graphics card, replace it with an Agp card.

Athlon 500

The Amd Athlon 500 is already pretty quick, so replacing it in the near future with an even faster chip doesn't seem a likely scenario. However, some Athlon boards, or more accurately, their chipsets, still have problems with some Pci hardware as well as with I/O performance.

With Version C6 of Amd's Irongate chipset, you can enhance the performance of an Athlon by up to 30 percent. The downside is that you'll have to swap mainboards.

If you want to replace the Cpu with an 1.1GHz Athlon for example, you should also update the Bios, but this shouldn't be a problem.

4 The Mainboard

Now that you know which Cpu serves your purposes best and which motherboard it takes to get it running, it's time to take a closer look at the mainboard itself.

Its significance is widely underestimated, for the mainboard is a key factor in assuring the stability of the computer and thus its suitability for professional applications. Unfortunately, you'll rarely be able to determine the make of the board when you buy a computer from a chain store or big computer dealer.

Besides, many vendors will cut corners here to save those 50 bucks that make the package deal such a bargain. After experiencing multiple nervous breakdowns because your computer constantly crashes, you'll know why those fifty dollars would've been well spent. In the following chapter, we'll take an in-depth look at the wild and wonderful world of boards and talk about the criteria by which to judge their quality.

Layout

Today, all the components (other than graphics-related stuff) that your computer needs to do its thing are soldered onto the mainboard. Some even feature onboard graphics and sound, which means that the chips that carry out these tasks are hard-wired onto the board. Fortunately this is not usually the case because as you shall later find out, you should avoid these boards like the plague.

You don't need to know every detail of the layout of a mainboard. Besides, if you're not a service technician, this knowledge won't do you much good—in a year's time it will be totally outdated.

Instead of x-raying every single component, we'll take a closer look at the functional groups or assemblies. These will still be around in ten years time and they're similar on every computer platform, not just on the Pc. Of course technology will have evolved over a decade, but the function that these assemblies serve within every computer will still be much the same.

The basic layout of a Pc

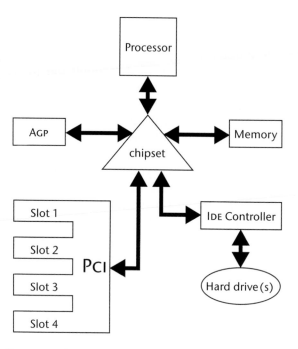

In the diagram above, you see the most important functional areas of the mainboard and by extension, those of the entire computer.

The processor is of course the brain of the board. The chipset—so named because it consists of set of cohesive components—is the nerve center of the mainboard. It provides the interface between the processor and its external environment. Most importantly, it talks to the main memory.

Every time the Cpu goes to read data, the message is re-layed by the chipset. The chipset also transports data from the memory to the Agp bus, to the Pci bus and to the Ide interface, i. e. to the hard drives.

Agp and Pci are two systems for hardware extensions: Pci is a universal standard and Agp was developed specifically for the display adapter. Both of these signals circuits are called a bus. This term describes the physical data circuits that carry electrical current as well as the set of rules (called the protocol) that determines how these electrical signals are interpreted.

If the maker of the mainboard and the extension card vendor stick to the standard, card xy will work with mainboard z. They never have to meet and hash the matter out over a couple of brews. Sounds practical, doesn't it? In theory yes, but in practice it doesn't always work out that way. More on this in the section ›The Pci Bus‹ on page 74.

Let's walk through the individual steps of hard disk recording to make this function a little clearer:

The Pci bus carries data from your soundcard to the main memory and from there to the hard disk. The chipset, Ide controller and Pci bus, with a little help from the soundcard of course, work together to execute this task. The chipset and Ide controller carry this data to the processor, which computes a reverb effect for example, then sends it back through the Pci bus and on to the soundcard so that you can hear it.

Picture the mainboard as a busy intersection with heavy traffic coming in from every side. The chipset serves as the harried traffic cop and the Pci bus and Agp are the roads on which it directs traffic.

The display adapter and soundcard as well as the hard drive and processor are the destinations for all the commuters on these busy roads.

One of musicians'
fave mainboards:
the Asus P2B

Chipset

As mentioned earlier, the chipset is the nerve center of the
mainboard. Every time the CPU addresses the memory, it
does so via the chipset. This is why the main memory must
be compatible with the chipset and enjoy its support. Indeed,
the chipset determines the speed and mode of memory access. In computerese, this is called ›memory timing‹ and you
can even control it within certain limits.

Since communication between the processor and its assistant is carried out at the external clock speed (through the
so-called Front Side Bus, FSB for short), the chipset also determines the speed at which the processor bus can be
clocked. The AGP and PCI buses are also served by the
chipset, and it also determines the top speed at which data
transfer can take place.

It would bore you to tears and keep me busy for years if I
listed all chipsets that have been produced for Pentium PII/
III and AMD CPUs. Besides, the vast majority of these are of
little more than historical interest. If you work with an older
system, you don't have any choice in the matter because the
chipset can't be replaced.

As far as older chipsets go, the only one worth mentioning
is the Intel Tx. This chipset could only handle 64-MB main

memory in the L2 cache. Back when the L2 cache was not aboard the processor (i. e. Pentium Pro and lower) the chipset was also responsible for this buffer (cf. the chapter ›The Processor‹ starting on page 37). If you install a memory unit that is bigger than 64Mв on this type of computer, be warned that you will most likely slow it down rather than speed it up.

For contemporary systems, we need to focus on just a few chipsets. For Intel processors of the PII/III class, there is the proprietary Bx. It is a mature, dependable and very fast chipset. However, it only supports external clock speeds of up to 100MHz. The new 133MHz technology requires its successor, the i820 (Camino). However, since it requires the astronomically expensive Rambus memory components to make the most of this technology, you're better off sticking with the proven Bx set. As mentioned in the chapter on processors, you should then select a processor with an external clock speed of 100MHz.

Other chipsets are also available for Intel processors, for example those made by a company called Vıa. Unfortunately, these chipsets either deliver poor performance or are incompatible with many Pcı cards, so ›hands off.‹

Some of these low-cost chips (which even Intel has seen fit to offer) feature onboard graphics. This option lets vendors put together bargain-basement computers since they're saving the bucks it would cost to install a display adapter. Beware, danger lurks. Say for example, you want to upgrade your rig with a better display adapter—with these chipsets there's no way of knowing whether you'll be able to switch off the onboard graphic function. Moreover, they also tend to squeeze the bandwidth of the Pcı bus.

If you opt for this type of system, be prepared for the raging migraines and nausea that comes with them. The vast majority of these systems are utterly unacceptable for audio and Mıdı applications.

The upshot is: For an Intel processor, select the Intel Bx chipset or the 820 I (Camino). Just ask your local computer dealer. If he can't provide a satisfactory answer, swiftly find a new one.

The Bx chipset on a mainboard

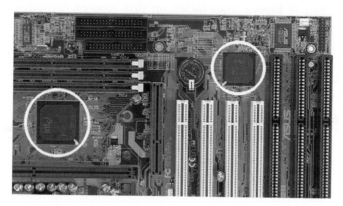

At the time this book went to press, the selection for the AMD Athlon was extremely limited. There's only one chipset available, AMD's proprietary ›Irongate.‹ Some mainboards do use a VIA chip to address peripherals (I/O). This chip has also been known to be used with Intel processors and mainboards. Alas, it is notorious for unreliability. If you opt for an Athlon mainboard, stick with AMD components.

▶ By the time you read this book, VIA will most likely have released a complete proprietary chipset. My soothsaying talents being somewhat underdeveloped, I can't predict if it will be any good.

Memory

The main memory is one of the computer's key components. It holds all the data that you want the processor to process. That's exactly what it is—a holding pen. This is where data is corralled for the CPU because it can't access data directly from the hard drive. This is why the quality and speed of the memory are important. On modern computers, you'll find just three types of memory:

Fp Dram

Also known as Ps/2, Fp Dram was for a long time the definitive standard for memory. Fp stands for ›Fast Page‹ mode, which back then meant that access time was less than 100 nanoseconds. By today's standards, this is pretty pokey.

Ps/2 is actually a design rooted in an Ibm standard, but with the 486 generation it was adopted by all manufacturers.

This type of memory ran at the external processor clock speed—at a maximum of 66MHz. Access time was some 50 to 70ns. Computers rarely use this type of memory anymore because it's simply too sluggish.

If, however, you have some of these modules lying around, you may be able to install them in your sampler. For example, these modules will work in the Emu Esi 4000 and some Yamaha samplers.

Edo Ram

Edo Ram is very similar to Fp-Dram, the components look identical and they fit the same Ps/2 base. Through a little routing trick, this memory type is a tad faster at reading data. Other than that, it's comparable to a simple Fp Dram. This memory is still employed in all computer types that run on a 66MHz external clock, in other words PII and Celeron processors that are clocked at up to 300MHz.

An older memory module featuring the Ps/2 design. The actual memory is Edo Ram.

SDRAM

This memory delivers significantly faster access times. In the best-case scenario, data can be accessed in a single bus cycle provided that a series of sequential addresses are accessed. This is called burst mode. However, in practice, speed depends how often this type of burst is possible, i. e. whether or not data is actually located at these sequential addresses. All new computers employ this memory and this isn't about to change because new memory technology is still extremely expensive and is therefore rarely used in mass-market products.

SDRAM no longer ships in the Ps/2 format. Instead, it is available on the DIMM modules routinely used for the Apple Macintosh. This means that this new memory does not fit into older computers. Vice versa, older memory modules do not fit in newer computers.

A current memory module, here a Pc100 DIMM. You can see that the design of this module does not fit into the same sockets as the older EDO RAM-modules.

Pc66, Pc100 and Pc133

A further category used to classify memory is the speed at which it can be clocked. Pc66, Pc100 and Pc133 indicate the clock frequency at which a memory module can run. It's no coincidence that these specifications correspond to the external clock speeds of standard processors and mainboards. You should always make sure that you opt for memory that matches the speed of the board and CPU.

Memory-related Problems

Memory errors are among the most ›celebrated‹ and vexing nuisances that your computer can throw at you. If just one of the millions of storage cells is defective, a value of 0 can unexpectedly become 1 and vice versa. If a program or a driver receives this incorrect value, all kinds of wild stuff can happen, but in most cases the system will simply crash and you'll have to restart Windows.

Memory errors are hard to pinpoint because it takes special equipment to analyze the problem. This gear is prohibitively expensive and not every dealer is willing to cough up the bucks to have it at hand.

Your only option is to hit on your friends, borrow some memory, install it, and see what happens. Much of the computer's inexplicable behavior can be attributed to defective memory.

If you come across a problem that you suspect may be memory-related, simply swap memories. Perhaps you can sweet-talk your local dealer into to lending you a replacement module to check for bugs. If your system no longer crashes after you've installed the new memory, you've tracked down the culprit.

If you have several memory modules installed in your computer, try de-installing one of them at a time. This will slow your system down, but once you've localized the defective module, you can replace it with a new one.

Does Memory Impact Audio Performance?

Yes, the speed and access time of memory are decisive. Modern CPUs perform much better, particularly in terms of FPU performance (see the chapter ›The Processor‹ on page 37), when memory is clocked at 100MHz. However, you'll also need a suitable board, so simply swapping memories isn't going to turn your box into a fire-breathing monster. What does enhance performance is the size of the memory.

The golden rule for memory is that you can never have too much. Consider 64MB the absolute minimum for an audio system—comfortable handling doesn't come until you have at least 128MB at your disposal. If you use software samplers or soundcards that use your computer's main memory, 256MB are very useful.

In this day and age, don't go for anything less than a Pc100 memory featuring the DIMM design. You'll be able to use these memory chips for a while. Pc66 and Ps/2 modules as well as EDO RAM are not future-proof investments.

IRQS

In the introduction to this chapter, I used busy intersections as an analogy for the activities on a mainboard and likened the bus systems to streets that lead to certain destinations (extension cards, processor).

To help you understand what the notorious ›interrupts‹ mean to your computer, I'll stick with this example. Imagine you've set off down the road to visit a fellow musician to talk shop. What do you do once you've arrived and are standing at the front door? Right, you ring the doorbell. This is exactly what a card does in the Pc when it wants to let the processor know that data is knocking at the door.

There is another technique used for this purpose called ›polling.‹ Here the processor checks at regular intervals if data is at the doorstep. To paraphrase the great Windows cynic Andrew Schulman:

›Polling is the same thing as getting up every ten minutes to see if someone is at the door. An IRQ is like having a bell.‹

This sounds simple enough, so you may wonder why even Pc pros occasionally speak of mysterious IRQ conflicts in comments liberally sprinkled with invectives. The reason is that here are just sixteen interrupts in a Pc which means that, despite the fact that your computer is more like a multi-story building with 100 apartments, there are only sixteen doorbells.

Way back when PCI was but a gleam in some computer nerd's eye, the ISA bus, then the standard for extension cards, wasn't designed to allow several devices to share interrupts. ISA is no different, and it still sees use today.

Every device had its own interrupt circuit—you don't share your doorbell with your neighbor either. To make matters worse, most of the sixteen IRQs are preassigned to standard components of the PC. So just a handful of IRQs are left over. If you look at the table, you can see that only four IRQs are available in a late-model standard PC.

Standard IRQ Assignments of a PC

IRQ	Device
0	System timer
1	Keyboard
2	IRQ Controller
3	Serial interface COM 2
4	Serial interface COM 1
5	Free
6	Disk drive controller
7	Printer port LPT 1
8	Real-time clock
9	Free
10	Free
11	Free
12	PS/2 mouse interface
13	Numeric coprocessor
14	IDE controller Channel 1
15	IDE controller Channel 2

If these available IRQs are insufficient for your purposes, you can ›free up‹ a couple more by changing some of the assignments shown here. If you don't use an IDE disk at all, you can reassign IRQs 15 and 14, if you use just one IDE disk, you can reassign one of these two IRQs.

If you don't own a PS/2 mouse, IRQ 12 is also at your disposal.

In many cases, you'll need just one of the two serial interfaces, so you may be able to free up IRQ 3, which is normally used for the second interface.

All of these possibilities will of course only work if the corresponding devices are actually deactivated. Otherwise, conflicts will be many and your grief great. These devices are deactivated in the BIOS of the computer. In the section ›BIOS‹ on page 81, you'll find instructions on how to do just that.

Go to the Device Manager to see which IRQs your PC uses and for which purpose they're being used.

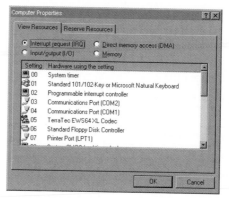

To check out which IRQs are used in your computer, go to the Device Manager and click on the Computer icon at the top of the tree. Windows will then display a by-device list of IRQs.

You may wonder how the board vendor can possibly know which IRQs are available in your computer when Windows doesn't even know which of the sixteen doorbells announces the soundcard, for example. Wonder no more—there are several approaches to configuring IRQs which we'll look at in the following section.

Bus Systems: ISA and PCI

I've belabored the point that a computer mainboard is the site of heavy traffic. Your computer consists of more than just memory and a processor; it is home to many peripheral devices that send data to the memory for the processor can read and process.

These bits and bytes also have to be ›buffered‹ somewhere while the computer turns its attention to other operations. Here I'm not talking about the tiny droplets that you peck in on your computer keyboard—although, strictly speaking, this is a bus system in itself—I'm talking about a deluge of information that washes in waves over the hard disk or soundcard.

There has to be a physical link between these components. These are the data buses, implemented in the form of circuits, on the mainboard of the computer that connects these devices. In addition, there has to be a set of traffic rules at the logical level.

Both participants in data traffic (the processor and the peripheral unit) must know how to interpret incoming electrical changes. They must also know the speed limits—how fast they can ›drive‹ information on this data highway? Beyond that, the right of way has to be determined—who comes first, when does one device have priority over another? Logistical concerns also have to be addressed—how long may a data shipment take? And there has to be a consensus on the format—how many characters may the transmitted computer word (bit depth or word width) have?

The IsA Bus

ISA slots

For the longest time, there was just one authority on all these matters: ISA (Industry Standard Architecture). The brainchild of some guys at IBM who probably make a fair living with a screwdriver, it dictated a speed of 8MHz and that communication took place on 16 data buses, in other words, using 16 bits.

It also cleared up the matters of who comes first and how a device announces itself. In other words, it declared those ever popular interrupts that we looked at previously to be the traffic cops. Incidentally, these IRQs are also dedicated circuits in which a change in voltage tells the processor that someone wants to have a word with it.

You can probably appreciate the disadvantages of such a system: data throughput is limited, configuration is a matter best left to a pro. Nonetheless, this bus gets the job done for pure MIDI interfaces and simple soundcards.

The PCI Bus

Here you see PCI slots. On this computer, the uppermost slot is Slot 1. There are also boards out there where the order is reversed.

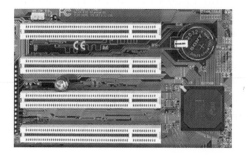

The faster processors became, the more obvious the drawbacks of ISA. With the advent of 32 bits, these became glaring:

◆ too slow,

◆ too narrow—32-bit data had to be broken down into two 16-bits components before it could be sent,

◆ and too inflexible, for every device needed its own interrupt.

Transitional solutions came and went until a new standard by Intel established itself in the Macintosh and Pc camps— Pci, featuring a higher clock speed of 33MHz, 32-bit width, the option of sharing interrupts and in theory, data through-put of 135Mb/sec.

This bus is well-suited to satisfy the professional data throughput requirements of multi-channel cards. This is why you'll find that these cards come almost exclusively in Pci versions.

How Does Pci Work?

To start with, up to four devices can be connected to the pro-cessor or memory via a Pci bus. To this end, there are four interrupt buses called ›Int A‹ to ›Int D.‹ However, these are not immediately available as soon as a Pci Int is used—the card must first be assigned an ›old‹ Isa Irq. This assures compatibility and the operating system knows what's really happening.

The four Pci buses have to be connected to all four Pci slots. When the computer is fired up, every card requests the resources it requires from the Bios, which then dishes these out as it sees fit. If several cards clamor for an interrupt, they can, for example, all be supplied by the Int A bus, which is then assigned to an available Isa Irq by the computer Bios. ›Plug&Play,‹ a standard for automatic configuration which was introduced along with Pci, actually carries out these tasks.

That's how the theory goes. In practice some board manu-facturers have in the past interpreted these specifications rather liberally. For example, in some cases a dedicated Int A bus has been routed to every slot, each of which must then be connected to its own Irq. Sometimes this done by setting jumpers, other boards offer software configuration only. This is why I can't make any universally applicable statements about how a board distributes Pci Ints to Isa Irqs. How the board executes these tasks is not necessarily decisive when you're configuring an audio card that you've installed, but it does explain the different setting options that these boards offer.

State-of-the-art boards largely comply with the official specifications. You can safely assume that there are indeed only four IRQs—namely, A through D—all of which are routed to all four slots.

Newer chipsets also support more than four PCI slots. Since there are only four IRQ buses available, at least two cards will share an IRQ, which, under normal circumstances, shouldn't create any problems.

Perhaps it's starting to dawn on you why problems rarely crop up in computers that are equipped with just a PCI display adapter. Often, these easy-to-please devices don't even require an interrupt. And they don't initiate data transfer— they're simply ›spoon-fed‹ data into their graphics buffer from time to time.

Here problems don't arise until sloppy, inconsistent drivers don't ›feed‹ the devices the way they're supposed to. This little irritation is discussed in detail in the section ›Installing Drivers‹ on page 18.

SCSI controllers, on the other hand, are not only required to report regularly to the processor (a task for which they require an interrupt), they also initiate data transfer, which means they act as a busmaster.

What's the Problem with PCI Cards?

To assure that everything runs smoothly when you fire up your computer, the BIOS must know which ISA IRQs are available in order to assign them to PCI INTs whenever they're required.

If an old ISA board interrupts your system, the BIOS won't know about it because this ill-mannered lodger will fail to announce itself. It won't leave its calling card until it's too late, that is when a conflict occurs. If the computer launches at all, you can at least check in the Windows Device Manager where the problem lies. Incidentally, some boards have a penchant for Isa Irqs 9 to 12 (because they're generally unassigned in a standard Pc). This means that your system may not gripe about if say, an old soundcard is assigned to Irq 5.

Nevertheless, your best bet is to tell the computer Bios about Irqs that are being used by old cards simply by selecting Used by Isa card. Often, depending on the given Bios manufacturer, you'll find this option under the Bios menu item Advanced/Peripheral Settings. The Bios will then know not to assign this Irq.

When resources are scarce, several Pci boards can share interrupt buses. For instance, Irq 11 is then assigned to Int A, and the Scsi controller and soundcard can coexist in harmony. This may work, but there's no guarantee. Just because the Pci can handle the situation doesn't mean that the card itself can deal with it.

An Scsi controller is a greedy little devil and generally wants an Int all to itself. And a soundcard named something like ›Hoontech SoundTrack 128 Pci Ddma,‹ for example, can't share interrupts because the chip used on the board is a native of the ›lost‹ Isa world.

You may also find on occasion that Pci boards will have to be forced to accept a specific interrupt. Ironically, this is the case with Isa Plug&Play cards—they will only run with specific Irqs. When they can't have them (because Pci boards come first during a boot sequence—first come, first served—and have already snagged these Irqs) they tend to pout.

Theoretically, Pci boards are only ›aware‹ of their Ints A through B, and not of the Irqs assigned by the Bios, which means that for most Pci cards, there's no way to configure the card itself.

How Can You Outwit Pci?

In this type of situation, you have to trick the system into doing what you want it do. The approach to doing that varies from board to board.

In many cases, the computer Bios will let you assign the four Pci buses Int A to D explicitly to Isa Irqs. If there is just one card in the system, Int A will generally be used and all you have to do is go to the Bios and set it to the desired Irq.

The first Pci slot is generally the top slot when you're looking at a board that has been installed vertically.

If several cards are on board (display adapters that don't need an Irq don't count), you can generally assume that the card in the first Pci-Slot will use Int A, the second Int B, and so forth. Here too, you can assign the desired Isa Irqs manually.

Some boards operate under the assumption that the Isa Irqs are assigned directly to the Pci slots. Although these cards march to the beat of a different drummer and there'll be no indication of the Ints, don't let this worry you. All you have to do is remember into which slots the different cards are plugged, then assign the desired Irqs in the Bios. Of course, you should first take a look in the Device Manager to be certain that these are really and truly available.

On some boards you can't change the assignments at all. In this case, your only option is to try plugging the card into different slots to see which Irq is assigned to it. This is tedious, but it will work.

Busmastering

Busmastering simply means that the card can initiate a data transfer. The processor gives the card a single memory address to which it then shovels data automatically. This does not burden the processor, meaning that it is free to take care of other business during this time. Most later-model Pci audio boards and Scsi controllers use this approach.

This is good news for the musician and his Pc because the card can convert audio data and load it into memory, where the Scsi controller can pick it up immediately and write it to the hard disk. During these operations, the Cpu can continue to carry out computations required for sequencer playback or feed the performance-hungry plug-ins.

It is necessary to distinguish between ›master‹ and ›slave‹ devices. Master devices can initiate data transfer on their own (busmastering), slaves respond only to write/read requests. Display adapters are typically slaves, Scsi controllers are generally master devices.

Way back when, Scsi devices were the only devices that could do this. This is why older boards had just one busmaster-enabled slot. In most cases this was Slot 1—usually the uppermost slot. If you want to install a busmaster card and own an older board, you should plug it into the first slot to be on the safe side.

There are also boards where the numbering is reversed. If the busmaster card refuses to run at all when inserted in the uppermost slot, you should try out the lowest slot. If you want to install a second busmaster-enabled card (say an ›Event-Layla‹) in addition to the Scsi controller, you'll have to invest in a new mainboard. On the upside, this problem is unlikely to crop up with boards manufactured within the last four years.

If several cards can initiate data transfer on their own, there have to be some rules determining how long one of these operation can go on—otherwise the other devices will never get their turn.

Murphy's Law dictates that the device getting the shaft would of course be the audio card, inevitably leading to drop-outs, crackle, phase shifting between the stereo channels and other equally unwelcome annoyances.

Making the Most of Busmastering

On most boards, you can adjust the value for Busmaster Latency, which is also called Pci Burst Latency. For step-by-step instructions of how this is done, check out the section ›Bios‹ on page 81.

The default on boards equipped with the Award Bios is often 32. This indicates the maximum number of Pci clock cycles that will be granted to a busmaster device at one go. If the card can't manage to get the job done in this time, tough luck, because the transaction will be interrupted. Your audio card will voice its dismay by either grinding its teeth (cracking noises) or sputtering (dropping out for a moment).

In this event, you can begin stepping up this value until you arrive at a point where the problem no longer occurs. Careful though: If you set too high a value, you may hamstring your system because a card will be able to hog the bus for whatever length of time you give it.

The idea here is to strike a balance. Some boards feature an option called Auto where the individual slots are given bus time according to their priority ranking. In this case, you should plug your busmaster audio card into that old standby: Slot 1.

Finally, there are computers where you can assign a different latency for every slot. This option certainly offers the greatest flexibility: You can set a higher value for the audio card and a lower value for the slot that holds the Scsi controller. Hard disk throughput will suffer somewhat, but that's just one of the pitfalls of life in a computer. There's just one bus, therefore there can be only one busmaster.

If the Scsi controller is your only busmaster device, try setting the Pci Latency to 64—you may be able to boost hard disk performance with this little trick.

The Isa bus also had a busmastering facility of sorts. On modern Pci boards, the Isa bus, with a priority well below that of the Pci bus, is the low man on the totem pole.

If you use vintage Isa busmaster Scsi controllers, your system's data throughput will suffer dramatically. In this case, replace the controller with a Pci version; at today's prices, you won't have to hock your family heirlooms to pay for it.

Ordinarily, Pci shouldn't give you tremendous difficulties. For an Ide system, just make sure that you plug the audio card into Slot 1 and the display adapter into Slot 2 (for Agp, your options are even clearer), and everything will be fine. You'll only need to fall back on the preceding tips if, for example, you use several audio cards, an Scsi controller and perhaps an Isa Plug&Play card.

Bios

Although the Bios is the first thing that pops up when you start your computer—it's the bearer of those cryptic tidings that clutter up your screen—I've deliberately refrained from focusing on it up to now. Why? Because in the preceding chapters, you learned a little about the individual components of the mainboard and their configuration options. Now that you know what these are and what their purpose is, I'll show you just how to configure them.

In a modern computer, the actual Bios doesn't do all that much. Bios stands for ›Basic Input Output System,‹ and this is precisely the task it once served.

Here we're talking about a very mundane program much like any other except that this software is not stored on hard disk or diskette, residing instead on a memory chip. Early operating systems such as Ms-Dos used Bios routines to handle data in- and output. For a long time, the hard disk was also addressed via the Bios. These programs are dinosaurs from the Mesozoic era of the Pc world. As you can well imagine, they're slower than frozen molasses. This is largely because they are programmed in 8-bit code.

This outdated stuff can't satisfy the requirements of contemporary hardware or software. Virtually none of the functions of the Bios are used anymore. Operating systems and programs work with their own routines and address hardware directly.

The role of the Bios is now pretty much limited to executing your computer's launch routine. Once you crank up your box, the Bios is torn from its slumber to carry out a couple of routine checks. Among other things, it seeks and identifies memory and any peripheral devices that may be lounging about your computer and makes these available for your processing pleasure.

▶ This is of special significance to Plug&Play configuration of components, which is why we'll take a closer look at it the issue in the up-coming section ›Hardware Installation‹ on page 98.

The Bios loads a precisely defined area of the hard disk into the memory. The operating system lives in this part of the disk and from this point forward, the operating system is solely responsible for carrying out the remainder of the start-up process. The Bios doesn't even need to know about other peripheral devices, even hard disks, that are not immediately involved in launching the system.

The other Bios function is to configure the chipset. The Cpu's assistants often have extensive configuration options, which isn't all that surprising when you consider the diversity of functions that they carry out. Not every Bios lets you have a say in the configuration of all parameters. This can be a huge drawback for a music computer, for example when Pci cards are giving you grief. If the Bios would only let you, you could solve many a problem by tweaking this or that parameter. Therefore, the rule of thumb is the more configuration options, the better. For an office computer, Bios configuration options are immaterial, for the music computer, they can spell the difference between satisfaction and frustration.

Now I'll show you how you can access the setup of the Bios and which options you have once you get there.

Calling the Bios Setup

You may be puzzled when I (or anybody else) talks about going to the Bios and changing its settings to fix a problem—you've probably never seen this rare beast before. Understandably so, for although the Bios is a program, it is burned onto a chip and you won't find it hanging out with the rest of the boys on your hard disk or a diskette. Therefore, you can't call it by clicking on an icon under Windows or launching it as you would any other orthodox program. Indeed there's only a brief moment when you can access the Bios setup—just after you start the computer, before it runs through its start routine.

Some corner of the screen will indicate which key or key combination you need to press to access the Bios. In many cases, this will be the [F2] or [del] key.

Whatever this key may be on your system, once you press it, you should see a screen that looks much like this screenshot:

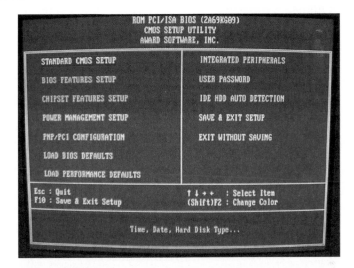

The main menu in the Bios

Don't let it bother you if your screen doesn't look exactly like the one pictured above, almost every computer will display something slightly different. The menu items may also vary, their names will be similar enough so that you can recognize them. With a little practice, you'll be able to locate the items that you need on every computer.

Use the arrow keys of your keyboard to go to individual menu items. To select them, simply press the Enter key of your keyboard.

Don't be alarmed, I'm not going to explain all options in the BIOS—you'd best not mess with most of these anyway. We'll look at what's of interest to us—the meat-and-potato functions, particularly those that are relevant to audio applications.

The BIOS pictured here is by a company called Award. It runs on a board featuring the Intel Bx chipset, an Asus P2B-S. Award supplies its BIOS to other board manufacturers, so chances are that you're looking at something very similar on your computer. Let's take a closer look at the individual menu items.

The standard CMOS setup

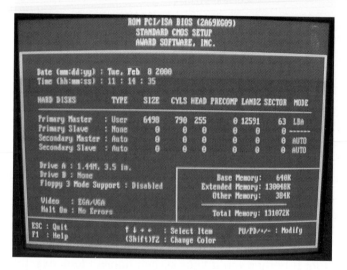

Standard CMOS Setup

Under this heading, you'll find some very basic functions like time and date. In addition, this is where the sizes of the disk drives are entered.

Other than the date and time, you should leave this part of the setup alone because the manufacturer has already taken care of it. (Otherwise your computer wouldn't start.) You'll only need to access this menu again when you want to install another IDE hard disk.

Scsi hard disks are not registered here. The computer's Bios wouldn't recognize these strange varmints anyway, so if you've bought an Scsi system, don't let it rattle you when you don't find the disks registered here.

Bios Features Setup

This menu is more crowded. Here you'll find all the special features that a Bios has to offer. Depending on the type of computer and how much the mainboard manufacturer skimped, it can also be a very lonely place. Virtually all options that you can fiddle with here won't do much to improve performance, but there are nonetheless two worth mentioning.

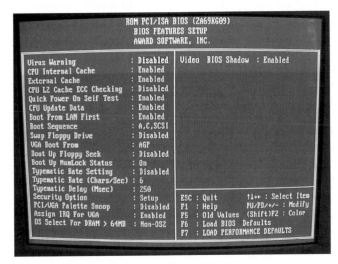

The Bios Feature Setup—not much here that will boost performance.

Boot Sequence

Here's where you can determine the precedence in which the Bios searches for disk drives that are ready to be launched.

In the default setting, the computer first scans a diskette (Disk Drive A) for an operating system, then the first hard disk (Disk Drive C). You can tell that this is so by looking at that the disk drive when you fire up your box—it is addressed first.

If the drive holds a disk that isn't bootable—and this will be the case with most of your diskettes—you'll receive a message telling you as much, for instance, Operating System Not Found. Perhaps you've already been the recipient of such disquieting tidings.

If in future you want to spare yourself the dubious joy of this greeting, simply select Disk Drive C for the menu item Boot Sequence. If however, at some point you want to boot from a diskette—for instance if your hard disk breaks down and you need to install a new one—don't forget to set Boot Sequence so that the computer will boot from Disk Drive A.

This menu item serves another important purpose: If you want to retrofit an Scsi controller and an Scsi disk and make the latter your No. 1 hard disk—perhaps because its blinding speed is such a thrill to behold—you may have to select the option Scsi when you're determining the start sequence. However, this may not be necessary depending on the Scsi controller.

IDE HDD Block Mode Sectors

Now here's an option that can actually accelerate the performance of your IDE hard disk. With it, you can tell the IDE controller of the chipset to transmit blocks to several sectors at the same time instead of just reading and transferring one sector at a time. This works with all standard disks that are currently commercially available. If you still own disks of a Stone Age vintage, you should set the option to Disabled. Otherwise, select HDD Max. This should make the most of what your disk has to offer.

Since a HD recording application will in all likelihood request data from sequential sectors, this option will jack up the performance of a music computer.

Chipset Features Setup

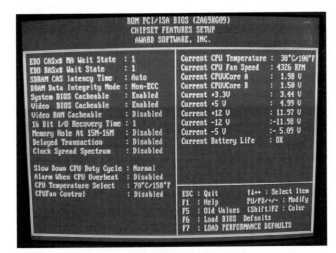

```
              ROM PCI/ISA BIOS (2A69KG09)
                 CHIPSET FEATURES SETUP
                 AWARD SOFTWARE, INC.

EDO CASx# MA Wait State  : 1      Current CPU Temperature  : 38°C/100°F
EDO RASx# Wait State     : 1      Current CPU Fan Speed    : 4326 RPM
SDRAM CAS latency Time    : Auto   Current CPUVCore A       :  1.98 V
DRAM Data Integrity Mode : Non-ECC Current CPUVCore B       :  1.50 V
System BIOS Cacheable    : Enabled  Current +3.3V           :  3.44 V
Video  BIOS Cacheable    : Enabled  Current +5 V            :  4.99 V
Video RAM Cacheable      : Disabled Current +12 V           : 11.97 V
16 Bit I/O Recovery Time : 1        Current -12 V           :-11.98 V
Memory Hole At 15M-16M   : Disabled Current -5 V            :- 5.89 V
Delayed Transaction      : Disabled Current Battery Life    : OK
Clock Spread Spectrum    : Disabled

Slow Down CPU Duty Cycle : Normal
Alarm When CPU Overheat  : Disabled
CPU Temperature Select   : 70°C/158°F
CPUFan Control           : Disabled  ESC : Quit        ↑↓←→ : Select Item
                                     F1  : Help        PU/PD/+/- : Modify
                                     F5  : Old Values  (Shift)F2 : Color
                                     F6  : Load BIOS Defaults
                                     F7  : LOAD PERFORMANCE DEFAULTS
```

Giving you some interesting tuning options, this menu lets you monkey with the features of the chipset.

In the section ›Chipset‹ on page 64, I explained that you can, within certain limits, influence the functions of this key mainboard component. You've probably been waiting with bated breath to find out how. Well, here we go, but proceed with extreme caution here, for you can put your computer into a permanent slumber from which it will never wake. Be warned and beware that I assume no liability for any damages.

Read closely the following paragraphs. If you feel that you don't understand exactly what I'm rambling on about don't change anything, skip this section and put it out of your mind forever. Remember, do the wrong thing here and you could lobotomize your box.

SDRAM Configuration

This is where key parameters for memory addressing are adjusted. A modern memory module usually communicates its specifications via SPD (Serial Presence Detect). Then the chipset will know just how to address the memory. If you are very sure that you own high-quality memory modules, then you can, with a bit of courage and nerves of steel, gradually and in small increments lower the values for the SDRAM parameters CAS Latency, RAS to CAS Delay, RAS Precharge Time and Idle Timer. These values indicate the clock cycles of the external CPU bus (FSB). The lower the value, the faster (i. e. more often) the memory can be addressed. This in turn influences memory performance, which of course is crucial for HD recording and software samplers.

If, however, you set values that are too low, the memory components will no longer be able to keep up with the chipset. This brings on the wrath of the computer gods; they will penalize you severely with punishments ranging from unsystematic crashes to total refusal of the computer to start. The default detection values for SPD are not always correct, but they're too rarely so inaccurate that you would be able to use this tuning option to turn the nag that is your computer into a fine Arabian charger.

▶ If the worst-case scenario does occur and your computer won't start, you should still be able to call up the BIOS. Then you can manually reset the parameter that brought on the disaster to its former value.

Incidentally, this worst-case scenario is not the only thing that can happen. Incorrectly adjusted memory timing can also lead to irregular, inexplicable memory crashes. It's entirely possible that the SPD detection routine reads out too fast a value and the BIOS or the chipset of your memory is addressing the memory too quickly. In this case, it's possible to slow the timing a down a tad by increasing the aforementioned values step by step.

Snoop Ahead

This parameter is used to adjust ›streaming‹ for the PCI bus. Data is sent as a steady stream rather than in separate small packets. The default for this parameter is Enabled, which is just how you should leave it. You should only disable it for trouble-shooting purposes or if a card can't keep up and then only as trial measure.

16 Bit I/O Recovery Time, 8 Bit I/O Recovery Time

These two cryptically-named parameters determine the rate at which old Isa boards are addressed (again in bus cycles). This option is usually set to one Busclock. If you have problems with a very old card (for example, an ancient Mpu interface), you can increase the value step by step. The card is then addressed at greater intervals, i. e. more slowly. At any rate, speed is neither here nor there in terms of the Midi interface's operation, so you can give one of these veteran Isa boards a new lease on life in a new computer by using it for Midi.

Graphics Aperture Size

Agp display adapters can use a part of main memory in order to file data for 3D textures when its own memory or buffer doesn't suffice. With this Bios parameter, you may determine the size of the memory area in which graphics data resides. In my experience, this doesn't have an influence on performance, so I suggest you use the default value.

If you're running short of main memory you can limit the memory allocation here and set the option to the lowest value. However, main memory is only used if an application explicitly asks for it and then only if the display adapter actually supports this function. This is not the case with all Agp boards and the only applications that will do this are DirectX games. You're certainly not going to voluntarily run games next to an audio program so you can generally disregard this parameter.

Video Memory Cache Mode

This parameter is among the most treacherous beasts in the Bios menu, for this is where you switch from Uc (Uncacheable) to Uswc (Uncacheable Speculative Write Combining) and back.

The standard setting is Uc, i. e. uncacheable. This means that graphics data is written directly to the main memory and not maintained in the cache of the processor.

›Write Combining,‹ in turn, means that specific data designated by the Cpu is loaded to an intermediate buffer, where it is collected and then written to the main memory in one big, dump-like operation. This can boost the performance of the display adapter considerably, but the card must be prepared to handle it. If it doesn't support this feature, your monitor will stay as dark as the blackest Stygian pit the next time you launch your system. To add insult to injury, you won't be able to call up the Bios and change this diabolical setting.

If you care to experiment with this parameter, you should have a second display adapter standing by so that, in the event of an emergency, you can install it briefly in order to expunge a setting that went thoroughly wrong. Up-to-date display adapters generally support Uscw, but older ones certainly don't.

Trifling with this parameter is as tempting as it is risky. If you do elect to try it out, beg, borrow or steal a state-of-the-art display adapter as a backup beforehand. You'll know immediately whether or not the operation was successful—if the computer starts and messages appear on the screen, heave a sigh of relief and thank your lucky stars.

The enhanced graphics performance affects audio applications too. In the section ›Windows‹ on page 145, you'll learn a bit more about the connection between graphics and sound.

Parallel Port Mode

The printer port on your Pc (Lpt 1) can be operated in different modes. Although this has nothing to do with the performance of your computer, it can be helpful if you're using music software that is protected by a ›dongle.‹ This oddly-named little gadget plugs into the parallel port to provide copy protection for software.

Sometimes software has trouble recognizing its dongle. In this case, simply run through all the modes that you find under this option. Depending on your computer' vintage, these may vary wildly. The option that will generally give you the least hassle is Standard (or Compatible) mode. On the downside, a state-of-the-art printer connected behind the dongle may voice its protest.

▶ If you can't resolve the conflict at all, buy a simple printer port in the form of a plug-in card. It will cost you the equivalent of a good meal and a couple of brews, but it's worth it to solve a pesky dongle problem.

Onboard Pci/Ide

Modern Ide controllers feature two channels to each of which you can connect two devices (hard disks or Cd-Rom drives). If you only have two devices, you can connect these to just one channel and free up a valuable Irq for other purposes. You must choose the option Primary to deactivate the second Ide channel. Some mainboards won't use the newly available Irq 15. Your best bet is to try it out.

▶ You can take this a step further if you own an Scsi system, which means that you need neither of the two Ide channels. Set the parameter to None in the Bios menu. Now you should have both Irqs 14 and 15 available for other devices.

Ide Ultra Dma Mode

In the chapter ›The Hard Disk‹ starting on page 109, we'll take a closer look at Dma mode. At this point we'll check to see if your controller supports Ultra Dma access. Older hard disks don't like this fast transfer mode at all and you can switch it off here if need be.

The default is usually Auto, which assures that the mainboard activates Dma as soon as it finds this breed of hard disk. If your hard disk is less than a year old, you can pretty much bet that it supports Ultra DMA. This significantly boosts hard disk performance, which is essential to HD recording and software samplers, so definitely enable this parameter.

IDE 0/1/Master/Slave PIO/DMA Mode

Next to busmaster DMA modes, IDE hard disks distinguish between different PIO modes. In the chapter ›The Hard Disk‹ you'll find more background info on this option. In a nutshell, it has to do with the maximum throughput and thus speed of your system.

Here too, the default is Auto, which means that disk specifications are normally detected automatically. However, from time to time a case of mistaken identity can crop up, particularly with newer disks. This is why you can select the mode manually for each of the disks. When in doubt, try out the individual modes step by step.

Power Management Setup

As laudable as it may be that modern computers will throttle their power to conserve energy when the computer is idling, for a music computer this can spell disaster. One of the measures that this power management facility likes to use to conserve energy is to switch off the hard disk. I recommend that you deactivate the very first entry in this menu—generally called Power Management—by selecting Disabled. However, there are two minor problems associated with this that you should be aware of:

In the Device Manager, a yellow exclamation mark may pop up next to Device Advanced Power Management. Feel free to ignore it.

Some computers won't shut off automatically when Windows is powered down. In my view, this not a tragedy of epic proportions since all you have to do is press a button to switch your box off. Some people, however, feel that this constitutes a dramatic downturn in the quality of their lives. If you absolutely must have your computer shut down automatically after you've sent Windows back to the virtual hell it came from, then you must enable Power Management. Do set all other options in this menu to Disabled or Off. In all probability, the exclamation mark in the Device Manager will also disappear.

Pnp and Pci Setup

This section of the Bios is relevant when you want to install a Pci card and are running into the problems that I addressed in the section ›The Pci Bus‹ on page 74. Typical nuisances here are ego-related—cards that don't want to share Irqs even though they've been told to as well as situations in which everyone wants to be the busmaster.

Lamentably, not every Bios offers the kind of extensive configuration options that the Asus mainboard presented here does. In these cases, you'll have to take the more work-manlike approach of plugging the card into other slots and ›groping‹ your way toward the best configuration.

If you're dealing with a mainboard that is up to snuff, you'll enjoy the following options:

Pnp Os Installed

You'll read more on the topic of ›Plug&Play‹ in ›Hardware In-stallation‹ on page 98. For the time being, suffice it to say that the Bios is responsible for detecting hardware automati-cally and assigning the notorious Irqs. It is, however, possi-ble to reallocate these resources. At the moment, the Osr 2.1 version of Windows 95, Windows 98, and Windows 2000 have mastered this little trick.

When in the Bios the option Pnp Os Installed is set to No, the functionality that reallocates resources is disabled. How-ever, you won't notice that this is the case in normal opera-tion. You'll find further information on this in the section ›Irq Steering and Plug&Play under Windows‹ on page 183.

Slot 1/2/3/4 IRQ

Here you can assign each PCI slot its own ISA IRQ. As discussed at length in the section ›The PCI Bus‹ (page 74), IRQ sharing can cause all kinds of headaches. If your computer's IRQ handling allows it, you may assign a dedicated IRQ to every slot. You may also assign an interrupt several times, for instance to cards for which you know there is no conflict.

For example, if you've limited the IDE controller to one channel in Chipset Features Setup, you can then assign the now free IRQ 15 to the slot that holds your audio card.

However, be aware that on most mainboards the slot of the AGP card gets the same IRQ as does the first PCI slot. If you plug a card into this PCI slot and at the same time use an AGP card, these two will always share the same IRQ. In this case, you can merely determine which IRQ this will be. As you may have already deduced, this means that you should never plug a card that is completely incapable of IRQ sharing into this slot.

PCI Latency Timer

This parameter crops up in several guises. Normally, this is where you'll determine the amount of time (in PCI bus cycles) that elapses between PCI accesses, in other words, how long the system will twiddle its virtual thumbs between completing one operation and starting the next. This option is a concession to old ISA boards, which panting and heaving, hang onto the PCI bus for dear life and need a rest between wind sprints.

Higher values spell poorer performance but possibly improved stability. If your box frequently drops out, hiccups like it has Windows stuck in its throat, or often sounds like it ate a platter of bean burritos when you're running audio applications and an ISA soundcard, then cautiously up this value in increments of five until the problems go away. Note that this may perceptibly diminish your computer's data throughput to other peripheral gear such as the hard disk.

Pci Burst Timer

With this menu item, you can set (also in Pci bus cycles) the maximum amount of time that a Pci busmaster device gets to hog the bus. Higher values result in better throughput during actual data transmission.

If you own more than one busmaster-capable card, say an Scsi controller and a Pci audio card, a compromise is in order. The reason for this is that the longer a device is allowed to engage the bus, the less time the bus will be available to the other devices. Therefore, I recommend that here too you take a step-by-step approach to finding the best setting and up this value gradually.

IRQ xx used by Isa

In ›Hardware Installation‹ on page 98, you'll learn that it can become necessary to exempt specific Irqs from the Plug & Play free allocation routine. You can do just that in this part of the menu when you choose the option Yes for the given Irq.

Usb Irq

If you want to use Usb, say to connect a Midi interface, you must select Enabled here. Under normal circumstances, this Irq may also be shared with a Pci board. If you don't require Usb, select Disabled to free up an Irq. A question mark may then appear in the Windows Device Manager next to Usb Device—just ignore it.

Vga Bios (Pci/Agp)

If you use both an Agp and a Pci board so that you can work with several monitors, here's where you determine which card is considered the primary adapter. Bios messages are sent to this card during system start-up and Windows also relies on this priority ranking. For further information on this riveting topic, check out the chapter ›The Display Adapter‹ on page 205.

Updating the Bios

Although it resides in a Flash-Rom, the Bios is really just another piece of software, so you can replace it with another version. This Bios update overwrites the content of the Flash-Rom with the new Bios routines. You should consider this option a last resort when all of my other brilliant tips have inexplicably failed and you're sure you can rule out all other causes for whatever the problem may be.

Also, be sure to check out the website of the mainboard manufacturer to find out whether or not the update will solve your problem. If it won't, leave well enough alone. A Bios update isn't something you should do simply to keep your system up to date.

If after careful consideration you find that an update is in order, proceed with extreme caution. Download the update from the website of the manufacturer, but be sure that you're importing the right file for your mainboard. Once you've made sure that it is the update you're after, double-check it. Then check it again. I can't stress enough the importance of being confident about what you're doing: If you load the wrong file, I guarantee that your computer won't start again, and it will take the costly services of a professional to fix the damage.

Updating itself is pretty straightforward—all you need is a boot disk that contains the Bios file and the right file for updating the Flash-Rom.

To install the version that you've just downloaded, you'll require a little utility that the maker supplies with the Bios. It should ship with every mainboard or all-in-one computer package. If you seem to have misplaced it, the dog ate it, or your significant other abused the diskette as a coaster, you're sure to find this tool at the website of the manufacturer. It too must match the board and the Bios version. Use only the tool that was designed specifically for your model, make and version of mainboard.

1   Right-click your diskette in My Computer and select Format.

2   In the next window that pops up, enable Full and Copy System Files.

3   Insert a blank diskette and click on Start.

4   Then copy the BIOS and utility to the diskette inserted into the disk drive.

Please remember the exact name of the flash utility; write it down if you must. Restart the computer. The Pc should now launch from the diskette.

5   If any mysterious messages crop up that ask you for the time and date, simply confirm by pressing the Enter key.

6   Then enter precisely the name of the program for updating the BIOS.

After this the program will indicate a BIOS file for you to selection. In all probability, this will be precisely the file that you first stored on the diskette in the previous step.

7   Follow the program's prompts and the update should get underway.

The new BIOS is ready to roll as soon as you reboot the computer. However, please bear in mind that all options are set to default values. Alas, you'll have to repeat all of those painstaking tuning efforts described the previous chapters.

If you feel anything less than utterly confident about this kind of tinkering, it's better to err on the side of caution. Ask an experienced buddy who knows the ropes. Should the BIOS update go awry, nothing but professional help is going to salvage your computer. If Lady Luck smiles on you and your Flash-ROM chip—which houses the BIOS—is not soldered but socketed, you'll be able to remove it, take it to an reputable electronics dealer and have him re-burn it. If not, you're out of luck.

Don't take leave of your senses and switch the computer off during this flash process. Also, refrain from all further actions (on the computer that is—you may breathe and move around a little) until the program tells you the operation was completed successfully.

Hardware Installation

Here we'll investigate three card installation processes:

Isa Cards without Plug&Play

Here we're talking about ancient Isa cards, soundcards and old Midi interfaces that were brought to market at time when Plug&Play hadn't been invented and Irqs had to be assigned manually.

If for whatever reason you're compelled to use this type of card, proceed as follows:

1 Check in the Device Manager (cf. ›Windows Quickstart‹ on page 15) to see which Irq is still available in your computer. To this end, double-click on the Computer icon.

A list will appear indicating which Irqs have been assigned for which purpose. If an Irq isn't listed here, it's available.

2 Find out if you have to set a jumper on the card to assign the Irq. (A jumper is a little U-plug that is placed on two pins to connect them. You should find this information in the literature that shipped with the card in the unlikely event that you still have this document. Otherwise, check the motherboard to see if there are any clues printed on it. If you see any post couplers jutting out anywhere and any mention of an Irq next to it, you've just struck pay dirt.)

3 Set the jumper so that the card is assigned the Irq that you selected a little while ago in the Device Manager.

Some cards are configured by means of a software driver rather than by jumpers. You'll find this information in the manual that came with the card.

4 Install the card by plugging it into a free Isa slot.

5 Start the computer and call the Bios setup (see the section ›Bios‹ on page 81).

6 Choose manual configuration in the Pci and Plug&Play configuration menu.

7 When a list will appears, enable Used by Isa for the Irq that you assigned on the card by means of the jumper. This configuration option may have a different designation depending on the given board.

8 Start the computer again. Windows won't recognize an ancient card without Plug&Play, so not much of anything will happen.

9 Now install the driver. Make sure that you employ the latest driver. Your best bet is to download the most recent version from the website of the manufacturer.

During installation, you my be asked which IRQ the card uses.

10 Indicate the IRQ that you jumpered in Step 2. If the card is configured by a software routine, this is the time to do it. Then indicate the IRQ that you identified in the Windows Device Manager in Step 1.

Now your card should run. Step 7 is particularly important to assure that Plug&Play cards run flawlessly.

▶ An old card won't acknowledge when the BIOS runs a Plug&Play query. This means that when you launch the computer, another card may be assigned the IRQ that your relic from another era habitually uses. Therefore, it's especially important to tell your computer to leave this IRQ alone. This is why you have to go to the BIOS and let it know that the IRQ is already in use.

ISA Cards with Plug&Play

Although it was originally designed to make life easier, this technology has always been derided as ›plug and pray.‹ It is supposed to do the following without your intervention:

◆ When the computer is launched, the BIOS' Plug&Play extensions query all cards.

◆ A Plug&Play card (ISA or PCI) will then acknowledge and tell the BIOS its resource requirements: the IRQs it intends to use and the amount of memory it needs.

◆ The BIOS then allocates its resources among the cards. Sadly each card won't necessarily get everything it asked for.

◆ Now the card knows which IRQ and which memory area it may use. The BIOS tells the operating system which resources were assigned to which cards. Everyone's in the know and theoretically, everything should work.

In my experience the Plug&Play mechanism works very well with Pci cards of any kind. Unfortunately, with Isa Plug&Play cards it's head-or-tails—half of the time it will work and the other half, it won't. The problem is that cards are often finicky—they can't handle it when the Bios assigns values other than those they ›desire.‹ In this case, the cards will insist on Irqs that the Bios has already assigned to other cards—danger lurks.

Configuring a Plug & Play Card Manually

Fortunately, you can also configure most of these cards manually. The procedure is much the same as the procedure for installing Isa cards without Plug&Play described in the previous chapter. Instead of setting a jumper, in most cases you'll have to configure the card by means of a software utility. Here's how:

1 Check in the Device Manager (cf. ›Windows Quickstart‹ on page 15) to see which Irq is still available in your computer. To this end, double-click on the Computer icon

A list will appear indicating which Irqs have been assigned for which purpose. If an Irq isn't listed here, it's available.

2 Install the card by plugging it into a free Isa slot.

Now you have to tell the card which Irqs it should use. For this purpose, you'll hopefully find a utility on the Cd or diskette supplied by the card vendor.

Copy this program to a folder and be sure to give the folder a name that you'll have no trouble remembering:

3 Click on the My Computer icon.

4 Double-click the icon for Disk Drive C.

5 In the view that appears next, right-click once (and only once) and select New ⇨ Folder in the menu. Create a folder and name it something like Tool.

The program that we're dealing with here will surely be a Dos program, which of course won't run under Windows. Therefore, you must restart your computer in the right mode:

6 Click on Start/Shutdown and Restart in Ms-Dos Mode in the view that appears next.

You'll now see a dark screen with a flashing cursor in the lowest line, in front of which is displayed a hieroglyphic that looks like this:

    c:\>

7 This is called an Ms-Dos prompt—enter the following:

    cd tool

8 Press the Enter key.

Now the Dos prompt should look like this:

    c:\tool>

9 Type in the name of the program and press the Enter key.

I can't tell you exactly what happens next because this depends on the program that ships with your soundcard, but you should find some option for assigning IRQs. The soundcard's manual should give you at least a brief explanation of the available options.

10 Always assign the IRQ that you identified in Step 1.

11 Start the computer and call the Bios set-up (see the section ›Bios‹ on page 81).

12 Opt for manual configuration in the Pci and Plug&Play configuration menu.

13 When a list appears, enable Used by Isa for the IRQ that you assigned for the card.

▶ This configuration option may have a different name depending on the given Bios.

14 Restart the computer.

Windows will now recognize a card featuring Plug&Play. A window will appear asking you about the drivers for the hardware that the system has just detected. The following steps are identical to the driver reinstallation procedure described in the section ›Windows Quickstart‹ on page 15.

Pci Cards with Plug&Play

This one's a cinch. Normally, it'll take just three steps:

1   Choose a free Pci slot and install the card.

2   Start the computer and insert the driver Cd or diskette that the manufacturer supplied.

3   Windows will now detect the new hardware and ask you for the drivers. The rest of the procedure is identical to the method used to install drivers as described in the section ›Windows Quickstart‹ on page 15.

One of the reason why Pci cards won't give you much grief is that they can share an interrupt. When an Irq is initiated, all drivers of the cards that use this Irq are addressed in sequence. One of these drivers of course will be the one for which the interrupt is intended. It recognizes that it has been called to handle a specific chore and will then take care of it.

This is what you'll see in the Device Manager when several cards share an Irq.

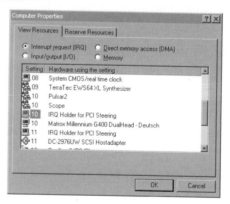

▶ Here's the rule of thumb for a stress-free system: Always use Pci cards. Bear this in mind when you're ready to go shopping.

There is of course a hitch—I can't promise that you'll never encounter any problems here. Be sure to read the section ›Bus Systems: Isa and Pci‹ on page 72 because not all Pci cards will perform as intended.

If a Pci card gives you hassles, for example if it becomes rudely flatulent during recording or playback or if Windows freezes up after you've installed the driver of the card, then try the following steps in sequence to trouble-shoot the problem:

1 Got to the home page of the manufacturer on the Internet and search for newer drivers for your card.

2 Install the card into another Pci slot.

3 Check the Device Manager to see which Irq the card uses. While you're at it, check that there Irqs available.

4 If the card shares an Irq with another device, then go to the Bios and set the slot that holds the card to the free Irq that you pinpointed in the previous step. For more info, refer to the section ›Bios‹ on page 81.

5 Your mainboard may assign busmaster priorities according to the numbers of the Pci slots. In this case, install the card with the highest priority (normally your audio card) into Slot 1. All other cards, Scsi controllers and the display adapter should then be installed to Slots 2 to 4—the display adapter goes in the last slot.

6 You may be able to achieve something similar by experimenting with different settings for the Bios parameter Pci Burst Latency. Unfortunately, not all boards offer this parameter.

7 An up-to-date audio card will definitely be a busmaster device. If you own an old board with just one busmaster-enabled slot (typically the first one), install the card into this slot.

UsB

The ›Universal Serial Bus‹—UsB for short—is a serial interface used to connect external peripheral devices to the computer. You may have wondered what that odd port located near the keyboard and mouse ports is good for. This is the UsB connector.

As its name would indicate, the UsB is another bus system. It was originally intended as a uniform standard, putting an end to the awful rat's nest of cables cluttering the area behind almost every computer.

Up to 127 UsB devices can be connected and the maximum data transfer rate is 12Mbit/sec. This means that it can move some 1.5MB of data per second which is sufficient for simple audio interfaces as well as MIDI. UsB was also intended to accommodate keyboard and mouse. The idea is that all devices be addressable by the one interrupt of the UsB controller on the mainboard thus freeing up a number of valuable IRQS.

In the real world UsB hasn't caught on. Although for years Pc mainboards have shipped with UsB chips and newer boards even feature the corresponding port, the peripheral devices that support this bus are few and far between.

Emagic offers two UsB MIDI interfaces, ›Unitor8‹ and ›AMT8,‹ but, only for Macintosh. Roland makes a UsB sound-card called ›Audio Canvas,‹ but it is fairly rare and its advantages over conventional solutions are few.

The good news is that on the other leading music application platform—Apple Macintosh—UsB has become standard. This breed of box no longer supports old solutions, so we can expect a greater number of UsB MIDI interfaces in the future.

To get the UsB to work, you must first activate the corresponding option in the BIOS (see the section ›BIOS‹ on page 81). In addition, you need an operating system that supports UsB. Windows versions OsR 2.1 and higher do so, but anything lower will give you headaches. (There is a patch available for earlier versions of Windows available on Microsoft's web site: http://www.microsoft.com/)

Just because a vendor promises that the mainboard is UsB-enabled doesn't mean that it will actually work. The ugly truth is that unless your board features Bx chipsets, it is unlikely that you'll be able to use the UsB port.

▶ A new specification was drafted a while back for Usb, which is with faultless logic called Usb 2. It is designed to deliver data transfer rates of up to 480MBit/sec. However, this standard has yet to be implemented by any manufacturer. It will definitely take some time for Usb 2 to see widespread use.

Firewire

Whereas Pci and Ide are bus systems designed exclusively for connecting internal components, Usb is an attempt to connect external devices. However, its bandwidth is too puny to seriously consider using it to connect multi-I/O audio devices to the computer, not to mention external hard disks.

External hard disks is not just something found in professional Dp and server applications. Modern hard disks are noisy enough that it is often desirable to locate them in another room. Because of its limited cable length, Scsi won't do for this application (for more on this, see the chapter ›The Hard Disk‹ starting on page 109), but Firewire will.

A few years back, Apple masterminded ›Firewire‹ (or Ieee 1394, as it is officially called)—a serial communication protocol. Firewire is designed to accommodate up to 63 devices. The maximum cable length is a whopping 72 meters (230 feet) and more yardage is possible with special cables.

Firewire offers three bandwidths or speeds—at its fastest, it can deliver up to 400Mbit/sec, which is approximately 50Mb/sec. The actual communication protocol is remarkably similar to what you would come up with if you combined the network protocols Ethernet and Tcp/Ip (Transmission Control Protocol/Internet Protocol). Here too, there are several layers in which communication can be executed.

As good as all this sounds, Firewire never really caught on. Part of the problem is the licensing—Apple is unwilling to simply give its innovation away. In fact, today Ieee 1394 sees widespread use in just a single application—for connecting digital cameras.

▶ Yamaha has announced its intentions to develop a technology based
on Firewire called ›mLAN.‹ In theory it will let us route MIDI and audio
over the same circuit and thus conveniently handle mixers, synthesizers and samplers on the computer. Unfortunately, this technology
has yet to find its way from the drawing boards of engineers to
dealers' showrooms. You'll find further information on this at http://
www.yamaha.co.jp/tech/1394mLAN/

What Should You Watch for When Buying a Mainboard?

I can't stress enough the importance of good hardware to the
stability of a computer. The mainboard plays a particularly
pivotal role. Although no-name boards often deliver poorer
performance, the differences between boards are no dramatic and performance is not the decisive criterion. More often than not, mysterious crashes are brought on by the PCI
bus, the graphics interface, or occasionally, by some problem
with the memory interface.

The bargain-basement mainboards that you'll find offered
at unbelievably cheap prices at your local discounter's or
even the supermarket are hardly suitable for music computers. For one thing, they are often equipped with onboard
sound and graphics. These are generally implemented either
by means of hard-wired chips or by the chipset of the CPU.

If graphics and sound are implemented with hard-wired
chips, you usually can't deactivate the onboard components
completely. Although you may find a corresponding option in
the BIOS menu, the hardware will simply refuse to free up the
IRQ. If graphics and sound are integrated in the chipset,
you'll find that the data transfer rate of the chipset is perceptibly limited. With a normal office computer, this is not a
huge obstacle—you'll eventually hear sound piped through
your speakers and see images on your monitor.

In a music computer—as we saw in the first chapter of this
book—all components of the system are being pushed hard

all the time. If the bus that addresses the memory is short of bandwidth, your software sampler will throw in the towel after you've activated just a few voices. Similarly, plug-ins of the Hd recording system will have your computer begging for mercy before you can get any serious work done.

A separate Pci controller requires an Irq too and a Pci bridge always serves as the interface, which in essence, is the same principle as a solution with a Pci card. The on-board Scsi controller does have an economic drawback: if you swap boards, the Scsi controller ends up in the bin along with your old board. If you are compelled to keep your system at the cutting edge of technology, this type of board will eventually put a dent in your budget.

In my experience, the motherboards made by the companies Asus and Gigabyte are worthy of high praise. The Asus ›P2B‹ and its successor model ›P3B‹ have proven quite effective and will serve as a solid underpinning for an audio system. Several versions featuring different options such as an integrated Scsi controller or integrated network card are available.

Of Gigabyte's offerings, I'd recommended the ›686-Bxs‹ and ›Bxe‹ mainboards. These boards use the Intel Bx chipset and support the PII/III class of processors. Beyond that, the Bios features live up to the standards discussed in the section ›Bios‹ (page 80).

To be fair, all vendors' flagship boards that are equipped with the Intel Bx chipset are luxury liners. If you opt for another manufacturer's Bx boards, you shouldn't have any problems. On all Bx mainboards, the Irqs may also be assigned freely to the Pci slots, which can be a key criterion for a music computer.

It would be a bit rash to recommend a board just for the Amd Athlon processor. Although Gigabyte and Asus offer boards, the Gigabyte board seems to be the company's red-haired stepchild—it gets shortchanged in terms of updates and support. On the Asus board, the chipset contains a component made by Vɪᴀ which can cause problems in conjunction with Event audio cards ›Event Gina,‹ ›Darla,‹ and ›Layla.‹

The only board I know of that definitely doesn't cause problems is the ›Biostar M7Mᴋᴀ.‹ On the downside, the Bɪᴏs of this board is the product of a minimalist mindset—it features few of the options that you would expect from a decent system. For example, you can't assign fixed Iʀǫ assignments for the Pcɪ slots and you can't adjust Pcɪ Burst Latency. In view of these shortcomings, there's no guarantee that this board will work with future cards.

▶ Since the pace of development is mind-boggling in the dog-eat-dog market for computer components, these boards may have vanished from the face of the earth by the time you read this book.

5 The Hard Disk

How Does a Hard Disk Work?

To understand the workings of a hard drive, you must distinguish what it does from what the computer (mainboard, controllers and operating system) does to it.

Layout of a Hard Disk

A hard disk consists of one or several magnetic metal disks (hence the name). Normally, these have a diameter of 3.5 inches and rotate at an invariable speed (in most cases, 5,400 or 7,200 revolutions per minute). Between the disks are magnetic heads which write data to these disks by magnetizing a tiny section of their surface. During a read operation, the opposite happens, the head registers data that resides in this magnetized area. This description of a hard disk's physical structure (the magnetized and non-magnetized areas) is quite an over-simplification—this is a highly complex piece of gear.

This is what a hard disk looks like on the inside.

Some parts of the hard disk have been around for a long time—heads, cylinders, tracks and sectors. The picture illustrates what these terms describe—specific areas of the disk.

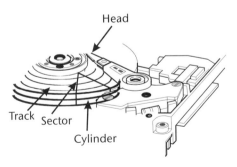

Head

Track Sector

Cylinder

Diagram of the hard disk's internal workings

Hard disks and their physical structure in the Pc have always been a rather involved topic—starting with the very first controller that IBM bought from Western Digital back in 1980 for the debut Pc. The sizes of the cylinders and tracks are dictated by the physical structure of the disk. This controller is restricted by an upper limit for the size each. At that time, it could address a maximum disk size of 512MB. Since the biggest disks available were typically 10 or 20MB, no one had reason to believe that 512MB would ever be insufficient.

By the early 90's disk drive technology had eclipsed this boundary and the physical format of the disk was augmented by logical sectors, cylinders and heads. Although the terms were the same, what they represented had nothing do with the actual layout or format of the disk. In order for operating systems such as Ms-Dos, Windows 3.11 and the first version of Windows 95 to deal with these new logical formats, they had to be translated by disk management software from outside firms such as Ontrack. Later on, the Bios was brought up to date with extensions that could detect and convert these logical formats.

Disparate Bios versions, software revisions and operating system limitations created all kinds of restrictions which limited hard disk utilization, often making part of the hard disk's storage space totally inaccessible. Fortunately, this nightmarishly complicated situation has been considerably simplified.

The latest Windows 95 versions (Osr 2.1 and 2.5) as well as Windows 98 and Windows Nt/2000 circumvent the Bios and address the hard disk directly. This has rendered the physics of the disk meaningless. For these operating systems, a hard disk is just a big collection of sectors. They could care less where these sectors are located and don't have to worry about finding them—that's the job of the disk's electronic components. The programs that are used to format disks run under Windows. Generally, these will recognize every new and older disk and deal with them accordingly.

You're unlikely to run into any problems here unless you're dealing with a totally stripped-down computer with a single hard disk. If your disk needs reformatting and you're using a version of partition software that doesn't recognize your particular hard disk, you're in trouble. You'll find some tips below for handling this unlikely situation.

Data Transfer Rate

Hard disk performance is crucial to your audio Pc. Two specs are decisive—data transfer rate and access time. If you take close look at the diagram of the hard disk, you'll probably recognize which factors determine these values.

For the data transfer rate, the disk rotational speed—how fast the disk revolves—is important, as is data density—how much data can be written magnetically onto the metal disk.

Manufacturers have made huge increases data density over the past two years, with improvements coming almost by the week. Accordingly, disks have became larger and faster. The average hard disk today offers mighty 12 to 16Gb of storage space.

In order to cram more data into the same amount of space, manufacturers work with different densities in different zones of the metal disk (Zone Bit Recording). State-of-the-art devices offer greater density in the outer zones, which makes these zones considerably faster.

Disk rotation speeds haven't improved as dramatically. Mid-class disks tun at 5,400rpm., faster disks at 7,200rpm. Only high-performance server disks achieve rotational speeds of up to 10,000rpm and these disks are so noisy that you can't use them in a studio computer.

When you look at data throughput specs, often you'll find that different values are quoted for one and the same disk. Many benchmark utilities don't measure the actual throughput, instead they read and write the same, generally very small file. Since hard disks also have a small cache, the value that these programs report is actually a measure of the cache and/or disk protocol. In many cases these values will be right up there with the theoretical peak value—the best that the disk can do when all stars are in proper alignment and the computer gods are in a benevolent mood.

The disk is not the only component to have a cache. Windows also reserves a cache in the main memory for its disk-related activities. This also corrupts the results somewhat when hard disk throughput is measured under Windows. The most accurate way to gauge performance is in Ms-Dos mode. The program cthdbench offered by the magazine *c't* does just that and has become the standard for this purpose. You'll find it on the Cd in the Tools folder.

The data transfer rate is not necessarily invariable. It depends on whether data can be read serially in one big go or if it is scattered all over the disk's surface. In the latter case, the heads have to be constantly repositioned, which slows data transfer down.

On disks that feature zone bit recording, throughput decreases as the heads move closer to the center. Therefore it is the average and not the peak transfer rate that will give you reliable specs on performance. Even this mean value is now more than 10Mb/sec, while the fastest disks may achieve 15Mb/sec or more. Since it takes 176Kbit/sec to play back or record a stereo file in 16bit, 44.1kHz format (the Cd standard), the faster disks will easily give you a whopping 64 audio tracks, maybe even more.

As impressive as these specs are, in reality there are obstacles that will slow your box down. First of all, the heads won't be able to read all the data in one go, they will often have to rove the disk in search of data. Secondly, data must routed into the memory of the computer by some type of bus. And from there, it has to be simultaneously fed to the audio hardware. All this takes time and of course limits the number of tracks.

The audio engine of the program that you're running also has an influence. If you own a computer that performs at least as well as a PII 350, you can figure on 30 to 40 tracks, far fewer if you use plug-ins liberally or use soundcards that read samples from the main memory of the computer.

Access Time

The other speed-related criterion for a disk is access time. This is not the amount of time it takes for you to secure a date with that gorgeous blonde in the marketing department—it is that blink of an eye between the moment a read command is sent out and the moment this data is delivered.

There are two different methods used to gauge this performance. As before, peak values sound good but are meaningless; the average access time is what we're interested in. Both the stepping motors that move the heads and the surface of the disk are factors here. The larger the surface area, the greater the distance a head may have to travel to find data. This slows the disk down.

▶ Low-cost computers are often equipped with a ›Quantum Bigfoot‹ drive, which uses 5.25-inch disks. This spells sluggish access, so give Bigfoot the boot.

The average access time of normal disks is around 10msec. Seek time can be as slow as 15msec. When you're shopping for a disk, this spec may or may not be important to you. If you work with long audio files, access time plays a subordinate role. If you work with just a few small files, you also won't have to give it special consideration because this data will often reside in the main memory of the computer. If, on the other hand, you work with very many small files, access time is crucial. Particularly if you're one of those, shall we say, ›untidy‹ types who rarely cleans house and defragments the disk. If this is you, buy a disk with the fastest possible access time.

The IDE Protocol

In the preceding section, one of life's great mysteries was revealed—how a hard disk actually works and which factors are important for studio applications.

Now we'll take a look at an equally thrilling topic—how the processor addresses a disk. After all, there must be some way to tell the read/write heads of the disk where to go and what to do once they get there. Of course standards have been achieved through consensus between hardware and software vendors.

Today, there are two standards that rule the Pc world—IDE and Scsi. In official computerese, these are called protocols. They stipulate both the physical (number of data buses, speed, data security measures) and logical (how the transferred information is interpreted) traits of data transport.

The Scsi communication protocol has been around longer and is not limited to hard disks, but IDE sees more widespread use. Indeed, every Pc built in the past 15 years or so supports IDE disks. For this reason, we'll look at IDE first.

You now know what happens in mechanical terms when a disk reads and writes data. Once the disk's electronic components have made data available, it must be transported using some protocol to a ›host controller‹ on the mainboard. From there it is sent to the main memory. These are two separate processing steps and can be executed quite differently.

Nowadays, the host controller (which no longer needs to know the physical topography of the disk) is responsible solely for transferring data supplied by the disk. A modern IDE controller features two channels to each of which you can connect two devices. The range of gear that you can hook up is limited to hard disks, removable disks, Cd-Rom drives and burners—IDE does not support other devices.

On your mainboard, you'll find two connectors that are designed to take the ribbon cables of hard disks. On each channel, one device serves as the master, the other as the slave.

These are definitions that date back to the humble beginnings of IDE. In terms of performance, it's irrelevant which device is the master and which the slave.

Contemporary boards will even boot from any connected disks and CD drives so that this configuration has no bearing on system start-up. The only thing you have to watch for is that only one master and one slave is defined for each channel. As you may have suspected, you can assign these roles by means of jumpers on the disk.

Next to the master and slave, you'll also find an option on most disks that goes by the name of Cs—Cable Select. When it is enabled, the position of the device along the cable determines its role.

▶ If you're having trouble getting your computer to recognize your new hard disk, then jumper it to Cs. This has helped me out of a bind many times.

PIO

Since the introduction of EIDE (Enhanced IDE) back in 1995, different modes for transferring data using IDE have been in use. The most common modes, which older hard disks should be able to handle, are called PIO (Programmed In Out) modes. And as the name suggests, here data input and output is programmed.

Unsatisfactory as that explanation may be, you really only need to know that the computer's CPU does the programming. The greater the disk's workload, the harder the CPU has to work. With PIO, you'll never achieve the kind of performance and track count that will make you the envy of your music-making friends. In the fastest mode (PIO 4), the peak data transfer rate is nominally 16.6MB/sec, but you'll never see this kind of speed in the real world.

Ultra DMA/Busmastering

In order to reduce the Cpu's workload, Busmaster DMA was introduced two years ago. Here the IDE controller is empowered to read and write data in main memory independently by PCI. This of course lightens the load on the Cpu.

The speed of hard disks has increased dramatically. Pio modes were unable to keep up and the new transfer standards Ultra DMA/33 and Ultra DMA/66 have recently been introduced. At 33.3MB/sec and 66.6MB/sec, they have certainly turbo-charged data transport. However, for now these protocols are only in force between the disk and controller—in other words, in and around the cable that you use to connect your hard disk.

These data transport standards place exacting demands on connecting cables. The controller and disk use checksums to confirm whether or not a transaction was executed flawlessly and in the event of an error, the area on the disk has to be read again. Generally this type of problem remains inconspicuous until the disk is pushed to its performance limits.

When the amount of data the disk wants to send exceeds the cable's physical carrying capacity lots of re-reads become necessary and performance suffers. It probably comes as no surprise to learn that this can and will happen in a music computer. Again, HD recording and software samplers are extremely demanding applications where mountains of data are ferried about.

▶ If you encounter problems with your hard disk and your new computer refuses to give you more than five tracks, first try replacing the cable that connects the hard disk to the IDE controller on the mainboard.

IDE Scenarios

Different combinations of Pio, DMA and busmastering may be used in the same computer. It is entirely conceivable, for example, that a controller acts as the PCI busmaster while it uses PIO modes to communicate with the disk. This schizoid situation shouldn't give you any grief—in most cases, there is method behind the madness. You're probably dealing with an older, non-Ultra DMA disk and a busmaster controller which is faster than the disk and this is not really a problem. The reverse case is less auspicious.

The hard disk may send its data to the controller by high-speed air mail delivery—Ultra DMA—while the controller in turn dispatches this data package by dog sled—the out-moded PIO—to main memory. This situation can take a heavy toll on disk performance because the disk has to constantly cool its heels waiting for the controller to catch up.

This is where the BIOS options start to make sense. You can usually enable Ultra DMA so that it applies globally to all data transfers from the controller to main memory and enable PIO/DMA mode for each of the four possible disk/CD drives separately. The latter options control data transfer from the disk to the controller.

Busmastering in Windows

The operating system has to cooperate for busmastering to work on the memory bus. Since all of the processes discussed above take place in the chipset, the operating system must ›know‹ the chipset of its mainboard for flawless busmastering. Windows often doesn't and here and there this leads to confusion. Any version lower than Windows 95 OSR 2.1 doesn't know busmastering from fly fishing. OSR 2.1 is the first version that acknowledges the Intel Hx chipset, which offer DMA busmastering.

With this Windows 95 version and higher as well as Windows 98, Microsoft supplies a driver for those decisive IDE busmaster chipsets, specifically ›Hx‹ and ›Bx.‹ With this driver, activating Busmaster mode is a cinch. Simply look for your IDE disk(s) in the Device Manager under Drives. Double-click the icon for each of your disks. A window will appear.

Open the tab called Settings, click on the little box labeled DMA.

There you have it; DMA mode is enabled for this hard disk.

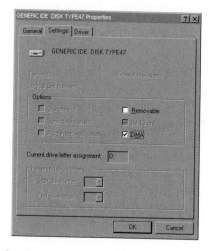

Customarily, the board vendor's driver ships with a main-board or new computer. You're free to install this driver irre-spective of which Windows version you may be running. But beware that you won't see the DMA box in the Device Man-ager and obviously can't check what you can't see. Neverthe-less, the driver will use busmastering whenever possible. In-cidentally, the same applies to AMD's Irongate chipset for the Athlon processor. Here too, busmastering only works with the proprietary driver since Windows doesn't acknowledge this chipset.

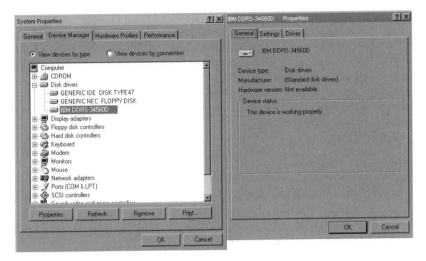

↑ Although it's not indicated here, this computer uses busmastering for IDE DMA data transport.

▶ Despite all this potential confusion, IDE is always both downwardly and upwardly compatible. You can run an ancient disk with a new mainboard as well as a new disk in an old computer. In the latter case, you'll hardly be able to make the most of the disk's major league performance potential since the other minor league components of the computer won't play ball.

Scsi

Scsi was born before the Pc in a time when the home computer was the smallest entity and small and mini computers were akin to what today would be called a department server. In those days Scsi (Small Computers Serial Interface, pronounced: Skuzzy) was developed as a standard for connecting external and internal peripheral devices. Accordingly, Scsi is not limited to hard disks. In the world of music, the sampler is an external device that is commonly connected to the computer via Scsi.

Let's look at hard disk applications first. You'll require an
SCSI controller to allow your computer to use SCSI and to connect SCSI hard disks. In most cases this will be a PCI card, although some mainboards have the requisite controllers and
connectors onboard.

SCSI Versions

As is the case with (E)IDE, several versions of SCSI are available:

- SCSI I: The oldest version features 8-bit technology. It en-
  ables transfer rates of up to 5MB/sec and can handle no
  more than eight devices, including the controller itself.
  The cable length (counting all internal and external connections) may not exceed 6 meters (20 feet).

- SCSI II (also called Fast SCSI): Long the most popular version, it delivers peak transfer rates of 10MB/sec and can
  take up to eight devices. Something of a trade-off between
  speed and convenience, the maximum cable length is limited to 3 meters (10 feet).

- Wide SCSI: Here the interface was expanded to 16 bits,
  which means it can take 16 devices. Throughput was
  upped to a respectable 20MB/sec, while cable length remained a paltry 3 meters (10 feet).

- Ultra SCSI: This offers the same throughput as Wide SCSI
  but can deal with just eight devices. Active termination is
  required. In addition, when five or more devices including
  controller are connected, total cable length may not exceed a truly underwhelming 1.5 meters (5 feet).

- Ultra Wide SCSI (UW SCSI): Predictably, here you get up to
  16 devices and a transfer rate of 40MB/sec. However, only
  eight devices actually run with any real stability. Yes, 16
  integrated IDs may be defined and addressed; whether or
  not this actually works is anyone's guess. The only way to
  find out is to give it a shot.

◆ U2W SCSI: This is the latest version with transfer rates of up to 80MB/sec, 16 possible devices, and a maximum cable length of 12 meters (40 feet). An external Ultra2 terminator must be connected to the end of the cable. The corresponding cables are generally part of the package, but external Ultra2 terminators are elusive and expensive.

▶ Good-to-know-stuff: The adapters will automatically switch to Ultra mode as soon as a non-Ultra2 device, for example, a sampler, is connected to the bus. In this case, a standard active terminator connected at the end of chain will suffice.

Shared Traits and Termination

The following holds true for all SCSI versions:

◆ Every SCSI device, including the controller itself, has a unique ID. The device is addressed and acknowledged exclusively by this ID. In the case of SCSI I/II/Ultra, this is a number between 0 and 7 and, in the case of Wide and Ultra Wide, it is a number between 0 and 15.

◆ SCSI is a bus with two ends. A terminal resistor (terminator) must be connected to each end, otherwise, electrical problems called reflections will occur. These can throw a spanner in the data transfer works. Only the first and last devices in the chain are terminated. If you connect internal devices only—all devices are connected to the SCSI controller by a ribbon cable—then the controller is the first device in the chain and must be terminated. Most controllers detect this situation automatically. On older cards, you may have to set a jumper. If this is the case, read the manual that comes with the controller.
In addition to the controller, you'll have to terminate the last device in the chain by jumpering it.

◆ This terminator may be active, meaning that it is powered by a voltage feed, or it may be passive, meaning that it is equipped with resistors that don't need external power. Ultra Scsi and later version require active termination.

♦ You may not tap into this bus using Y- or T-adapters. Therefore, you're dealing with a single a ribbon cable that is connected to all devices. You might argue that, at heart, there's no difference been these connectors and these prohibited adapters, and you'd be right. This is a little loophole—they may be used for a distance of up five centimeters (two inches), to include the circuits of the disk's electronic components. In any case, keep this connects as short as possible.

♦ The actual plugs for these internal devices come in two different forms: either as 50-pin or 68-pin connectors, depending on the Scsi standard. However, there are adapters available for both directions if you must connect devices featuring one standard to a device with another. Be aware that these adapters are quite expensive.

If you follow all the rules, Scsi will run smoothly and reliably. On the one hand, it's a very tolerant system. Even if you bend these rules—by for example, exceeding the maximum allowable cable length—you won't necessarily encounter problems. On the other hand, even seemingly trivial changes can wreak havoc: It's entirely possible that changing the position of a cable within the computer can cause a heap of trouble.

Troubleshooting the Scsi System

If you run into Scsi-related problems, start troubleshooting them by looking for violations of the rules described above. If something goes awry, say the hard disk goes on strike or the computer freezes when it tries to access a Cd-Rom drive, proceed as follows:

♦ Check that every device has an unique Id. During the computer startup routine and before Windows is launched, almost every controller carries out a search of devices called a scan. All Scsi devices should be listed by ID. If a device does not appear on the list or the message is garbled, two devices probably have the same ID. In the case of internal devices, the ID is determined by jumpers. It's not always clear how these have to be set. Again, check the manual to make sure. If you don't have any reference material on the disk or Cd drive, go to the websites of the manufacturers, you'll always get the scoop there.

▶ There is no disk out there whose specifications can't be found over the Internet.

◆ Check the cable connections. Often, a cable may be plugged in upside down or may have come loose.

◆ Be sure that you terminated the first and last device only? Assuming that you're using internal devices only, the controller itself is the first device and must be terminated. A controller usually recognizes this condition automatically. If it failed to detect that it is the first device, it must be set manually. An Scsi controller has a Bios just like the mainboard. And just like with the Pc's Bios, you can access it via the key combination that the controller indicates during the startup routine. Often, this will be [ctrl][S]. Set the parameter Termination to Enabled in the controller's setup.

◆ If none of these measures works, swap cables. In the case of Ultra, Ultra Wide and U2W, much hinges on the quality of the cable. Although well-meaning, a cable that was Dived by your friendly neighbor who is very handy with a soldering iron may be the source of a whole lot of aggravation.

◆ As a last resort, you could crank up the power to the active terminator by switching on Termpower on the last device in the signal chain (which has to be terminated anyway). Again, you'll need to set a jumper. You'll find this jumper labeled on all devices that I'm familiar with, so you won't even need to consult the manual.

ASPI

In any SCSI system without further drivers, only the first two hard disks can be addressed; you'll even need ›outside‹ help to address CD-ROM drives. The good news is that this help is available in the guise of the ASPI programming interface.

Originally the brainstorm of the mad scientists at Adaptec, a manufacturer of SCSI controllers, this standard is now used by all vendors of SCSI controllers. Programs that address an SCSI device use the ASPI instruction set.

Back in the days of MS-DOS, drivers that loaded by the boot file config.sys were used for this purpose. Take a look at the examples listed in the section ›Windows‹ on page 145. If you inadvertently installed these drivers for your controller, you'll find out how to get rid of them in the same chapter. These old Dos drivers can be a real fly in the ointment and cause all kinds of headaches.

Windows 95 features its own ASPI interface that it falls back on automatically as soon as a controller is detected within the system. However, this Windows ASPI interface has a catch: it does not support all the options that have been developed over the years and are now made available by Adaptec Dos drivers. Therefore, without suitable extensions, you won't be able to address older SCSI devices, in particular, the Akai samplers S-1000/2000/3000.

For this reason, Adaptec controllers ship with a dedicated ASPI software for Windows, which is installed automatically. A while back, you could download this software from Adaptec's web server and use it to excellent effect with other controllers. Unfortunately, the company changed the installation routine so that the program will only run if it detects an Adaptec controller in the system. This is why some makers of burner software and editing programs recommend in no uncertain terms that you use Adaptec controllers for samplers.

However, in my experience, critical programs will run just as well with cards made by the companies Symbios Logic and Dawicontrol. I wouldn't bet the farm that this is the case with no-name controllers.

▶ Software will often overwrite the ASPI layer with other files. You'll know that this is the case when, after you've installed a program or the software for a removable disk drive, you're suddenly plagued by all kinds of problems.

The ASPI layer consists of four files:

◆ windows\system\wnaspi32.dll
◆ windows\system\winaspi.dll
◆ windows\system\iosubsys\apix.vxd
◆ windows\system\aspienum.vxd

Search for these in the indicated folders and right-click the file name. Then select Properties in the menu that appears.

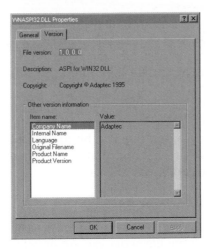

If you click onto the tab labeled Version, you will—as shown in the diagram above—see a number. It must be identical for all four files. If it's not, a file was overwritten. This isn't necessarily a problem; if your system works fine, leave everything as it is. If however, your system is having trouble communicating with your sampler, you must recover the original files.

You can restore files from the original Windows-95/98 CD. This is easy enough in the case of Windows 98. Use the program ›System Information,‹ which you'll find under Start ⇨ Programs ⇨ Accessories ⇨ System Tools. Under the menu item Tools, you'll find the entry System File Checker.

Here can you restore selected Windows files from the original CD.

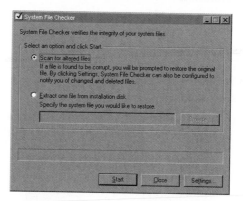

Enter the name of the file here and Windows will restore it from the original CD.

As luck would have it, Windows 95 does not offer the System Information utility. You can of course copy the files ›by hand‹ from the CD, but this is a bit too complicated. I'd recommend a sure-fire method that, although more time consuming, is foolproof: reinstall Windows.

Reinstalling Windows 95

Fear not, for this won't hurt a bit. Insert your Windows CD and double-click the file setup.exe. An assistant will take you through the installation routine. Windows also detects all available devices, and the drivers should be linked up automatically. The system will ask you if you want to keep the very ASPI files that we're trying to get rid of. Click No, for the whole purpose of this little ritual is to copy the original files from the Windows Cd.

Which Scsi Controller Is Best?

If you want to run just one hard disk or one sampler, an Scsi II (Fast Scsi) controller will do the trick. It won't take too big a bite out of your wallet (typically less than 50 bucks). Just make sure that you opt for a Pci card. The following controllers, among others, warrant investigation:

◆ Dawicontrol 2974

◆ Symbios Logic 20810

◆ Tekram Dc-310

◆ Asus Sc-200

The peak throughput of Scsi II won't make the grade if you're planning on running several hard disks. Ultra Scsi or Ultra Wide Scsi have set standards for multiple-disk applications. These controllers are more expensive, with price tags ranging from around 70 to 200 Us dollars, which of course may vary from country to country.

In any case, the following cards will deliver the goods:

◆ Adaptec 2940 Au, 2940 Uw

◆ Dawicontrol 2976 Uw

◆ Symbios Logic 8750 Sp U, 8751 Sp Uw

◆ Tekram Dc-395 U/Uw

Hard Disk Installation

Installing an additional hard disk is a breeze, configuring it is a tad trickier. The following directions should guide you safely home:

Installing an IDE Hard Disk

If you want to add a new device to an IDE channel that already has a disk or CD-ROM drive connected to it, you must first jumper the new device to Slave. If you have already connected two devices to the same cable and channel, then you'll have to use the second IDE channel. In this case, the new device must of course be jumpered so that it's the Master.

1 Set the jumpers accordingly.

2 Install the disk and connect the power cord and the ribbon cable for the data bus.

The connectors of ribbon cables are generally designed so that you can only connect them in one way. For this purpose, there's a tiny ridge located on the side of the connector and a corresponding notch in the port on the disk drive. Some cables aren't so ›encoded‹ and in this case you'll have to rely on their colors to ensure that the connectors are inserted properly. One side of the ribbon cable is color-coded, usually in red. The golden rule that this red wire must face the side of the disk where the socket for the power supply cable is located.

3 Start the computer, go to the Bios menu and select IDE Auto Detect.

The Bios will scan your new disk and read out its configuration data. It may prompt you to confirm this data with ›Y.‹

▶ For all non-Us readers, bear mind that the Bios is programmed for American keyboard assignments. What in the Us is the Y key may be located elsewhere; in Germany, for example, Y and Z are reversed.

The new disk is now installed, but it will not appear under Windows because it has not yet been partitioned and formatted.

Installing an Scsi Hard Disk

Before you connect the disk, start your computer and watch as your controller is being initialized. This routine will indicate which Ids have already been assigned.

1 Choose an available Id.

2 Jumper the disk or Cd drive to this free Id.

Be sure to check the manual because the labels on the device are not always intelligible.

3 If the new device is connected at the end of the Scsi bus (as the last device on the cable), you must terminate it with—you guessed it—a jumper.

4 Now connect the Scsi ribbon cable to the disk.

▶ Keep in mind the golden rule: the side of the cable that is color-coded (generally in red) must point to the electrical connector of the disk or Cd-Rom drive.

5 If you want to make life easier for yourself and avoid terminator-induced confusion, connect the device somewhere in the middle of the cable, not at its end or behind the device that has to date been terminated. Then of course you won't have to terminate the new device.

When you reboot your box, the system will detect the new disk. You are now ready to experience the boundless joy of configuring it.

Partitioning and Formatting Hard Disks

Now that we're experts on the mechanics and logic of data transfer, we will learn about a third level called the file system. It doesn't actually affect the disk as such, it's simply a method for determining how the operating system organizes its files.

Let's look at an analogy: Picture a desk in the real world. Everyone arranges it in their own order (or perhaps disorder). The hard disk is the physical desk, the operating system would be you, and the file system is the order in which you array your files, pens, pencils and erasers on the desktop.

Before you can create a file system, you have to divvy up the disk into sections called partitions. Windows will regard these partitions as individual disk drives despite the fact that they are all physically on one disk.

Partitions mainly serve organizational purposes. They let you assign one area of the hard disk to data and another to programs. However, this is not the law. You may also configure a single partition which takes all of the disk's real estate.

Windows can only handle two partitions per disk, a primary and an extended partition. The primary partition is Disk Drive C and may not contain any ›logical‹ disk drives. (Other operating systems allow logical drives.) Depending on the partitioning software that you use, you can configure all kinds and combination of partitions. Windows, however, will always ›see‹ only one primary and one extended partition.

↑ This is what a partitioned disk looks like schematically.

To make things even more complicated, modern disks feature different sectors with different densities, so you can distinguish between faster and slower partitions for an audio computer.

When you create a partition, a program called Fdisk that runs in Windows and is responsible for this partition will work from the outside in (i. e. from the perimeter towards the center). If you're partitioning a disk from which you want to boot the system, your best bet is to create two partitions, a primary and an extended partition. In the extended partition, you can then create two logical disk drives so that you end up with three disk drives:

◆ Disk Drive C, which is the primary partition and the fastest one,

◆ and Disk Drives D and E, which are both in the extended partition, whereby D is the faster of the two.

If, on the other hand, you want to install an additional disk, create just an extended partition in which you can then define two or three logical disk drives. You thus end up with disk drives distinguished by their different speeds. Use the fastest for audio data, the others for program data and the like.

Partitioning a New Disk

For the purpose of this example, we'll assume that you're installing a second disk and that, once you have installed the disk, your computer will boot in the usual manner even though the disk hasn't yet been formatted:

1 Click on Start, then on Run.

2 Type in fdisk and press the Enter key.

If you're running Windows 95 Osr 2.1 or Windows 98, Fdisk will let you create partitions larger than 2Gb. You can enable this extension if you respond with ›Y‹ to query shown below. However, caution is in order: Only these operating systems can read these partitions, meaning that you can't access these disks in Dos or Windows Nt. If you're dealing with a disk that has more than 4Gb, you don't have any choice but to create one primary and one extended partition.

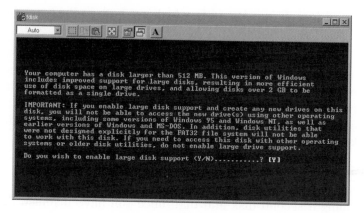

In the following menu, you should first go to the other hard disk.

3   Select Option 5 in the menu. Proceed very cautiously here: If you end up on the wrong hard disk while you're carrying out the following steps, you can kiss the data on it goodbye forever, for it will be irrevocably lost.

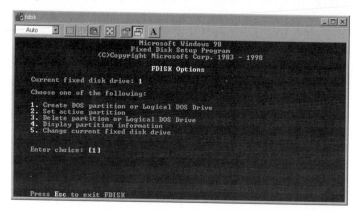

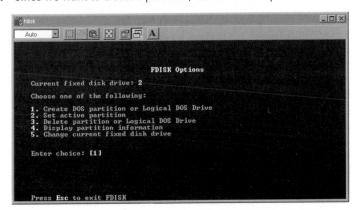

You can now select exactly what you want to do.

4 Since we want to create a partition, we'll choose Option 1.

In the following menu, you can select the type of partition that you want to create. You only need a primary partition if you want to boot from this disk. However, we don't want that, so we'll select the extended partition.

5 Select Number 2.

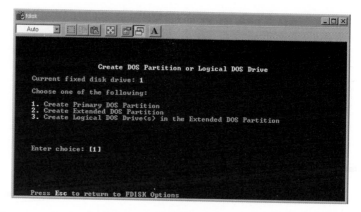

You must now indicate the size of the partition you want to make. I can't give you any advice on this one. However, you can only create one primary and one extended partition, so you should dish out all the available disk real estate to the extended partition. Incidentally, this is the default.

Now that you've created a partition, you must create logical disk drives within this partition. This gives Windows a structure on which it can base its file system.

6 Therefore, select Option 3: Create Logical Dos Drive(s) in the Extended Dos Partition

Here too, you must indicate the desired size of the new logical disk drive. You can create as many logical disk drives as you want. Since you presumably don't want to get lost in a maze of drives, you shouldn't opt for more than two.

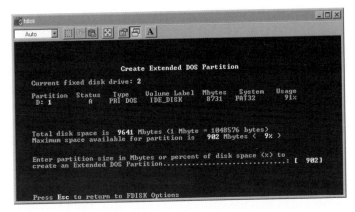

7 To this end, indicate half of the disk capacity in MB. Now you've created a new partition on your disk and given it a disk drive.

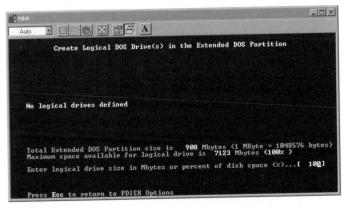

8 For the second disk drive, simply repeat steps 6 and 7.

9 When you've finished, exit Fdisk by [esc].

10 Reboot the computer so that you can ›see‹ the new disk drive.

After you've started the system, you can see the new disk drive indicated in My Computer under Windows as one or several letters. However, you can't use it just yet because it hasn't been formatted and doesn't have a file system.

11 Right-click on the disk drive icon of the disk that you want to format. Select Format from the context menu. You can then use the hard disk.

Perhaps you're wondering what the term ›format‹ actual means in this context. The process of formatting creates the actual file system. Sticking with our desktop analogy, this determines the layout of the desk, telling the operating system where it can file away all those odds and ends.

A file system is largely operating system-specific, although some state-of-the-art systems can read other file systems.

FAT File Systems

Windows uses two file systems, ›FAT 16‹ and ›FAT 32.‹ The two are quite similar and both are quite long in the tooth.

FAT stands for ›File Allocation Table.‹ This means that a table (the FAT) is located at the beginning of a partition. Information locating the ›cluster‹ in which a file starts is entered in the table.

In the case of FAT, the hard disk is divided into logical units called clusters. A file is written into these little units. Since a whole file rarely fits into one cluster, Windows distributes files across several clusters—not necessarily located next to each other. Perhaps inspired by a paper chase, at the end of each cluster is a ›pointer‹ to the cluster where the file is continued.

FAT 16 indicates that the clusters are administered with a 16-bit number, which means that there can be no more than 65,536 clusters. That limits the system somewhat. To circumvent this restriction, the sizes of the clusters themselves is variable depending on the size of the partition. However, no more than 65,536 clusters each with a size 65,536 bytes are possible. This totals 4GB—the FAT16 simply can't address disks any larger than that.

Two file segments may not reside in a single cluster (the paperweights wouldn't work then). This means that for every file of less than 64 kilobytes, the remainder of storage space in its cluster is squandered.

Fat 32 compensates for these disadvantages by doubling the number of administrative units—it does so by allowing 32-bit addresses. Everything else remains the same. Partitions with many more clusters can be created and the cluster size can thus be set smaller to reduce the amount of wasted space.

Fat 32 is what you're switching on when you respond ›Yes‹ to the question about the extensions in Fdisk as described in Step 2 of the partitioning procedure (see above). In fact, it's the only option available. You also can't influence size of the clusters, which is determined automatically.

Although there are undocumented parameters that let you fiddle with these values, I strongly urge you to resist this temptation. These parameters were not documented for very good reason: undesirable side effects are highly likely when you change their values.

▶ You can conveniently and safely adjust this parameter with hard disk utilities such as the excellent program, ›Partition Magic.‹

When Fat 32 was introduced (with Windows 95 Osr 2), there was much debate about which of the two systems' performance was better, particularly for audio applications. In the case of large files (which audio tends to generate), throughput is indeed better with Fat 16 because Windows doesn't have to address clusters quite as often (bigger clusters means fewer clusters). This in turn reduces the amount of time it takes to access data. Fat 32 features smaller clusters so that your box has to dedicate more computing power and seek time to finding the cluster containing the rest of your guitar solo.

This Fat 16 versus Fat 32 issue is rendered moot by newer and larger disk drives. Fat 16 can address two partitions of 4Gb each and that 8Gb is all she wrote, folks. Today's budding audiophile won't opt for a disk any smaller than this, so Fat 32 is literally the only way to fly.

Having said that, if you own an utility such as Partition Magic and don't mind wasting storage space on bigger clusters, you can create a Fat 32 partition and bigger clusters. This will boost performance by a couple of percentage points, but don't expect miracles.

This threshold of 8Gb also applies to older Bios versions, for both mainboards and Scsi controllers. True, you only need a Bios when you're not working under Windows, where the disk is addressed directly. But when you want to install a ›boot‹ disk, you can only do it in Ms-Dos mode. When you re-install Windows and start it from the boot diskette that ships with the Os, the computer will also be in a Dos mode. This all boils down to one thing—ordinarily, you can't use more than 8Gb.

There are two ways to solve this problem:

◆ You can obtain a Bios update for your Scsi controller or your mainboard, provided of course that such a beast exists.

◆ You can temporarily install the disk in another computer that supports bigger disks; partition and format it there; then reinstall it in your computer.

Defragmenting Disks

As you can well imagine, this makes for a rather chaotic system, kind of disk version of a bachelor pad with junk here, a mess there, and nothing at all in its proper place. Indeed, the more use the disk sees, the more the data gets chopped up into tiny fragments. You may end up with files that are distributed over thousands of clusters scattered all over the disk like so many unmatched dirty socks, pizza boxes and beer cans. After a period of weeks or months, your disk will become perceptibly slower until at some point it begins to crawl at a snail's pace. This phenomenon is called fragmentation.

You can remedy the problem by a process called defragmentation. Here files are reorganized so clusters that belong together follow each other in sequential order. This lends your disk wings so it can fly again.

To this end, proceed as follows:

1 Click on Start ⇨ Programs ⇨ Accessories ⇨ Disk Defragmenter

2 In the following window, you can select the disk drive that you want to defragment and launch the process.

Defragmentation, a key maintenance chore for the Pc-wielding musician.

I can't sing the praises of defragmentation too highly. Many audio evils are rooted directly in lethargic hard disks. Usually these aren't slowed down by mechanical shortcomings—it is that diabolical fragmentation that undermines hard disk performance.

Make a habit of knocking out this little maintenance chore at least once a week. Be aware that with today's huge hard disks this can take hours, so it's a good idea to do it overnight. On the other hand, the more you do it, the less time each ›defrag‹ takes.

Running Several Hard Disks

When the number of audio tracks that your hard disk allows you to work with becomes too meager to meet your needs, you may begin entertaining the notion of running several disks in parallel. By all means, go for it—all HD recording programs let you distribute audio tracks over several disks.

In theory, you should be able to double performance with two disks, triple it with three, and so forth just like back in the days when engineers hooked up further 24-track tape machines when the tracks of one had been exhausted. Unfortunately, this not the case in practice. Performance can only be multiplied when the disks can truly operate in parallel.

Only SCSI gives you the tools to do this. This protocol is able to deliver commands to one disk and then immediately address the next device before the first disk has supplied data. Once the second disk finally gets around to doing this, the SCSI can for the moment turn its attention back to disk no. 1. This process is called ›Disconnect/Reconnect.‹ Unfortunately, IDE doesn't do this. Here a task must be carried out before another device can be addressed.

By running several SCSI disks you can up track performance, by running several IDE disks, you can merely up storage space. There is an exception to this rule, namely when you combine SCSI and IDE. An SCSI task can be carried while the IDE disk is being addressed. This works well in practice, so you can considerate it a budget-friendly upgrading alternative if you don't have the spare change for a another SCSI disk.

Recommended Hard Disks

For what seemed like eons, the only sensible option for audio applications was to buy an SCSI system. Among the reasons for this was that, IDE used to require the processor to handle all data access. This meant that connecting several IDE disks to slower computers defeated the purpose of having all this hard disk real estate—it could actually limit the maximum number of possible tracks as well as the maximum number of plug-ins. The CPU workload generated by IDE was substantial. Since the advent of Busmaster DMA, this is no longer an issue because file access under IDE is just as resource-sparing as it is with SCSI.

The ability to address several devices independently is today pretty much the only advantage that SCSI has IDE, at least when we're talking strictly about disks. Bear in mind that premium disks that deliver state-of-the-art performance are largely SCSI devices and these are so prohibitively expensive that you may not enjoy them once you've sold your significant other's prized collection of pre-War World II bottle caps to foot the bill. In the interests of curbing domestic violence, cheaper SCSI disks are the more reasonable choice. However, if you're on a tight budget, IDE disks are a cool way to go for home recording. For some 200 bucks or so, you get a plenty of pie with a healthy helping of speed to satisfy your music-making sweet tooth. The rule of thumb is:

If your gig calls for external devices such as samplers and you lust for top performances in terms of oodles of tracks and lighting speeds, your dilemma is solved: you have no choice but to opt for SCSI. For anything less demanding, a standard IDE system will do.

If, however, your system is older or you don't want to use busmastering or can't use it because your controller doesn't support it, you should weigh the advantages of SCSI. In this case, it is the only way that you can eke out more disk performance from your computer. Chances are that an SCSI controller will be cheaper than a new mainboard with a current IDE controller. And you'd have to buy a new disk in either case.

Virtually every hard disk on the market today is suitable for audio applications. That special qualifier ›Av‹ which manufacturers in the past made you bleed for, has since been rendered meaningless. OK, I'll cut the vendors some slack—in the old days, the heads of hard drives had to re-calibrate regularly and Av disks didn't do this while the disk was in operation, so in that sense the extra cost was justified.

I've listed the fastest disks below for you to ponder. Be aware that these disks run at least 7,200rpm and are therefore rather loud.

High-performance IDE disks:

- IBM DPTA
- IBM DJNA series
- Maxtor DiamondMax Plus series
- Quantum Fireball Plus series
- Western Digital Ac418000 Expert
- Seagate Barracuda ATA

High-performance SCSI disks:

- IBM DRVS Ultrastar
- IBM DMVS Ultrastar
- Quantum Atlas IV
- Western Digital 8310 Enterprise
- Seagate Barracuda SCSI
- Seagate Cheetah

You'll only need these disks if you require studly track performance, from say upwards of 30 to 40 tracks. Otherwise, a cheaper disk that is a tad slower or a combination of two mid-class SCSI disks will do just fine.

6 The Operating System

What Does an Operating System Actually Do?

The Dim and Distant Past

I'm not going to bore you by expounding at length on the nature of the beast known as an operating system—you're a musician and have other stuff to worry about. However, a little background on the fundamentals of an Os (operating system) will help you ferret out errors should they occur.

The Os is the great mediator. So that not every program reinvents the wheel—in other words, recreates the hard disk in its own image—the operating system provides some essential functions that are universally applicable. Among these are such exciting things as storage management, file access and hardware communication. The Pci processes described in the previous chapter, for example, have to be controlled somehow.

Without an Os, each programmer who cooked up a text processor would have to spice each meal with his own routines for mouse control, keyboard input, and writing, saving and loading files. You can imagine the complications. This is why the operating system takes care of these administrative chores. When an Os makes available uniform, precisely documented functions, all the Bill Gates wannabes in the world can write programs. (Of course will only run on the platform for which they were written.)

What exactly the mission of an operating system is and what it is not has been the subject of heated debate and the general consensus has changed over time. Back in the days of embryonic systems such as Cpm and Dos, the jurisdiction of the Os was limited to the boot routine, memory addressing, keyboard input, hard disk and floppy disk drive. Every program had its own routine for printing documents. Audio output too was left up to the poor programmer. This is hardly surprise, since any Dos program supported only a handful of audio cards. Usually, only the most common card, Soundblaster, was supported, which certainly must have made Creative Labs' shareholders happy. To this day, the notorious issue of Soundblaster compatibility plays a pivotal role because it has been around for so long that it is now considered the industry's lowest common denominator.

When Windows 3.0 finally offered a graphic interface for the Pc, the range of tasks that this operating system handled had to be extended considerably. Whereas the display was limited to a single standard—a Stone Age solution in terms of resolution and refresh rates—the new graphic interface demanded higher resolution and thus many special display functions. Of course all of these had to be addressed by uniform code.

The same applied to printers. While every program initially controlled its own printout, Windows created a uniform standard for all. It was originally up to each program to generate type font—not until the advent of Windows was font handled uniformly.

All of these tasks as well as storage and disk management are still dealt with according to the same blueprint. And this is where that dread term ›driver‹ comes into play. A driver is a small piece of software that serves as the make-or-break link in the chain from the application to the hardware.

The following illustration gives you a very simplified view of the processes that have to be carried out so that a program is able to prod the hardware and peripheral devices of the computer into doing what it wants:

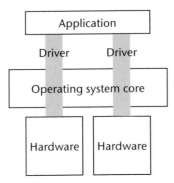

Communication between software, operating system, and hardware

You may have never seen anything but Windows 95/98 grace the screen of you Pc. (If you're getting on in years you may have some recollection of Windows 3.11.) These are by no means the only operating systems out there and certainly not the best for audio and Mıᴅı applications—they are merely the most widespread. The reason for this is that as increasing numbers of computers shipped with soundcards, the powers that be decided it would be a good idea to standardize audio in and output and let the operating system handle it.

All subsystems for audio and Mıᴅı were tacked on as an afterthought—they were made to suffer for the sins of their fathers, so to speak. Indeed, there were all kinds of ›genetic‹ flaws that could only be offset by clever programming and steadily increasing computing power. We'll take a look at these hereditary drawbacks as well as the tricks that will help you overcome them in this chapter.

Windows

Before Windows 95 reared its lucrative little head and extended Microsoft's license to print money, the company faced a dilemma: on the one hand, its predecessor—Windows 3.11—had won widespread acceptance, particularly in the revenues-spewing field of business. On the other, its techno-logy was hopelessly outdated. Windows, you see, was a 16-bit operating system (32-bit extensions were available, but these don't merit further discussion). If the ›best was yet to come‹ for Bill & Co., something had to give—you guessed it, your wallet.

In the chapter ›The Processor‹ starting on page 37, you learned about bit depth and the differences between 16 and 32 bits. What was said for the processor applies equally well to the operating system. When a feed bag full of data has to be processed, the operating system can't peck at it, it must gulp it down in one go. This is not, however, the only impor-tant aspect of 32-bit operating systems and programs.

Multitasking and Multithreading

Much more important than pure speed—which can be in-creased even for 16-bit programs by meticulous optimization and crafty tricks—is the breaking up of programs into small units that allow the best possible distribution of computing power.

You know how your significant other gripes when you take the latest issue of your favorite 'zine with you for a lengthy session in the bathroom? That's multitasking, the ability to do two things at the same time. Here a single central pro-cessing unit executes two or more programs at a time. This was first possible on the Pc with Windows 3.0. Every pro-gram is a task, several of which can be active simultaneously, hence the name. Strictly speaking this is not true, since the processor can't actually do two things at once. What happens is the same as when your significant other tells you to wash the dishes when what you really want to do is watch the swimsuit face-off of the Miss Universe competition. You of course wash the dishes but stop to see the good bits. In the same way, the processor temporarily stops a task to turn its attention to another program.

Up to Version 3.11, multitasking was cooperative. This meant that another task didn't get its turn until the first program voluntarily relinquished control of the operating system. Windows had no way of slapping an uncooperative program's greedy little mitts if it refused to take them out of the cookie jar, so when a program froze or crashed, it took the entire system down with it.

Windows 95 introduced preemptive multitasking. Here the operating system controls all simultaneously active tasks all the time and has no qualms about preempting one program for the greater good of the system. This makes running several programs in parallel a lot more stable and smooth.

Multithreading takes this a step further. A thread is a fiber in the cloth of a program. Almost all state-of-the-art 32-bit programs consist of several threads. This approach allows the increased computing power of modern processors to be exploited even more efficiently. Multithreading is only possible with 32-bit technology because it provides ›reentrant-proof‹ program code. Put simply, this means that the program code is self-conscious—it has to know who it is and what purpose it serves in life. And it has to be self-confident—it better not suffer stage fright and fail to perform when it's time to shine. In view of the diverse processes that a sequencer must carry out simultaneously, modern audio programs probably wouldn't be possible at all without multithreading.

Compatibility and 16 Bits in Windows 95

According to a purist's interpretation of the doctrine of multitasking and multithreading, Microsoft Windows 95 should have been written from scratch. Of course, then all of the old programs would have been rendered instantly obsolete. You can bet that the business world would not have been amused. In all likelihood, it would have boycotted such a system because this would have meant that all legacy software and hardware needed replacing. Thus a compromise was in order.

Windows 95 makes amends for many of the disadvantages that marred previous versions and introduces more modern technology. However, to assure compatibility with older applications, 16-bit code can still be found at key junctures in its central nervous system. Graphics output and multimedia—in other words, everything that has to do with audio and MIDI—are among these. At the lowest level, the system still runs at 16 bits. Be aware that the 16-bit code can't simply be interrupted and restarted at random—only one 16-bit process can run at any give time.

Since the graphics and multimedia engine chugs along at 16 bits, the old Windows 3.x drivers will still work. However, you should avoid using these whenever possible.

When you instead employ a Windows 9x driver, a 32-bit program will actually be looking at a data bus that is 32 bits wide. This applies for example, when it wants to send audio data to the card. This is something of an optical illusion however, because Windows is actually duping the program into believing that it is working in 32 bits. In the course of further processing, data transactions are converted back into 16 bits. This has both advantages and disadvantages.

On the downside, the display card driver can slow down MIDI data output. On the upside, you can turn this into an advantage by granting MIDI processes priority. On the downside, this may open up another Pandora's box—the system's efficiency may suffer, for example, when you're playing audio back simultaneously.

Most software vendors exploit steadily increasing computing power and nifty programming tricks to get a handle on these problems, but there is a high price to pay in the form of ›latency.‹

Buffers and Latency

In the previous chapter, you read about the many imponderables involved in audio and MIDI applications. The huge amount of data is of course a critical consideration. A conscientious programmer can't simply assume that his program will compute every sample and send it to the driver in time, all the time. This is why all audio programs that run under Windows use buffers.

What happens here is that a big payload of data is computed in advance before it is sent on its merry way. If a part of the program can't keep up with the real-time playback for a tenth of a second, you won't hear it falter for as long as data remains in the buffer. The straggling thread can take its sweet time to catch up with the output queue.

This buffer system is the source of something you'll come to know and despise—latency. You'll notice there is an ever so slight pause between the moment your mouse clicks the playback button and actual playback gets underway—this is the length of it takes to fill the buffer. The same thing occurs when you want to manipulate an event during playback. If for example, you move a virtual fader of a software mixer, the system begins a calculation operation that is sent to the buffer's input. Before you can hear the results of this computation, all the data that's still hanging loose in the buffer has to be kicked out. And there you have more latency.

Latency depends on the size and number of available buffers. It thus varies from audio program to audio program, which of course means that program x and program y won't have the same latency even when they're running on identical computers.

Buffers are variable in most programs. As you may now surmise, smaller buffers mean less latency, but they also require more computing power because there isn't as much buffer to play with—the program has to dedicate more resources to handling time-critical data.

You won't automatically reduce latency by buying a buff new computer. At best, with a new processor you can gradually reduce the size of the buffers in your program and ›feel‹ your way to your system's performance threshold. To be sure, you'll know it when you get there: the program will stutter or gurgle rudely because samples were lost somewhere along the way.

Latency is irksome, but if and when it will become truly maddening depends largely on the application. Many users feel that they can live with a recording program whose latency is as high as 500msec, but don't expect to be able to created delicate fades or sophisticated sweeps with equalizers in real-time. On the other hand, these aren't a problem if you create these effects using a static mix.

Latency Problems during Recording

Where latency has the power to drive you barking mad is during monitoring—the process of patching an input signal thru a mixer channel and on to the output so that you can hear the audio results immediately. If you've worked with an analog mixer and a real physical tape machine, you're probably accustomed to hearing lashings of compression or effects on the input signal while you're recording.

▶ If you've always wanted to know what a prima donna is, try routing the vocal signal of a singer to his or her headphones without slapping on some reverb. The first words will be, ›I can't work like this,‹ followed a detailed description of entirely new and imaginative things that you can do with your anatomy.

Latency is not only generated during playback, it also rears its ugly little head in the course of recording. The vocal track of our example also has to run through one or several buffers. Even if your program offers good reverb effects or stunning delay, your vocalist will always hear the effect a bit later—how much later depends on the given latency. And your singer is right—she really can't work this way.

This is why even for ›casual‹ home recording, you'll need an external mixer. In a bind, you could use the hardware of the card, for most cards offer an onboard mixer of varying sophistication that controls the card directly. You can at any rate feed the input signal to the output right there on the card so that you'll at least have some type of monitor signal. You won't be able to patch in effects unless you own a card with at least four inputs and outputs. If this not the case, it's time for your piggy bank to make the acquaintance of a hammer, for you will need an external mixer.

Latency Problems with Software Sound Generators

Latency is also an aggravation when you're working with software synthesizers. You of course would like to be able to actually play your synth with your master MIDI keyboard. Anything more than 10ms of latency is perceptible and a will wreak havoc with your timing.

▶ Personally, even 10msec throws me, but many users are not bothered by this amount of latency and it's probably little different than playing a hardware synth.

Reducing Latency

The options you have at your disposal for reducing latency depend largely on the driver architecture of the operating system, meaning the complexity of the processes required to spoon a morsel of data into the soundcard's muzzle.

Under Windows, we can class these architectures into three categories: MME (Multimedia), DirectX (Microsoft's proprietary 32-bit interface) and extensions by third-party manufacturers (ASIO, EASI). The more direct the architecture, the fewer the reserves—smaller buffers spell less latency. So, let's a closer look at these architectures.

Mme

Mme interfaces are the oldest that run under Windows and remain the Os's lowest common denominator. These interfaces are a manifestation of the compromise—some might say deal with the devil—that the company made to assure retrograde compatibility.

As the name ›Multi Media Extensions‹ so succinctly points out, Mme consisted initially of extensions in order to equip Windows 3.0 with multimedia capabilities. To permit a program to access its audio and/or Midi hardware, a hardware manufacturer must merely supply an Mme driver.

And so the unholy circle closes: The software calls up an Mme function from Windows, for example ›Play the following audio file!‹. Windows acknowledges this polite request and passes it on to the driver which in turn, assures that the requisite data is sent to the audio hardware, where it is translated into sound. The program needs only know the Mme functions, not the hardware that these address.

You can probably see the problems coming a mile away: Mme has a 16- and a 32-bit code, the latter which serves solely as the ›front end.‹ All of a program's Mme calls are forwarded to the 16-bit code. An entity of an Mme driver is just such a 16-bit process. If you're dealing with the eight stereo devices of a standard multi-I/O card, this tallies to eight separate 16-bit processes.

Since the same holds true for the user interface and display activities, the 16-bit section of Windows 95 is as crowded as a Tokyo subway at rush hour. And it simply can't be avoided because 16-bit code is not designed to be called and addressed repeatedly.

Again, Windows 95 contains 16-bit components for reasons of backward compatibility, so Microsoft had to devise a mechanism (Win16Mutex) that would prevent multiple calls, which can only work if all 16-bit processes are stopped until the one that is toiling away finishes whatever it was tasked to do.

If the 32-bit code of MME or the display has to wait for the reply of a 16-bit process, sound and graphics will of course also be held up.

▶ Mind you, real 32-bit routines that don't call critical operating system functions aren't bothered by the delay. They'll continue toiling merrily away in the background. Hard disk access is one of these routines.

You now know why you'll often get advice that has to do with the display adapter to solve your audio problems. Although at first glance, they seem to have as much to do with each other as Hank Williams and Neil Armstrong, the 16-bit connection between them creates a bottleneck.

The labyrinthine mess that is the architecture of MME requires several larger buffers. The latency of every program thus pushes far beyond the boundaries of what is tolerable. For instance, in this MME scenario Cubase has a typical latency of 500 to 750msec, Cakewalk and Logic a few milliseconds more. The soft synth Generator/Reaktor limps along at 60 to 100msec rather than at the 10msec that it could, given the right conditions, deliver.

In this day and age, MME is only bearable when you're working with pure audio editors where latency, on account of the few real-time functions that these programs offer, plays little role.

MIDI and MME

Under Windows, MIDI is also addressed by the MME interfaces. The requirements in terms of computing power aren't nearly as demanding and the amount of data isn't nearly as overwhelming, so you don't really need buffers for MIDI. Some software manufacturers do without, while others use buffers.

One noteworthy example hereof is the famed System Pre-Roll in Cubase. Results can be very good with or without buffers, but problems can also crop up. Users often complain about poor MIDI timing, but everyone has his own ideas about what this means. In order to get to the bottom of these nebulous problems, we'll look at them systematically to see what actually takes place when software (in most cases a sequencer) sends out MIDI information.

The Path of MIDI Data in the Computer

When the sequencer sends out a Note On event, it will in the best case scenario (running status) consist of two bytes. The small amount of data shouldn't be much of a challenge for a contemporary computer. On the other hand, the driver of the MIDI interface, if poorly programmed, can cause problems because the driver alone is responsible for data flow.

From the computer the data flows to the hardware of the interface. From this point on, our two bytes travel serially, meaning that the individual bits line up to form a procession, albeit a very short one. The speed at which it travels is dictated by the MIDI specification to be 31,250bit/sec. From this figure, we arrive at a travel time of 0.64msec for our MIDI event. This adds up faster than you might think. If you play a 16-voice chord for example, some 10msec will pass between the time the first note and the last note sound.

The last stop is the receiving MIDI device. MIDI processing and voice rendering of course takes some time, so the response of different samplers and synthesizers varies markedly.

When you consider that modern audio sequencers such as Cubase and Logic need to maintain constant synchronization between MIDI and audio hardware, you can appreciate how many factors affect MIDI timing.

▶ If you run your sound generator in Multimode and like to use lots of voices, you shouldn't be at all concerned about the timing of your sequencer, you'll most definitely have other, more pressing problems to worry about.

Some programs—Emagic Logic Audio comes to mind—use little tricks to render overweight MIDI arrangements. The secret lies in the output logic, which follows a complex algorithm. Events are not treated equally, instead they are prioritized and transmitted according to their ranking. In this case, the chronological sequence within a track is not affected. This means, in practice, that the tracks are not serviced from top to bottom; instead, the track that contains the currently most significant event gets first turn. Naturally, note-on commands number among these VIP events, as do program changes so that sounds actually change when you want them to. In other programs, MIDI output stubbornly follows the order dictated by track numbers and simultaneous events are serviced from top to bottom.

Also the audio hardware and its timers have an influence on MIDI timing. Since the MIDI part is constantly being synced up—incidentally, just like it was once synced up to the tape machine by SMPTE—MIDI output also marches to the beat of the audio card. At one time you could actually see the timing fluctuate in the tempo display, but today, variations are usually so minor that they're not indicated at all. Beyond that, professional audio hardware doesn't influence timing perceptibly. However, there are no-name cards that will cause it to fluctuate wildly. If you're running one of these bargain-bin mutants and it makes MIDI timing seesaw savagely, there won't be much you can do.

Multi-channel Audio

MME-compatible soundcards used to largely ship in stereo versions. The newer multi-channel cards rely on a ruse to trick Windows—they simply introduce themselves to it and thus the audio application as several stereo cards. Even in the virtual world, the tailor makes the man, so this will work in most cases, provided that the software can handle several devices.

›Work‹ is perhaps too forgiving a term, all it means is that something will definitely arrive at the outputs. That's about all you can say with any assurance because this approach has serious disadvantages:

Launching a further copy of the driver is a new task for the operating system. A little micro manager called a ›task scheduler‹ is responsible for controlling and parcelling out Cpu time. It constantly interrupts such tasks to allow others to run for a few milliseconds—even a state-of-art Cpu can't chew gum and walk at the same time.

Suppose you click on the play button after the system launches one of the driver entities, but before it can start the next entity. The graphical information for this event has to be relayed to the screen, so by the time the next entity kicks off, the delay between the audio channels can range up to several milliseconds. Unfortunately, Windows 95 has no power to influence this, so this delay may vary with every start.

Multi-channel Interleaved

This is another example where crafty programmers came up with an approach to leapfrog these obstacles.

Soon after Windows oozed out of the primordial swamp of its creator's minds, there were different soundcards with different options—for example, some were mono and others were stereo. Mme provides functions that ask a program exactly what the hardware can do. If the programmer did his job, the program will automatically detect that the hardware has eight channels. Fair enough, but what happens next?

Before we get into this, let's back up a bit and see how stereo is reproduced. In a stereo file, the information for the right and the left channel is by turns lined up in a row (Stereo Interleaved). The first byte is for the left channel, the second byte for the right channel, the third for the left and so on. Although much simplified, this is the gist of it—everything follows the same ›one left, one right ...‹ knitting pattern that grandma once used to drive grandpa out of the house.

›Multi Channel Interleaved‹ is the logical extension of this principle. Grandma might find it hard to follow this pattern with her knitting needles, but modern audio hardware handles it just fine: The first byte is for the first channel, the second for the second channel and so it goes on through to the final channel that the hardware is able to acknowledge.

And so the application knits its little audio stream and sends it off to the driver, which decodes it accordingly and routes the signal to the physical outputs.

The Upside

♦ There's only one driver entity and one audio stream. Problems caused by delayed starts of the different devices are precluded.

♦ If the 16-bit subsystem decides to become obstinate, it will obstruct just one (audio) process and not eight (which is an especially nightmarish scenario if it impedes these at random). It's easier to compensate for one delayed process using buffers.

♦ The effort involved in syncing different components falls by the wayside because the accuracy of the channels' timing is dead-on down to the last byte.

♦ It's easy to tell the drivers apart—there is, after all, just one.

The Downside

♦ This method requires more resources because the individual channels have to be packed up, whipped into line, and sent to the driver, where they have to be unpacked once they arrive. This chows down on both Cpu and memory performance.

♦ Individual outputs can no longer be addressed in parallel by several programs. In other words, you can't run Logic and let a soft synth like Rebirth noodle away at the same time. In all fairness though, Asio drivers won't let you do this either.

You'll enjoy the best of both worlds if your card speeds up the process by means of hardware support. Under the right conditions, this can compensate fully the drawbacks of poorer performance. RME Audio's card offers this feature.

▶ Bear in mind that both the driver and application must be able to handle this format.

Who Delivers the Goods?

After all of this background info, you're probably yearning for some hard facts. On the hardware side (and/or the corresponding drivers), the following cards can currently handle ›Multi Channel Interleaved‹ format:

◆ Emagic Audiowerk 8 (MME Driver 2.0)

◆ Frontier Design Group Wavecenter

◆ RME Audio DIGI 32/8 and DIGI 96

◆ Sonorus StudI/O

◆ Creamware TDAT 16

◆ Creamware Pulsar

Wavecenter, StudI/O, TDAT 16, Pulsar, and DIGI 32/8 can also run as ›Multiple Stereo Devices.‹

The following software supports these formats:

◆ Cubase VST 3.55 and higher

◆ Logic Audio 3.6 and higher

◆ Samplitude 4.0 and higher

Clearing Up the Details

So how do you recognize a ›Multi Channel Interleaved‹ driver in Windows 95/98? To put it bluntly, you can't. You'll be able to track down this elusive beast by looking at the software. You'll know it's there when an output device shows eight channels rather than two. You can actually select these in the same pop-up menus and windows that you use to select the left or right channel.

If a card offers both Interleaved and Multiple Stereo Devices, you have two options:

♦ You can switch between the two in the driver setup. The card will appear on your screen featuring either stereo or eight-channel visuals. This is, for example, how Audiowerk 8 works.

♦ The card simply registers several devices: one Stereo and one Multi Channel Interleaved. This is the approach used by Wavecenter, StudI/O and TDAT 16.

Is Multi Channel Interleaved support a selling point? Multi Channel Interleaved makes the most of MME and is thus an improvement in terms of synchronization and multi-channel reproduction, but it hasn't yet become a standard. Cubase and Logic, both of which are leading applications, offer their own, considerably more powerful architectures—ASIO and EASI. In short, Multi Channel Interleaved support shouldn't be a feature you focus on when, armed with a credit card and wild-eyed gear lust, you're ready to shop.

ASIO and EASI

You now know how problematic MME is in practice. As nice as the notion might be of being able to somehow run every card under the sun, the operative term here is ›somehow‹— in this case is more a threat than a promise.

Audio software vendors have long understood that ›by hook or by crook‹ won't do. They're in the business of moving products, but even the best virtual studio won't sell if you the user can't get it to work as fast as its real-world counterpart.

Clearly, if the root of all evil is the architecture, the obvious thing to do is design a new, improved architecture. Steinberg was at the vanguard of this development and, with ASIO, turned up a driver architecture that was initially reserved for it proprietary Cubase VST. ASIO has now been licensed to card and driver vendors as well as to other manufacturers of audio software (which in computerese is called the host software). Emagic's Logic Audio now also supports this architecture and can work with ASIO drivers. Since these two programs represent a big slice of the market, ASIO has become an important criterion in selecting a soundcard.

Cubase VST was the first application to support ASIO drivers.

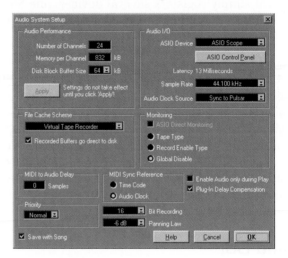

ASIO is a pure 32-bit architecture, which is why it doesn't have to vie for the attention of Windows and the CPU with the rival 16-bit subsystems of display adapters and MIDI. ASIO, like every driver, consists of two parts: the ASIO driver of the audio card and the part addressed by the host software (sequencer, audio editor) that is responsible for audio output. Here a virtuous circle is closed: recording and playback are made possible by a signal chain made up of the hardware, ASIO driver and audio software.

Virtually every audio card worth its salt ships with ASIO drivers and, yes, this is a key selling point when you're looking to buy hardware. Powered by the 32-bit system, the architecture is extremely efficient, which means latency can be as low as 3msec. Beware though, that buffers this small spell a bigger workload for the Cpu, so here too you'll have to poke and probe to find the best setting for your computer. With the average card and PII 300 or higher computer, you can expect latency to range from 10 to 30msec, which is some twenty times less than the listless Mme will give you.

Asio was ready for multi-channel audio from the start, so you won't be needing tricks such as Interleaving. However, Asio drivers can only be used by one program at a time. This means that if the driver of the card doesn't let you run Mme devices in parallel (unfortunately, this is sometimes the case), you will only be able to work with one audio program at a time.

How Do You Know Asio Is Available?

Unfortunately, there's no hard and fast rule here. Under Windows, you won't recognize it at all because Asio is not a Windows interface. Asio is used solely by the host software and the hardware's Asio driver. The installation procedure for Asio drivers also varies widely. Some cards install it automatically along with the normal Mme Windows driver. With other cards, you'll have to first establish certain conditions for it be installed.

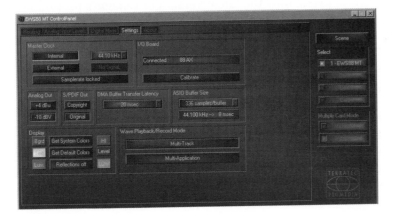

Ews88Mt features a window in which you can set the Asio parameters. However, this is not the case with all cards.

Exactly how Asio is interfaced with the host program also varies. In the case of some cards, the Asio driver is configured in the host program itself (Event Gina, Layla, Darla), other cards offer a window dedicated to this purpose (Terratec Ews88Mt). Then there are cards such as Creamware's Dsp platform Pulsar/Scope that won't let you fiddle with any Asio settings.

Who Supports Asio?

Software

First among software that supports Asio is of course, Cubase Vst. Emagic Logic Audio and Native Instrument's Reaktor also deliver support Asio.

Hardware

Almost every professional audio card supports Asio, even Isa soundcards such as the Ews64Xl now feature Asio drivers. The word is that Asio drivers will soon be available for the world's bestselling soundcard, Soundblaster.

Easi

Easi is a new standard by Emagic. At the time that this book went to press, only the latest version of Emagic's proprietary sequencer Logic supports Easi.

The only cards that support it are Sonorus StudI/O and Ego Systems Waveterminal 2496. Creamware's Pulsar/Scope should also be Easi-enabled by the time you're turning these pages.

Comparing Asio and Easi, the latter is the better documented of the two. Beyond that, it is an open standard that also supports sophisticated hardware features—for example, it will let you integrate a card's onboard effects. Should it win the support of hardware manufacturers, Easi could give rival standards a run for their money. But this is impossible to predict, so Easi drivers are only a selling point if you own

Logic. Since this sequencer also supports Asio, Easi shouldn't necessarily be your topmost priority.

DirectX

Microsoft too was quick to note the disadvantages of the old Mme interface under Windows 95. All of the most popular products in the lucrative games market were still being released as Dos versions because Windows was simply too slow in delivering graphics and sound.

Soon after the introduction of Windows 95, the new 32-bit interface DirectX was released. The idea behind it was to cut down on the number of operating system levels (and therefore intermediate processing stages) so that hardware would be addressed more directly thus speeding up the whole process. DirectX uses an output utility to access hardware directly with DirectX drivers. This is a functionality which Windows wasn't originally designed to deliver.

Another feature of DirectX is that it detects the features of the hardware and executes only those functions that the hardware does not offer. It does so by means of software emulations. Although these emulations are excruciatingly slow—the flow of frozen molasses comes to mind here—they do work.

Initially, DirectX consisted only of DirectDraw, the interface for graphics. This reason for this was simple enough—Windows' display powers were too puny for games, so this was the first attempt to boost it. Today DirectX is the moniker for a grab bag of interfaces for markedly different applications. DirectInput is responsible for controlling of joysticks, DirectPlay for playing games via a network, Direct3D for 3D rendering in games.

The bag holds three items of particular relevance to music applications:

DirectMusic

This is a MIDI interface. Regrettably, at the moment there is neither a MIDI interface available that supports DirectMusic nor software able to address such a MIDI interface should once actually exist. To date, DirectMusic consists merely of a software synthesizer (an emulated Roland Sound Canvas) which can only be addressed by an included test program.

However, DirectMusic has enormous potential because it offers powerful functions that solve a big problem with MIDI output. With DirectMusic, MIDI events are given a time stamp which gives the system precise control over the output signal. Without this, a MIDI program has to simply ›trust‹ that the MIDI message will be delivered on time.

DirectSound

This is DirectX's audio interface. Like ASIO, 32-bit processing has worked miracles, although ASIO is the better of the two in terms of latency. In HD recording, the latency of DirectSound drivers ranges from 100 to 200msec—much better than MME, but certainly not good enough to give anybody's mojo a rise.

Another handicap is its approach to recording. Microsoft unwisely decided that when DirectSound is running, recording is carried out by the MME driver. This means that a program designed to record and play back simultaneously—and this is absolutely the rule—is faced with the enormous problem of having to work with two different architectures at the same time. (Not the least of which is that playback and recording have a different latencies.) For obvious reasons, this ›innovation‹ didn't exactly sweep the planet. Audio software vendors disabled DirectSound recording in their programs.

Annoyingly, your audio application will nonetheless present a DirectSound input to you. But the program has a surprise in store for you if you actually attempt to record: the track will remain blank. There is a way to get around this in practice: simply activate MME for recording and DirectSound for playback and mixing.

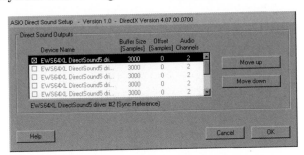

A look at Direct-Sound's output. Note that you can't play back and record at the same time.

DirectShow

You probably won't know this component by this name. And it is a bit out of the ordinary, for it has nothing whatsoever to do with hardware. Instead, the interface is designed to deal with data streams in real-time. It's probably beginning to dawn on you that we're looking at one of those infamous plug-ins here.

Virtually everyone calls this software extension a DirectX plug-in, although, strictly speaking, this is incorrect. This interface was once a separate program called ActiveMovie. Evidently to facilitate distribution, Microsoft threw it into the DirectX package. Audio software often still refer to it as ActiveMovie, so don't let this confuse you. You may think that you can only use this ›DirectX plug-in‹ with an audio card that supports DirectX. This is not the case.

Again, DirectShow has nothing to do with hardware—it's simply a way to assure some uniformity to make life a little easier for software and plug-in vendors. What you will need is a place into which to plug the plug-in—a program that supports DirectX. Which audio card you use is totally irrelevant.

Here's an example of a DirectShow plug-in that is commonly called a DirectX plug-in: Waves True Verb

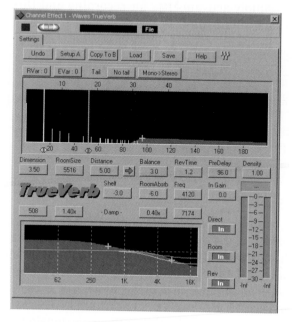

Who Delivers the Goods?

Let's back up a bit and look at who supports DirectShow plug-ins. All leading HD recording programs such as Cubase, Logic and Cakewalk do. The audio editors Wavelab, Sound-forge and Cool Edit Pro also support DirectShow. Future re-lease of the software synthesizer Reaktor will have DirectX support, however, here the situation is reversed: it will run as a DirectX plug-in.

Although DirectSound is also supported by all leading au-dio cards, it is not nearly as impressive for HD recording as is Asio.

DirectSound is all the more important for software synthe-sizers. Generally, you'll want to run several of these with your sequencer and Asio can't (at least not yet) be used by several programs simultaneously. Makers seem to have come to an unspoken consensus that DirectSound will serve as the output medium.

DirectMusic, on the other hand, doesn't to date enjoy the support of even a single application or MIDI interface.

▶ DirectMusic will be the key to MIDI operations under Windows 2000, the long-awaited successor of Windows NT. By the time you read this book, it's likely that the situation will have changed to the benefit of DirectMusic.

Problems with DirectX

The fundamental problem with DirectX lies in the different versions that are available. Over the years, Microsoft updated DirectX much more often than Windows—version 7 is current. Depending on which version you started with and which updater you used, you can end with an unspeakably vile mix of versions that can be the agent of the strangest, cruelest and most unusual phenomena in your computer. To make matters worse, you can't simply reinstall DirectX because Windows' version management won't let you.

▶ The kind-hearted folks of *c't* magazine mercifully offer a little tool that lets you reset the version numbers of all DirectX files so that a subsequent reinstallation will work out and you'll end up with a ›clean‹ system again. You'll find this program at
ftp://ftp.heise.de/pub/ct/listings/9903-204.zip

WDM

Microsoft has come up with another approach designed to once and for all get rid of that old 16-bit junk cluttering up the virtual landscape. Called ›Windows Driver Model‹ (WDM), this is a 32-bit driver architecture that is supposed to replace all old Windows 95/98 drivers. The aforementioned problems with the 16-bit subsystem will then fall by the wayside. The corresponding audio and MIDI drivers would serve as a substitute for MME, as it were.

WDM is supported by Windows 98 and Windows 2000 (NT 5.0). This provides the Microsoft's two disparate operating systems with a common driver platform and Windows 2000 with the broad hardware base that its predecessor Nt 4.0 never had.

Up to now Wdm drivers are available for just a few sound-cards (Soundblaster) and as a beta version, for one display adapter (Matrox). All is quite on the Wdm front: news of up-coming Wdm drivers for Isdn cards, Midi interfaces and other thrilling peripheral components have yet to be an-nounced. Therefore, I can't share with you any glossy pic-tures or profound practical experiences. Check out the Wizoo website every so often to see if this has changed.

What Makes Audio and Midi Act Up?

So far, we've taken a guided tour of many of the obstacles that Windows can throw in the intrepid musician's path. You can hurdle these by selecting the right hardware—display adapters and soundcards. All the same, in Windows' depths lurk all kinds of monsters intent on ruining your day.

As you can well imagine after our stroll through the archi-tecture, to assure trouble-free operation, you must switch off everything that could run in parallel with your audio/Midi program. Starting with utilities for the display adapter and virus scanners, and including indexing programs that a cer-tain office software package known far and wide installs without asking your permission. In short, you have to nip all potential troublemakers in the bud.

To the average Jack or Jill, an installation program might as well be Mandarin Chinese. Few know what they need and don't need, and the rare user who does know often doesn't have a choice in the matter—the program installs whatever it damn well pleases. So, unfortunately, there's no getting around tidying up the installation by hand.

Windows has a total of four mechanisms that detect pro-grams at system start-up and launch automatically. And you may never know that an application is running. Some stealthy virus scanners run in the background without you ever seeing a window or icon indicating as much.

Autostart

The Autostart group is located in the Start menu, which does seem a rather obvious place for it. Programs with links filed in this folder are launched automatically.

I can't tell you exactly what you'll find there, but if you've installed an Ms Office package, in all probability you'll be looking at something like the screenshot below. By all means delete these two links. They launch a search program that runs in the background and searches for Word files, Excel files and the like so that they appear that much faster in the File/Open dialog.

You can live happily ever after without this feature, but its hard disk scanning activities can certainly inconvenience your audio recording aspirations. Say goodbye and dispatch it to the virtual limbo where it belongs.

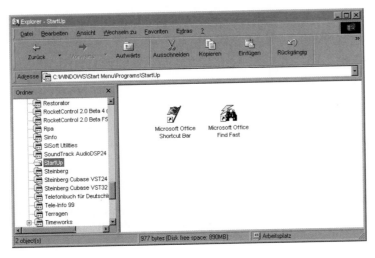

The indexing routine of Microsoft Office. You can with extreme prejudice off both entries.

Registry

The registry is a central database in which Windows stores configuration settings. It consists of two files, user.dat and system.dat, that you can edit only via a special program that goes by the name of ›Regedit.‹ This is one of those areas where angels fear to tread, so don't rush in foolishly. The registry contains very important information that, should you unintentionally delete it, will cause very, very bad things to happen. Please limit your actions exclusively to the steps that I'll show you and leave everything else exactly as you found it.

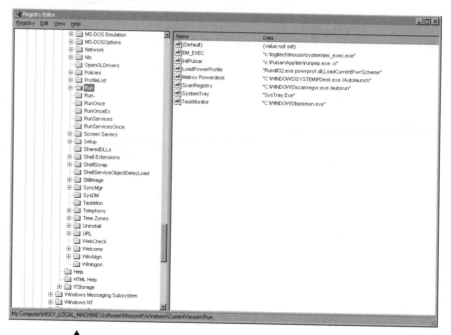

↑   This is where you can determine within the registry which programs will run in the background. Much but not all of this stuff can be deleted without causing harm.

1   Click on Start and Run.

2   Type in regedit and press the Enter key.

Now you're looking at the registry. In the left window, you'll see so-called keys arranged in a tree structure much like files in the Explorer.

3 Click on down to the key Hkey_local_machine\Software\Microsoft\Windows\Currentversion.

Here you'll find four critical keys, Run, Runonce, Runservices and Runservicesonce. Some of the stuff in here is quite beneficial. Generally, you can—and I do hate to use this term here—guess what the purpose of an entry is by deciphering the combination of file names that it contains.

Before you continue, you should make a backup of the branch of the registry tree that you want to edit by exporting it.

4 Say you want to edit the Run key. Click on it and select the command Export Registry File from the Registry menu.

Now you can determine what you want to export, the entire registry or just the selected branch. When in doubt, select All, which means you'll be saving what is called a ›Reg‹ file. If something goes wrong, you can later restore the old settings by simply double-clicking on the icon for this file.

Now you're ready to do some serious invasive surgery, so let's not make it of the exploratory variety. The gee-I-wonder-what-will-happen-if-I-delete-this approach is not the mindset you should adopt here. Sticking with our little exercise with the Run key, Em_Exec supports my particular mouse, Microsoft IntelliType Pro is a utility for my keyboard. ScanRegistry is a special service courtesy of Windows 98. As you would expect, it scans the registry for errors and fixes any that it finds. This service runs once only during start-up and not constantly in the background, so it's not a problem. Init-Scope initializes my soundcard, which means it stays. The Matrox Powerdesk utility, however, has to do with the display adapter and is therefore dispensable.

5 Delete this type of entry by clicking on it once and pressing ⌞del⌟.

The task monitor, which carries out maintenance tasks at specific intervals, is another troublemaker. Although some of these tasks are quite useful, you should start them manually. For example, defragmentation is one of these tasks and it's not a great idea to defrag while recording audio. Feel free to delete the registry entry called TaskMonitor.

The RunOnce key should contain no entries at all. This is where installation programs register entries that are processed immediately after the first reboot and then deleted automatically. If you do find an entry, the installation routine of some program did sloppy work and you can safely delete it.

RunServices and RunServicesOnce should also be empty on a standard computer. If you find something here, you'll have to find out whether or not the entry is required by the system just as you did for the Run key.

Of the four keys discussed here, this one is unique in that you may delete an entry even if you don't know precisely what it is. Windows will start even when nothing is registered here. Again, this is the only key that lends itself to speculative bonzaiing. If you delete something important, you can restore it with the backup that you created in step 4. In all other parts of the registry, you can't do this because Windows may not launch when you delete some entries. In this case your backup copy is useless so proceed with restraint and caution when you're working with the other keys.

win.ini

This file dates back to Windows 3.11, Windows 9x also uses it for reasons of compatibility. It contains two entries that can also start programs. win.ini is a text file, but the more convenient editing option is to use a file that goes by the name of ›Sysedit.‹ Click on Start ⇨ Run, and type in sysedit.

Here's how you call
the Sysedit file.

You'll now see a view of old files that date back to the days of
Dos and Windows 3.11.

1 Click on the window of the file win.ini and you'll see the two critical
entries Load= and Run=

Whatever you may find doesn't belong here, for it is part of
an old program.

2 Delete everything following the equal sign.

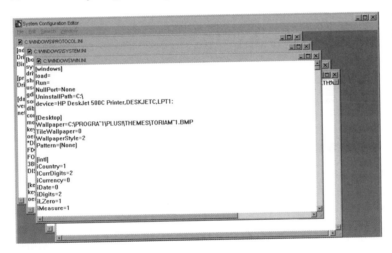

This is what the
win.ini file should
look like: Load= and
Run= is followed by
nothing at all.

autoexec.bat and config.sys

These two files are relics from the stone age of personal computing, the operating system Ms-Dos, and they too have survived for reasons of compatibility. Windows 9x will start even
if these files are unavailable, so in principle, you can delete
them. Nevertheless, I recommend that you don't.

These two files contain functions of the Ms-Dos input prompt under Windows. Even if you couldn't imagine for what purpose, you may need these someday. Notably, the files translate the layout of non-Us keyboards so that the computer interprets your input properly, which, for the obvious reasons, is good if you're using another type of keyboard.

The two files should look much like the one in the illustration below. Anything beyond what you see depicted is highly likely to be irrelevant and probably extremely annoying. Dos drivers, for example are not only superfluous, they're actually quite treacherous under Windows. And since autoexec.bat and config.sys are loaded before Windows is actually started, the Os can't do a search-and-destroy number on these mischief-makers.

autoexec.bat and config.sys should look like this.

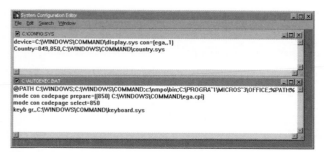

Conveniently, there's a safe method of checking what happens when you edit these files. Simply type Rᴇᴍ in front of the line in question, store the edited file, and restart your computer. The computer will ignore all lines starting with Rᴇᴍ, which lets you find out if this change will cause weird things to happen. If it does, delete Rᴇᴍ and everything will be back to normal.

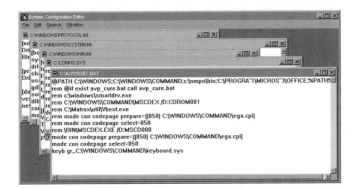

A few lines that have been commented out (labeled with REM).

In the picture, you'll see some lines that have been ›re-marked‹ or ›commented out‹ by typing REM into the lower portion of the files. These were inserted by Dos installations, in other words, by Scsi Dos drivers and the Dos installation routine of an IDE CD-ROM drive. These Dos drivers can be a huge thorn in the side of your hardware.

For example, the popular soundcard Terratec Ews64 responds with the most bizarre crashes if Dos drivers are loaded for an Scsi controller in config.sys. Hard disk performance under Windows also suffers considerably. These old drivers can slow your new high-performance disk down to a snail's pace.

▶ The rule of thumb for autoexec.bat and config.sys is that you should comment stuff out liberally by typing in REM. Your audio applications will definitely show their gratitude by delivering better performance.

How Do You Make Windows Fit for Music?

If you've followed along with all tips thus far and haven't turned your box into an inert zombie in the process, you should have a rather stable system for music applications.

Allow me to recap the most important measures:

◆ Although this doesn't concern Windows directly, you should opt for quality hardware and avoid no-name, bargain-bin gear.

◆ Tweak the Bios as described in the imaginatively named section ›Bios‹ on page 81.

◆ Without fail, install the drivers for your mainboard under Windows. These should ship with your computer; if they don't, ask your dealer for them or download the drivers from the website of the manufacturer. The focus here is not so much on the actual drivers for the mainboard, but rather the drivers for the chipset. Typically, new chipsets were released after the current Windows version hit the market, which means that Windows won't recognize them. Also, many computer dealers don't bother to install these drivers. Your computer will probably run Ok until the time comes that you install a new audio card or start demanding more hard disk performance. As soon as you want to run an audio application, the Os must be able to identify the chipset to assure flawless operation of the Pci bus.

◆ Switch on Dma hard disk mode in the Device Manager of Windows for every disk drive that you're running (for details, see the chapter ›The Hard Disk‹ on page 109).

◆ Switch your box's power management facility off (see ›Bios‹ on page 81).

◆ When you're ready to buy a soundcard, be sure that at least Asio drivers ship with it. The best you could hope for would be a everything-but-the-kitchen-sink deluxe edition featuring Asio, Easi, DirectX, Wdm and Windows Nt drivers. Sadly, this is only the case with pricey professional products.

◆ Avoid all programs that run in the background. Track these down and eliminate them as described in the previous section.

◆ Defragment your hard disk at least once a week.

There are many more optimization tips that I'll share with you. In the following section, you'll find a hodgepodge of tricks that, although they defy categorization, can be anything from useful to vital for your music-making ambitions.

Disabling CD Detection

After a standard installation, Windows will habitually check the CD drive every now and then to find out if a new CD has been inserted. You can well appreciate what a nuisance this can be if it happens while you're recording audio to disk. This is above all the case with an IDE disk drive because, as explained in the chapter ›The Hard Disk‹ on page 109, the IDE controller can't address two devices simultaneously. If Windows fires up its CD detection routine, your disk will grind to a sudden halt. Your program may suddenly stutter like a talk show host on an amphetamine bender or it may turn obstinate and freeze up altogether.

Since it can cause these bad things to happen, we'll disable this detection routine:

1 Go to the Device Manager, look for your CD-ROM drive and double-click the corresponding icon.

2 In the following options window, click on the tab labeled Settings.

Just like in the diagram below, the option Auto Insert Notification should not be check-marked. If you use several CD-ROM drives or a separate burner, repeat this step for each drive.

Switching off auto-detection will have a side effect. You're probably accustomed to an installation routine or some other utility that explores the content of the CD starting immediately and automatically after you insert a CD-ROM into the disk drive. This will no longer be the case when you disable the automatic detection function. Personally, I consider this an advantage because, after a while, these automatic start windows are more a burden than a blessing.

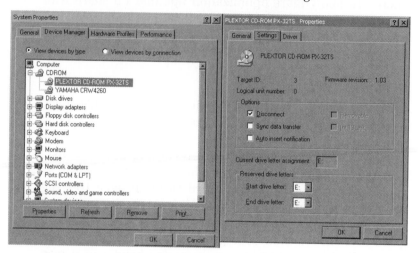

↑   This is what your screen should look like: Auto Insert Notification (for the CD-ROM) should be switched off.

Beefing Up Hard Disk Write Performance

Windows doesn't offer many accessible tuning options. One of the few that you can fiddle with is hard disk management. The operating system can request data in advance from the hard disk if it expects a program to request successive data. You can determine how far it looks ahead as follows:

1   Open the Control Panel again.

2   Double-click System.

3   Now select the tab labeled Performance instead of the familiar Device Manager.

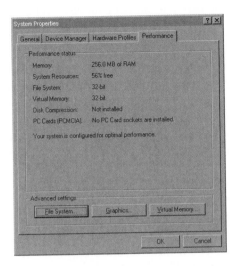

This time it's not our friend the Device Manager that we're going to visit. Now we want to edit Performance.

4 At the bottom of the window you'll find a button called File System. Click it and you'll see the following window:

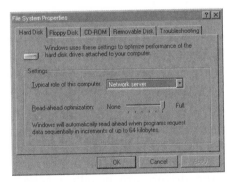

Optimizing the file system.

In this example, I set the option to 100%, which means that Windows will snoop ahead and read up to 64 kilobytes of data in advance. This value should be adjusted to deliver the best results with your HD recording program.

▶ If your program works with smaller blocks, Windows may see exactly what we all see when we look into the crystal ball—nothing. In this case, back off the value step by step and see if hard disk performance improves. The best you can hope for is to wring one or two extra tracks from your system.

There is another tuning measure shown in the above screen-shot. The option selected for Typical role of this machine is Network Server. This setting tells Windows to consider data throughput to and from the hard disk a priority, which is beneficial to HD recording. However, you'll have a bit less computing power left over for plug-ins and soft synths. Select Desktop Computer if this is primarily how you use your computer.

(By the way, this setting is flawed in Windows 95. Some programmer with mayhem on his mind flip-flopped the names of the options Mobile or Docking System and Network Server. This means that if you want to select the Network Server option, you'll have to enable Mobile or Docking System in the window. This bug has been exterminated in Windows 98.)

Virtual Memory

Windows 95 lets you use part of the hard disk to simulate main memory. This assures that programs are always executed even when there isn't enough physical memory available. The mechanism can be bothersome in two situations:

♦ When a software sampler or a soundcard accesses the memory, there's no time for fooling around. If the samples that it wants are loitering about on the hard disk rather than in Ram, there's going to be trouble. Commercial applications and drivers are usually programmed so that data is not transferred to the hard drive, but this is not always the case with shareware.

♦ Windows adjusts the amount of required hard disk dynamically and you can bet that it will to so at precisely the wrong moment, for example, when you're recording the most heart-felt, soulful vocal performance ever. When the system drops out at this critical juncture, thoughts that involve Microsoft's headquarters, 500 gallons of gasoline and a book of matches may cross your mind.

Before you are driven to commit mahem, you should adjust the settings for the virtual main memory (Swap file).

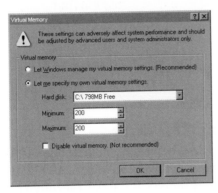

When you set the upper and lower limits to the same value, Windows won't tamper with the Swap file any more.

1 Go to the Control Panel and click on System, then the tab labeled Performance.

At the bottom you'll find a button labeled Virtual Memory. It is the key to the Swap file.

2 In the user-defined settings, enter an identical value for the top and bottom threshold.

This dupes Windows so that it will no longer adjust the amount of hard disk dynamically. Enter a value that's roughly triple the size of your main memory, but no less than 150MB. If have 256MB or more of main memory, simply enter the actual size of your memory.

▶ With 256MB of RAM, you could also try switching off the virtual memory altogether. To this end, simply click on the corresponding box in the above window.

This is how you switch off virtual memory. However, you shouldn't try this if you have less than 256MB available, otherwise—rather than the start screen of a program—you'll often see a message telling you that there's not enough RAM available.

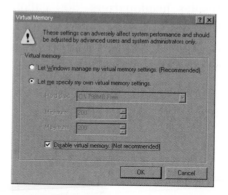

Tweaking Hard Disk Cache

Another topic closely related to the Swap file is the disk cache of Windows, which we'll look at now. This is an area of the memory that buffers the most recently read data of the hard disk. The reason to have a cache is that in all probability, some data will have to be read several times. Having this data in the cache is highly efficient; in fact, it catapults performance by several hundred percent and has done so since the days of Ms-Dos.

Windows 95 and 98 are able to adapt—just like virtual memory on the disk—the size of this cache dynamically. Normally, this is a nice-to-have feature, for it assures that the physical memory is put to better use. If you're an old hand at computing, you may recall with a shudder the trial-and-error ordeal that tweaking cache size was under Windows 3.11.

The problem with music applications is that when Windows changes the size of the cache, it also reorganizes the memory and typically does so at the most inopportune moments. Therefore, you're well advised to switch this mechanism off under Windows 95/98.

This is a bit more involved and you can't actually do it in Windows. The trick is that Windows 95 also scans the file system.ini, which is another one of those Windows 3.11 relics that has survived for reasons of compatibility.

Open the file in ›Sysedit,‹ which you can launch by typing in sysedit under Start ⇨ Run. Now look for a file called system.ini and enter the following three lines:

```
[vcache]
MaxFileCache=32768
MinFileCache=32768
```

These entries define the maximum and minimum size of the disk cache. By assigning two identical values, you are outwitting Windows and disabling this dynamic resizing feature.

The numbers in the example are in KB and apply to a main memory with 256MB. This gives you a cache with 64MB, which is also the upper limit. You should dedicate no more than a quarter of the available RAM to the cache. Use the table below to figure out which cache size is best for your computer:

Vcache Settings in system.ini

RAM size in MB	Entry in the file system.ini
32	8192
48	10240
64	16384
96	24576
128 and more	32768

IRQ Steering and Plug&Play under Windows

As you recall, we took a closer look at Plug&Play in the chapter ›Hardware Installation‹ on page 98. You may be surprised to see it pop up again here in a chapter dedicated to Windows, but there is method in my madness.

In Versions OSR 2 and higher, Windows 95 can reconfigure Plug&Play resources such as IRQs and memory addresses even after the BIOS has assigned these resources. Windows 98 also has this capability. To this end, Windows install a special driver called IRQ holder. It reroutes all calls to and from the hardware to the given IRQ.

If in the Device Manager you click on the Computer icon, you may see something similar to this screenshot. Two entities of the IRQ holder that controls IRQ sharing are available.

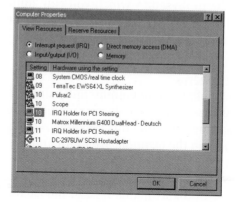

You can see this IRQ depicted in the screenshot above. Bear in mind that the IRQ holder can also use the resources of the card that are distributed by the BIOS. However, it may also mask the fact that the card actually uses another interrupt because you won't see this assignment mirrored in the Device Manager.

This little song and dance is called ›IRQ steering.‹ The mechanism costs valuable time when hardware is addressed directly—especially when Windows actually reroutes IRQs and each of these interrupt requests arrives with a delay of some nanoseconds because the IRQ holder has to first figure out for which destinations these interrupts are intended. Worse, if several cards share an IRQ, then all drivers have to be called up until the right one is found.

The influence of this mechanism in practical has been the subject of some controversy. The problem is that Windows is able to redistribute resources, but it is not compelled to do so. Quite the opposite is true: normally, the resources will be controlled by the BIOS. If, however, you deliberately assign the PCI slots to specific IRQs manually in the BIOS, you certainly don't want Windows to tamper with these resources and confuse the issue.

This is why you can switch off PCI Steering in the Device Manager. Simply click on the System Devices icon and look for an entry called PCI bus.

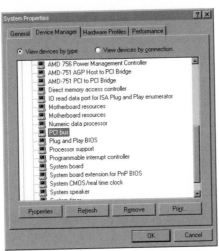

You'll find the icon for the PCI bus in the Device Manager.

As usual, a double-click will take you to the Options window. There you'll see a tab labeled IRQ Steering. Unlike so much computerese, this doesn't take an engineering degree to decipher. Here you can fine-tune exactly where Windows gathers its information on Plug&Play. In practice, the benefits are negligible—leave it as it is or switch off IRQ steering altogether as shown in the screenshot.

Here's how you disable IRQ steering.

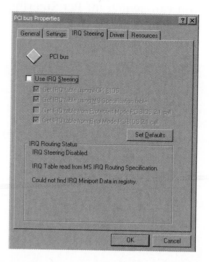

If you've resolved the PCI and resource conflicts described in the section ›Bus Systems: ISA and PCI‹ on page 72, there won't be any drawbacks when you disable IRQ steering in Windows. On the contrary, performance may improve. To be honest, the improvement won't be perceptible on every computer.

Audio Mapper and MIDI Mapper

Windows itself also has rudimentary options for managing MIDI and audio. These were designed for very basic programs that don't offer their own setting options for playback and recording.

You want to be able to determine freely which devices will render audio—for instance, those annoying system sounds—or which MIDI device will play a standard MIDI file from the Internet. Enter the mappers.

Ignore the MIDI mapper. It isn't configured upon installation anyway, so it won't get in the way, which is just the way we want it.

The audio mapper is another story. Windows will crash when a card that does not support 8-bit playback is selected as a device. Eight bits is an entirely insignificant format for musicians, but it was used in old games and still sees wide use on the Internet.

Some professional cards no longer support this mode. This may cause Windows to freeze when you boot it for the first time after you've installed the card. To prevent this unwelcome situation, enter the following settings to Windows 95:

◆ Click on the Multimedia icon in the Control Panel. In this window, select None for Preferred Device for Recording and Playback. You'll have to kiss the system sounds goodbye (what a shame), but you can be sure that the mapper won't give you any more grief.

▶ Windows 98 doesn't offer the option Option None, there you'll find an entry called Use Any Available Device. On the up side, this bug has been exterminated in Windows 98.

The drivers of some older cards won't let several programs access the hardware simultaneously. If the audio mapper commandeers the card, your audio program may sulk since it can't address the soundcard. You can also prevent this problem with the above settings.

Disabling Window Animation

Windows is able to animate menus and windows, for example, when you zoom a window smaller or click on a menu item. This stuff may look neat, but it chows down on performance power. Besides, on account of Windows' architecture, animation can also cause all kinds of trouble in the multimedia subsystem. Your best bet is to simply switch it off.

For Windows 98 users, this is a cinch: go to the Control Panel, take a look in Display and the tab labeled Effects. There you can disable animation by deactivating ›Animate windows, menus and lists‹ as shown in the screenshot.

Here's how you can switch off something you can well do without—animation.

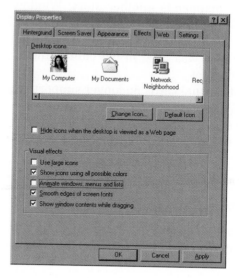

Windows 95 users must resort to an additional utility, Power Toys by Microsoft. You'll find this useful program suite at http://www.microsoft.com/

Double Buffer

If you employ an Scsi controller for which Windows failed to supply a driver during installation, chances are that a double-buffer was installed for this controller. This serves the purposes of data protection for older controllers and you can switch it off if you're running a more recently-made card. Double-buffering takes a big bite out of the performance pie by slowing down hard disk access.

You'll find the setting that controls the double-buffer in a hidden file. Obviously, to change this setting you'll have to make the hidden file visible. You can then delete the entry that activates double-buffering.

1   Open disk drive C in My Computer.

2   Click the menu item View and then Folder Options.

3   On the tab labeled View you'll see a setting that lets you view hidden files. Select ›Show all files.‹

4   Now when you look at disk drive C, in addition to all of your folders, you should see a file named msdos.sys.

5   Right-click the file icon and select Properties. A window will appear; deactivate write protection in it.

6   You can now open the file by double-clicking it. You should see the following entry:
    DoubleBuffer=1

7   Delete this entry, store the file and close it.

8   Enable write protection.

9   Restart the computer.

If you should ever re-install Windows, this entry will be reset to the default, which means you'll have to repeat these steps.

Windows 3.11 Drivers under Windows 95/98

Believe it or not, the retrograde compatibility of Windows allows it to use old Windows 3.11 drivers. These drivers can bring on many of *the* vile things a computer can do to make your life miserable—for example, system crashes or total refusal of a program to work with your hardware.

How Do You Recognize Windows 3.11 Drivers?

You'll recognize Windows 3.11 drivers by, well, not recognizing them: you won't find them in the Device Manager, they're listed under Multimedia under Control Panel. And this is the only place that you can configure and delete them.

Old Windows 3.11
drivers are picky
about where they
hang out—you'll find
them only in the
Control Panel under
Multimedia.

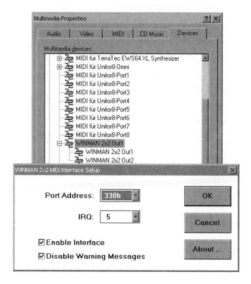

1   Click the Multimedia icon in Control Panel.

2   Select the tab labeled Devices in the window.

Here you'll find a list of all devices that are available for multimedia applications. If the list contains a device that doesn't appear in the Device Manager, you've pinpointed one of these pesky drivers.

▶ Typically, you may find the MIDI interface drivers Midiman Winman 1×1 and 2×2.

What Can You Do about It?

First you should try to get the Windows 95/98 drivers from the hardware vendor. Then you can delete the device from the Multimedia window and install the Windows 95/98 drivers in the usual manner.

If it routinely gives you problems and the manufacturer is unable to provide real Windows 95/98 drivers, your best bet is to do without the hardware. There's simply no way that you can tweak the system to deliver decent performance.

You'll have to bite the bullet and invest in a soundcard and a MIDI interface that ship with genuine Windows 95/98 drivers.

The Different Windows Versions

Windows 95

Over the years, a number of quite different Windows 95 versions have been released. You can find out which system you own by clicking System in the Control Panel. This window indicates the Windows version number.

The very first version, the mother of all Windows 95 versions so to speak, is called 4.00.950. It was followed successively by the versions 950A, 950B (also called OSR 2), OSR 2.1 and OSR 2.5. These of course allowed Microsoft to incorporate changes, bug fixes and support for new hardware. Examples of the latter are the Bx chipset (OSR 2.5) and USB and DMA support in OSR 2.

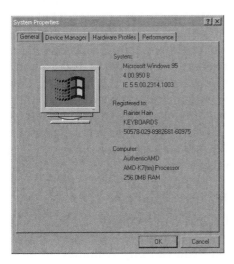

The version number of Windows, here the version 950B.

Unfortunately—and please feel free to express your outrage as you read this—there's no way to legally replace your Windows 95 version with a newer version. Oh yes, all versions that followed the original Windows 95 were offered for sale, but only if you spent trifle extra on an inconsequential piece of gear—a new computer. On the upside, chances are that your computer already runs one of the newer versions.

For older Windows versions, you can download the changes from the Microsoft website individually, so that you're not left out in the cold if you want to install your operating system to a new computer.

Things about Windows 95 that Drive Musicians Nuts
The first that musicians will notice problem with Windows 95 is a bug in the MME system. Only eleven MIDI ports can be addressed, even if nominally you could install more. This applies to virtual MIDI ports designed to allow communication between programs as well as the drivers of a soundcard or software synthesizer.

You'll know this bug is there when you simply can't address specific MIDI ports—no matter what you do, nothing goes in and nothing comes out. In the worst case, this will cause MIDI programs to crash.

The Multimedia Control Panel is also a bit idiosyncratic. It will go on strike when it feels that too many soundcards have been installed. Although this doesn't affect audio programs—these don't use multimedia as an intermediary, communicating instead directly with the driver—you may encounter problems with system sounds or when you're playing back sounds from the Internet.

Windows 98

To belabor the patently obvious, Windows 98 is the successor to Windows 95. Here, unlike Windows 95, you have an upgrading option—you can buy Windows 98 on the market in the form of a normal update.

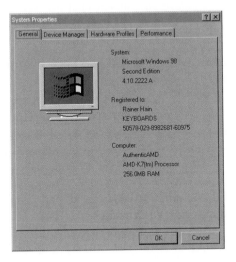

Frankly, you should do that. Although 98 is not any faster, a vast number of bugs have been exterminated, for instance, the bug that limits you to eleven MIDI ports. You also get a central system management tool that makes it much easier to carry out administrative tasks for your computer. Beyond that, system files are afforded better protection—it's not nearly as easy to overwrite these when you're installing new software. For my money, that alone is worth the cost of an update.

Windows 98 also supports a completely new driver architecture called WDM. For the time being, this isn't cause for celebration because few of these drivers are available, but that is bound to change in the future. Notably, WDM drivers run under Windows 98 as well as Windows 2000 (the successor to Windows NT 4.0), which stands to simplify the development of drivers and eventually make them significantly more versatile. Particularly for MME, the pesky problem with the 16-bit artifacts, which plagues Windows 98 as well as Windows 95, will finally be resolved.

▶ Be aware that Windows 98's fundamental architecture is no different to Windows 95. This means you can use older Windows 95 drivers without jeopardizing your sanity.

A Brief Discourse on Windows 98 and Musical Applications

On the upside, the bug that limited you to eleven MIDI ports has been fixed in Windows 98. On the downside, this Os still has to be tweaked to suit the purposes of the musician.

The problem is that Windows 98 lets you configure something called an ›active desktop,‹ which lets you plaster your interface with Web content. This extension has a voracious appetite for memory and resources. The installer will ask you during the installation routine if you want this active desktop as your standard interface.

If you missed my little monologue or your dealer meant all too well and installed it for you, you should put a stop to this resource-devouring ›convenience‹ now:

◆ Click on Display in the Control Panel and then on the tab labeled Web.

The settings on your screen should look just like those depicted in the screenshot, i. e. there shouldn't be check-marks next to Show Active Desktop as Website and Internet Explorer Channel list.

This is what your screen should look like when you want to do without an active desktop.

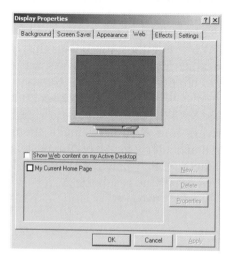

By contrast, the Fat32 file system is a welcome innovation in Windows 98. Windows 95's Fat16 limits files to a maximum size of 2Gb. Usually, this is plenty, but there are applications—for example, loading a lengthy live recording from Dat to edit it on your Pc—when it's not.

Although Windows 98—or more accurately its file system—no longer has this limit, you will have to configure a partition to hold a file of this size. You'll find further info on this in the chapter ›The Hard Disk‹ starting on page 109.

Alternative Operating Systems

There is life beyond Windows—it is of course not the only operating system that will run on a Pc. Indeed, hardly a computer platform offers you as many operating systems to chose from.

In addition to Windows 95/98, Windows Nt/2000 and Os/2, there are diverse Unix variants—the most popular being Linux—and BeOs. As you learned in the chapter ›The Operating System‹ on page 143, the fact that an operating system is available doesn't necessarily mean it will serve your purposes. The decisive factors are whether or not programs that you want and need have been written for it and if drivers for the Os are available for the hardware that you want to use.

This means that, for all practical purposes, there are only two alternatives to Windows 95/98 for audio/Midi application—BeOs and Windows Nt/2000. All other systems are not suitable for making music either because of their design or technology, or because they haven't evolved to a point where musicians who don't have advanced computer skills will be able to handle them.

Linux freaks will most decidedly disagree and, true enough, installing and running Linux for routine chores in the average office environment is no longer an arcane science. Finding the right programs and configuring audio and

MIDI is, however, a challenge that even the seasoned pro might find daunting. Although some applications are available for Linux, as virtuous as the Os might be, I can't recommend it to the musician.

BeOs

BeOs is a 32-bit operating system designed specifically with multitasking and multithreading in mind. MacOs and Windows make the same claim, but now you know that they are watered down to assure retrograde compatibility.

The basic idea behind Be's approach is to ›lighten up‹— throw the unnecessary ballast of so much ›legacy code‹ overboard. Every application is a client that can address different servers depending on the task the program is executing. In this respect, it is similar to the Internet, albeit much smaller and much faster. There's nothing in between the operating system and the hardware core to slow things up. The data paths are shorter than with MacOs and Windows and thus more efficient. This gives BeOs a fundamental performance advantage and it has proven its suitability for multimedia time and again.

What's So Different about BeOs?

Well, everything and nothing really. You could say that the interface is the product of cross-pollination, a composite of all known operating systems—a touch of Apple here, a pinch of Windows there, all topped off with a dash of Unix. Whatever the user may be accustomed to, he'll find enough familiar trappings so that he won't feel lost. The Apple menu is called Be menu, and the Windows user can open the usual context menu with the right mouse button. Although at heart it has to nothing to do with Unix, there is also a bash-compatible shell, which will bring to joy to the heart of command line fetishists.

BeOs doesn't ›feel‹ much faster than Windows 98, NT or Linux when you're running routine applications on a PC.

However, when you start putting a Pc through its paces and push it to extremes, you'll be amazed at this Os's response. Where Windows would slow to an excruciating crawl, Be's windows simply open a little slower, but it continues soldiering on bravely. You'll never know that sinking feeling of twiddling your thumbs for minutes at a time waiting for a mouse click to be carried out.

Be's onboard features include just about everything you need to have fun—even getting connected to the Internet is a piece of cake. Alas, the same thing I said for MacOs and Windows holds true here—man does not live by the operating system alone, which brings us to the bad news:

Applications for BeOs

Unfortunately, although Steinberg and Emagic have announced that applications are in the offing, other than the odd utility, they haven't turned up anything of substance yet. No serious recording program that runs on Be is available at this time. In fact, Emagic has abandoned its development for BeOs and Steinberg may be soon to follow.

Hardware for BeOs

The hardware compatibility list is about as long as a list of fun things to do in North Point, Alaska, in winter which is to say quite short.

The onboard Scsi interface is not supported by the Asus P2B-S used by many musicians. There are also no drivers for any of the professional Midi interfaces. A rumored BeOs driver for the Event/Echo-Layla card is supposedly in the works and the situation will be much improved with its arrival. But, as it stands, I won't be wasting much ink on a compatibility list.

▶ If you want to learn more about what's happening with Be, check out
http://www-us.beeurope.com/support/guides/
beosreadylist_intel.html.

Should You Gear Up for BeOs?

Many moons will come and go before you can work professionally using BeOs. Microsoft has released Windows 2000 and solved a lot of that Os's problems, so it seems likely that hardware and software manufacturers will first scurry to provide support for the Microsoft product.

▶ Don't bet on seeing this situation change in the near future. The question is not when Be will be looking at brighter future, the question is if it is looking at any future at all. Be's recent decisions indicate it does not consider BeOs as its future.

Windows 2000

Windows 2000 is by no means the successor to Windows 98 even if its name suggests as much. Perhaps baffling everyone but Microsoft's marketing masterminds, it's actually the successor to Windows Nt 4.0, Microsoft's professional product. Windows Nt has been around for years, but it is (or was) generally an ›enterprise‹ operating system.

What looks and smells like Windows 98, but is an entirely different critter? Windows 2000.

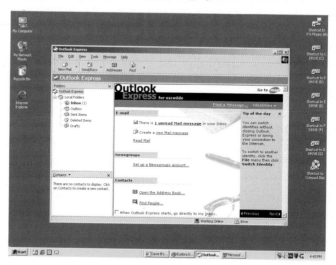

As discussed in the section ›Windows‹ on page 145, Windows NT (and thus Windows 2000) are completely different operating systems that have to nothing with the Windows 95/98 architecture.

With one exception, none of the 95/98 drivers will work, you'll always need specific NT drivers. The exception is WDM (Windows Driver Model)—these drivers will run on both Windows 98 and 2000.

Most real 32-bit programs also run under NT/2000, as do many old 16-bits programs. These programs are executed in a dedicated subsystem, which in turn is handled by the system exactly the same way it deals with 32-bit programs. This means that the 16-bit system can't, as so often is the case in Windows 95, hog the system and edge out all other applications. No program is able to access the hardware directly or overwrite important components of the system in the memory.

All of this adds up to one thing—Windows NT is incredibly stable. Should a program crash—which isn't all that far-fetched—nothing much will happen except that the system will mention it to you in passing. You won't have to reboot the computer—just launch the errant program and you can get straight back to work.

Multitasking and multithreading are part of the package, only these processes run a lot smoother. And true enough, an NT computer has a cool vibe—it actually ›feels‹ a lot smoother than a Windows 95/98 computer.

As usual, there's a bit of a catch, in this case memory requirements. Don't give Windows 2000 or NT another thought if you're unwilling or unable to find enough green in your wallet for at least 128MB.

What's So Different about 2000?

The interface of Windows NT is very similar to that of Windows 95/98. Although some things, including the Device Manager, did go AWOL for a while these familiar elements have reported back for duty—undoubtedly due to the fact Windows 2000 now supports Plug&Play. The look of Windows 2000 is a little more futuristic and professional than that of Windows 98.

Some tips also work for Windows 2000, e. g. limiting the virtual memory size.

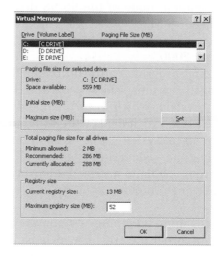

Experienced Windows 95/98 users won't have any difficulty adapting. The majority of handling techniques translate well. The installation procedure for drivers is very similar. Some of the tweaking tips of this book will apply, for example, the trick by which you can limit the size of the virtual main memory. The Plug&Play tips will also work.

And you won't have to worry about obstinate 16-bit MME subsystems or display adapter drivers because they've all been sent back to the virtual hell from whence they came.

There are also some differences. Windows 2000 features a user management system governed by an extensive and detailed set of user rights. You have to log in to your own computer before you can get to work. A normal user is not empowered to change system settings. Smart move, if you ask me. In any case, only users with administrator privileges can fiddle with these rights. You can open up an administrator account during installation and can add further users later on.

As a normal user, you can install an application, but not a driver, as the instructions that come with NT drivers routinely point out.

Windows 2000 also offers services that run in background without your being aware of them. These processes carry out many basic operating system functions. You can access these services using the Control Panel, which you'll also find in Windows 2000. This is where you should look for processes that could spoil your audio pleasure. On the upside, it's much easier to shut down and restart these services with Windows 2000's graphic interface than it is with Windows 98.

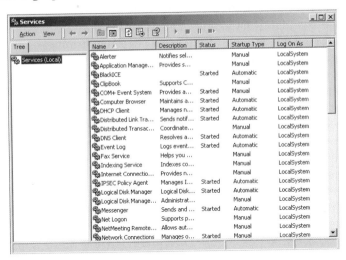

Windows 2000 background services: This is where you'll find the pesky ones.

A complete tour of Windows 2000 is well beyond the scope of this book. So instead I'll regularly post the most important tips and tricks on the WIZOO website for you as soon as I am more familiar with Windows 2000 and I can check and see what happens when I tweak this or fiddle with that.

Applications for Windows 2000

As you may recall, most Windows 95/98 software also runs on NT/2000. However, there are exceptions. Some programs use hardware dongles for the purpose of copy protection. These have to be addressed by drivers since NT/2000 doesn't allow direct hardware access.

A Windows 95 driver won't work—you need a driver that was developed for NT/2000, which in many cases means you're out of luck. The current versions of Cubase VST and Logic do support NT/2000.

MIDI timing is a real headache in Windows NT. The design of the task scheduler—a mechanism that NT uses to allocate computing power to threads—is rather lax due to its somewhat coarse resolution. Left to its own devices, it interrupts processes just every 20msec. MIDI timing may suffer considerably, which is why Steinberg and Emagic advise against running their sequencers on NT.

It appears that Windows 2000 will solve these MIDI timing problems. For one thing, the task scheduler's resolution is finer and for another, WDM drivers and DirectMusic make up the MIDI architecture. It stands to reason that this will constitute a workable solution for MIDI, but we'll have to wait and see. Much looks promising and provided that a hardware driver is available, you can already work with the leading programs.

Pure audio programs run smoothly on NT. Wavelab and Soundforge audio editors also work well with NT/2000, in fact, the Os comes highly recommended for these applications. If you ever have a chance to try it out, you'll find that they are stable and run smoothly—certainly more so than on Windows 95/98.

Hardware for Windows 2000

All the usual components such as mainboards, chipsets, SCSI controllers and display adapters are supported by NT/2000. In the case of MIDI interfaces, the situation isn't quite as bright, but the classic Unitor 8 has an NT driver that you can use for Windows 2000.

The selection of soundcards is somewhat greater. The RME DIGI 96 series cards support NT, as does Terratec's EWS88MT and Sonorus' StudI/O. According to Creamware, drivers for its Pulsar card are in the works.

Although Windows NT drivers will run on Windows 2000, this won't do you much good if you can't install them. Some of these drivers won't install simply because the installation routine is slightly different. You can be fairly sure the vendors will come up with modified drivers soon after Windows 2000 debuts because the effort and overhead involved in adapting these is within reason.

WDM drivers would of course be the preferred option. These are available for Soundblaster cards, but support for professional audio cards has yet to be forthcoming.

Should You Gear Up for Windows 2000?

You'll probably be able to scrape together all the programs that you need for Windows 2000, particularly in view of the fact that the market leaders' Windows 95/98 programs run on NT/2000. Hardware is a bigger problem. Since it's considered good form for a vendor to supply Windows NT drivers for the hardware he is touting, you can rest assured that your gadget of choice will support Windows 2000 at some point in the future.

Windows 2000 has what it takes to become the leading audio and MIDI platform, but only time will tell if it makes good on this promise.

7 The Display Adapter

What Does a Display Adapter Do?

You may be wondering what a chapter on display adapters is doing in a book about music applications. Sure, ergonomic refresh frequencies of more than 80Hz and high resolution and color depth are just as critical to working comfortably on the music Pc as they are to the office workhorse. And speed is of essence so that it can deal with the ever more sophisticated interfaces of MIDI and audio programs.

All display adapters made in the last four years provide performance galore. Modern cards deliver refresh frequencies and color depth—the number of colors that can be displayed simultaneously—to die for. The latter depends directly on the size of the graphics buffer, which has become so inexpensive that price is no longer an issue.

So we're in display adapter paradise, right? Not quite, because display adapters pose two major problems that can degrade audio performance and monkey with MIDI timing.

Problems with Display Adapters

You may encounter two problems with display adapters, the dreaded bus blockade and the Windows 16-bit GUI, as I began calling it in one of my less inspired moments.

Bus Blockade

Some display adapter drivers demonstrate truly bad form by habitually blocking the PCI bus and by extension, the ISA bus behind it. This is bad. In order to understand how bad, let's take a look at how all those neat graphics are actually sent to your monitor.

As you may have observed, the image on your screen consists of a bunch of dots called pixels. Each of these dots in turn consists of three lesser dots (in red, green and blue), the position and color of which is determined by their relative brightness.

Thus your monitor is able to represent millions of hues. However, to display any given color, the display adapter has to compute and tell the monitor the position of every single dot as well as calculate x different color values. Now here's the crux of the matter—x may be very large, for example, 16.7 millions colors—each dot can represent any of these colors. Therefore, even if any given dot has just a single value at any given time, the memory for every dot must be large enough to hold all other 16,666,669 million colors because as soon as the display changes—say when you move a window—the dot immediately changes its color.

The card has to have plenty of memory to accommodate this amount of data, which today is no longer a problem. What is, however, a problem is the fact that this data has to be constantly shuttled to the card—this obviously requires a great deal of bandwidth on the bus. This is one aspect of the bus blockade problem because this graphical data vies for bandwidth with audio data and MIDI signals.

In the days of Standard VGA (sixteen colors and 640×480 pixels), an image was calculated by the computer's processor dot by dot and written to the main memory, where the driver stopped by to pick it up and truck it on over to the display adapter. The seasoned user may shudder to recall how very long all this took with programs that were heavy on graphics (of which Windows in all its versions is one).

Then arrived the day of the so-called ›Windows accelerator cards,‹ which carried onboard processors. Contemporary display adapters no longer answer to this name, but the principle has remains the same. In many cases the driver no longer transmits the entire image pixel by pixel from the main memory to the memory of the display adapter. Instead, it sends a command like ›draw a line with a thickness of A from point x to point y.‹ Left on its own again, the display adapter generates the image in its memory exactly the way it was told to.

Thus the amount of data that has to be shifted over the bus is considerably reduced, as is the workload of your processor.

The card has small memory buffer to which these commands are loaded to be serviced in sequence. When this command buffer is full, trouble is on the horizon. A tiny status bit is set to let the system know what's going on. Much like you knock before you enter a house, a ›clean‹ driver will politely check the status bit before it transfers data. This of course takes time. Some manufacturers have discovered that they can garner more brownie points in benchmark tests if they simply do without this status query.

When the buffer is full—and this is often the case with big windows and high resolutions—the Pci bus transfer will fail because the receiver refuses to accept data. The Pci bus then closes down, causing the Isa bus that follows it to the same. And well it should, for if it didn't, the data that has just been sent would be lost.

So if a soundcard wants to send data at this moment, it's out of luck. It can't because the bus is already engaged. Unfortunately, this data is lost. You'll know that this is the case when you hear those telltale clicks in an audio signal.

Infuriatingly, the same thing can happen when large bitmaps that can't be represented as graphics commands are loaded bit-by-bit from the memory of the computer to the corresponding memory on the display adapter.

How to Identify a Problem with the Display Adapter

It's fairly easy to find out if your card is beset by this problem: Simply play back a Wave file with your audio program, open the biggest window you can find, and navigate wildly all over the interface. If audio playback remains unaffected, congratulations, you're home free. If, on the other hand, you hear clicks or the signal momentarily drops out, you own one of these problematic cards.

How to Fix It

The often recommended solution to simply slow down graphics acceleration is a lame joke. It works, but only because substantially fewer or even no commands will be sent, which of course makes it impossible for the buffer to fill up. Instead the computer's CPU has to take on this chore. This little trick puts the processor of the display adapter out of business and you end up with a defacto standard VGA card that delivers precisely the kind of ›speed‹ for which these cards are notorious.

If the following tips won't work for you, you can do this as a last resort. Personally, I'd just invest the 100 bucks or so in a new card and ›accelerate‹ the old one right out the window.

On the other hand, the Microsoft drivers on the included Windows installation CD can be an acceptable solution. They are a tad slower, but at least they're ›clean.‹ If you can't find a driver for your card on the Windows 95/98 CD, consult the table on the next page for a ›fix‹ that will work for your system.

Card	Fix

Matrox Millennium/Mystique	Insert a new section into the file containing the following:
	`[mga.drv]`
	`PCIchipset=1`
	The best driver for audio applications is Version 3.80, which you should definitely use. This release is also referred to as ›Ms-certified‹ on the Matrox website.
	In addition, you should go to the Control Panel. Under Display, select the extended MAG setting and deactivate the parameter ›Use PowerGDI acceleration.‹ This option may be called something different or missing altogether depending on the driver version. You may find a parameter called ›PCI-retries.‹ If you do, enable it. The 3.80 driver doesn't offer this option. Instead, simply disable ›Use Busmastering‹ and ›Use Write Combining.‹

Card	Fix

Cards equipped with an S3 chip
(This tip pertains to generic drivers that the chip manufacturer S3 delivers, but it will also work for many of the drivers supplied by card vendors since they are based on the generic drivers.)
	In the system.ini, insert the following parameter to the section [display]:
	`[display]`
	`busthrottle=1`

#9 Imagine 128 Series 2	Driver Version 4.102.36 is available; it should fix this problem.
Trident Cards 9685/9682/9680/9440	Use the standard Windows drivers instead of card manufacturer's drivers.

As you can see, we're dealing with old cards here, old at least according to the standards dictated by the dizzying pace of development in the Pc universe. Frequently, the reason that these survive is because many users are on a tight budget—when they do hand over the green stuff for a system upgrade the old display adapter stays, often outliving several computers.

The onboard graphics solutions discussed in Chapter 3 are also potential troublemakers. They can squeeze bandwidth on the bus connecting the processor and main memory because they're effectively ›hard-wired‹ into the chipset of the computer.

The Windows 16-Bit Problem

The second category of problem has to do with the architecture of Windows. As you may recall from my ramblings in the chapter ›The Operating System‹ on page 143, Microsoft apparently chose the two-faced Roman God Janus to be the godfather for Windows, for it too has two faces, one with 32 bits and the other with 16. Most regrettably, the graphics interface suffers from this schizoid dementia, as does audio and MIDI playback.

The 16-bit section is a bottleneck. If a graphics driver de-cides to get mule-headed, the system's MIDI timing may lurch like a seasick landlubber after a day on the open sea. The utilities supplied with display adapters like to get into this same groove. They run in the background—sometimes even imperceptibly—and like nothing better than to throw some dirt into the gears of your musical workflow.

In a nutshell, this is the kind of problem that a musician can be faced with: an ineptly programmed driver requires more computing power. While it is active, it holds everything else up, including audio and MIDI output.

How to Identify a 16-bit Problem

Since few will have the skills and tools required to disassem-ble and examine a driver, this isn't all that easy. The rule of thumb is that once you've checked and ruled out everything else, the trouble you're having is almost certainly caused by the driver.

In other words, if audio playback with Asio or DirectX driver runs perfectly, but pure MIDI playback tends to wob-ble, you could be looking at this problem. However, you should first try applying the tips from the preceding chap-ters.

What Can You Do about It?

Unfortunately, not much. If a newer driver is available for your card, by all means try it out. Even an older driver can be some relief. It may not be optimized yet, but perhaps it's less of a millstone around the card's neck.

Mind you, I'd advise you to purchase one of the cards rec-ommended below. If your mainboard has an AGP slot, you won't have to mortgage the house—even AGP cards that go for less than 50 bucks will help you out of this mess.

Another common tweaking tip is to reduce color depth to 256 colors. However, if you opt for this measure you may be shooting yourself in the foot. In up-to-date current programs, those pretty little pictures of mixers or synthesizer control panels that you see on your screen have greater color depth. If you force the program to display these so-called bitmaps with fewer hues, the enter images has to be converted. This is no help because it guzzles computing power like college kids guzzle beer on spring break.

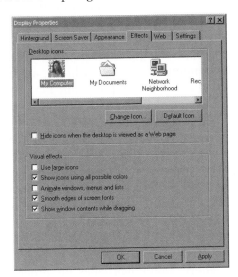

Set this option to ›Show window contents while dragging.‹

Windows 98 (or Windows 95 with Plus Pack) gives you another option you can try: In the Control Panel under Display, you'll find a tab labeled Effects, and in it the option Show window contents while dragging. The alternative is that you only see the frame while you're dragging a window. The window is generated anew when you release it in a new position. Depending on the content of the image and its color depth, this may mean that a large amount of data must be shifted to the card. If, on the other hand, the picture is dragged along with the frame, fewer pixels have to be computed. The latter option may make your system run a bit smoother. In addition, this process is carried out in several steps, which leaves a little time for the soundcard to transmit data between each step.

Pci and Agp

Since mid-1998, a new bus has been all the rage in the Pc computing world. Called Agp, it was designed exclusively for communication with the display adapter. The system, which features its own control logic and a different physical format, is entirely independent of Pci. Accordingly, an Agp slot looks different and you can't simply plug your Pci display adapter into it. You'll have to do your patriotic part in driving the economy and cough up the bucks for an Agp card.

The clock frequency of the Agp port is 66MHz. As is the case with Pci, it is derived from the external clock frequency of the processor. This means that there are fewer division ratios to mess around with, so the Agp card generally doesn't like it when you attempt to speed up a processor by increasing the external clock. At worst, this kind of experimentation can fry the hardware. This is my cue to caution you once again. If you boldly want to go where no one has gone before, do it elsewhere. Don't over-clock the processor!

An Agp slot on a mainboard.

As you may recall from my ruminations on the nuts and bolts of the Pci bus, its theoretical peak throughput is impressive, certainly more than enough to meet our purposes. So you may be wondering if the world really needs a special graphics bus. The answer is it doesn't. The Agp architecture indeed delivers even more throughput, however as long as the potential of Pci hasn't been exhausted, this won't be much of a benefit in an office computer.

Sure, the technology is a bit different. Agp boards can, for example, abuse parts of the computer's Ram as a graphics buffer. Normally, this option is used to the benefit of 3D graphics, whose interface textures are real memory chow hounds and hardly fit in the card's onboard Ram. And future applications' appetite for more bandwidth, particularly those of the 3D variety applications, will grow ever more voracious.

So what does Agp do for the average music computer?

Quite a bit actually. Just contemplate for a moment the problem with bus blockades: With the benefit of Agp, we could care less if the programmer is an avid disciple of the ›Lsd, virtual reality without the expensive hardware‹ school of thought. If a lame driver jams the Agp bus, your audio card and hard disk can continue to maintain a spirited dialog over the Pci audio highway.

Beyond that, ever more Pci Masterbus cards are setting up camp on mainboards, so it certainly won't do any do harm if the display adapter, a notorious bandwidth hog, feeds at another trough. As far as resources such as interrupts and I/O addresses go, Agp behaves just like a Pci slot.

To be able to enjoy the services of Agp, you'll need Windows 98 or, at the very least, Windows 95 Osr 2.1, the update featuring Usb support. The latter can be downloaded separately from the Microsoft website, provided that you are the proud owner of Osr 2. All you have to is install the Usb support and studiously ignore the fact that Usb has nothing whatsoever to do with Agp.

Time for a war story: I once attempted to install an original Windows 95 version on a computer equipped with an Agp card (Elsa Victory Erazor). To my eternal amazement, it actually worked, although I had to fudge a bit using the drivers for the Pci version of the card and a patch for the Pci bridge of the Asus P2B-S motherboard. This may not mean much to you, but it does go to show that manufacturers at times use the same drivers for Agp and Pci. However, I wouldn't wager a dime on this working all the time.

▶ If you own an (old) Windows 95 version, feel free to try it out—you have nothing to lose. If it doesn't work, your only option is to update to Windows 98.

Recommended Display Adapters

The following recommendations are based on my own experiences with display adapters. Obviously, this isn't the last word on these cards. Since development in this field takes a quantum leap at near weekly intervals, by the time you read this there may be an entirely new generation of cards vying for your hard-earned.

Remarkably, I've never come across an AGP card that gave me any grief, so I can recommend these across the board. If your computer is equipped with such a slot, buy an AGP card.

In terms of PCI cards, the following cards are verifiably hassle-free:

◆ Elsa Winner 2000/Office

◆ Elsa Victory Erazor/II

◆ ATI All-in-Wonder-Pro

◆ ATI Rage series

◆ Diamond Viper V330/V550

If you're on a budget and have the opportunity to score an old card cheaply, I recommend the intriguingly named Diamond Stealth 64. These are cards equipped with an S3-864 or -964 chip; they don't even require an interrupt so that you conserve valuable resources.

By the way, the same can be said of nearly all cards that feature 2D or pure Windows acceleration. These haven't been spotted in stores for many a moon, but you may still find them in some discounters' ›fire sales.‹ You can also put the word out and maybe some pal of yours will leave it to you as a token of his friendship when he buys a brand, spanking new Ultra Voodoo accelerator for his Doom game.

▶ If you're the hapless owner of a Matrox Millennium, this present just might deliver you from digital audio hell.

Installing a Display Adapter

I can't provide you with a detailed installation manual for every display adapter under the sun here, but I can draw your attention to a couple of points well worth remembering.

Either you'll spy a program by the name of setup.exe that you have to launch with a double-click or onboard Windows mechanisms will carry out the installation routine for you. In the latter case, Windows will detect the new card when you launch the Os and ask you for drivers. Generally, a window will pop up to which you must enter the drivers' location by simply selecting the appropriate CD or diskette drive.

If you're given the choice of versions—either Windows 98 or Windows 95—during the installation routine, be sure to select the driver that matches your version of operating system. As discussed at length in the chapter ›The Operating System‹ on page 143, Windows 98 sports a new and improved driver architecture. If there are drivers available for it, use these. If not, you can use the drivers of the previous version for Windows 98.

Another possibly is that during the installation routine you'll be able to determine which components will be installed. Next to the actual drivers, you'll be offered tools and utilities of dubious usefulness. Select just the drivers, don't let these ›helpers‹ hang out on your disk. These little troublemakers run in the background and—inevitably at the least opportune moment—spoil your work on the sequencer. Generally, you can tell that such programs are active when an icon appears in the right corner of the Taskbar.

▶ If my warning has come too late, you can disable these utilities as I described in the section ›Autostart‹ on page 169.

Multi-monitor Systems

Yes, several monitors can be driven by a single computer. Well-heeled Macintosh users have enjoyed this option for years, Pc users have had to wait until Windows 98.

If you want to get any serious work done with a sequencer while simultaneously running another application, there's hardly any getting around a second monitor. Be it a software synthesizer/sampler, the interface of the soundcard hardware or the editor for the synthesizer, all programs' looks have become extremely sophisticated, if not downright opulent. Fortunately, most of this stuff has also become fairly easy and intuitive to handle, but all of this high-resolution visual splendor simply won't fit on the screen of a single 21-inch monitor.

So the idea of dusting off that old 15-inch monitor and a display adapter you retired long ago to gain a little more screen space to work with doesn't seem all that far-fetched.

Windows 98 will let you connect a whopping nine monitors and an equal number of display adapters. Nine does seem a bit over the top for even the most avid home recordist—the average Jill or Jack will be happy with a setup sporting two monitors. One of the two is the primary, the other the secondary display adapter. The primary display adapter issues the Vga messages during the boot routine until the graphic interface appears. DirectDraw screen modes for games, for example, are only routed to the primary adapter.

Microsoft didn't draft any special conventions concerning the primary adapter for Windows 98, so you can use older Windows 95 drivers to this end.

The second card, on the other hand, must offer Windows 98 drivers and among other things, the computer must have some way of switching its Vga mode off—otherwise it wouldn't know where to send the Bios messages while it's booting.

Since VGA mode can't be disabled on most older display adapters, you'll see your aspirations of recycling an old card and using it as a secondary adapter crushed. Catch 22 time: Older cards often can't be employed as a primary card either because the driver wasn't designed to handle this role.

The PCI slots' priority rankings decide which display adapter is detected as the primary and which as the secondary device. If you want to determine which of the cards comes first, the only way you can do this is by plugging them into the slots in the desired sequence. If you're dealing with a combination of AGP and PCI, the AGP card is by default the secondary adapter, but for most AGP cards, you can change this in the BIOS.

Who Gets Along with Whom?

For multi-monitor setups, using two cards of the same type or at least cards made by the same manufacturer is not a bad idea. In addition, you should ensure that the manufacturer's drivers support multi-screen mode, which, amazingly enough, can't be said of all drivers on the Windows 98 CD.

For example, despite a statement to the contrary on the maker's website, the Diamond Viper V330 won't let you use it as a secondary adapter. Windows simply reports (and I'm sure I detect a note of grim satisfaction in the message) that the drivers aren't multi-monitor-capable. This hold true for both the drivers on the Windows 98 CD and those on the Diamond website.

The Matrox Millennium II seems to take it as a personal insult when another maker's card is plugged into the computer as the primary adapter. Windows responds by deactivating the Matrox and you have to reactivate the card by hand. (The card eventually ran on my bunch test computer, but I wouldn't bet the ranch on it. Also, the card only worked with the ›Unified‹ Version 4.11 driver in a multi-monitor setup. If you use a more ›audio-friendly‹ driver, you might run into difficulties.).

Conversely, the Matrox G100 and G200 will work in perfect harmony with other vendors' products in either role—both the primary and secondary adapter. The same can be said of the Elsa Winner 2000/Office; both AGP and PCI versions are perfectly compatible with cards other than the aforementioned mischief-makers.

The ATI Rage and the excellently named All-in-Wonder may also serve as both primary or second adapters. On the Hercules Dynamite, you'll have to set jumpers to switch off VGA mode and the fixed VGA address. Most annoyingly, you'll have to figure this out for yourself by studying closely the illustrations for there's no mention of this in the manual.

The Elsa Victory Erazor will, on the other hand, be initialized, but the system freezes while it's configuring the screen. So if you own one of these and want to enjoy all that extra interface acreage, you'll have to wait for the driver update that Elsa has promised to roll out soon.

The selection of cards that deliver sure-fire multi-monitor mode performance is quite limited at the moment. Cards that will be released after this book will certainly offer this feature. In my experience, cards that can will run as both primary and secondary adapters can be combined with one another. Experiments with older cards that are only suitable for use as primary adapters may succeed every now and then, but generally the pain of pulling this feat off is greater than the pleasure of seeing it work.

In my experience, most computer dealers are not a great help. Typically, they don't know the first thing about multi-monitor mode, but pretend that they do and give you the wrong scoop.

Since a PC is equipped with only one AGP slot, when you plug in two cards you have no choice but to run one of them as a PCI display adapter. This gives rise to all of the problems discussed above. Therefore, the best multi-monitor mode solution is to opt for an AGP card with two monitor connections. Matrox offers this type of card called the G-400 Dʜ, whereby Dʜ stands for Dual Head.

▶ Heads up: The only thing that distinguish this card from the single-monitor port version are these two letters.

The G-400 Dʜ card is available in different versions featuring 16- and 32-Mʙ memories as well as in a deluxe ›Max‹ version with a high-frequency graphics processor. Since, as musicians we simply want more working area rather than 3D fireworks, the simplest version (without Max and with 16Mʙ) will do just fine. Beyond that, this card isn't plagued by the driver problems described above—the ones for which Matrox cards were notorious. However, you should definitely stick with the ›Certified‹ drivers available from the Matrox website.

The company's Internet sites offers different categories of drivers:

◆ ›Certified‹ drivers—certified by Microsoft and free from the kind of programming trickery that inspired the punch line, ›Programming is an art form that fights back,‹

◆ ›Unified‹ drivers—an all-in-one package for all Matrox cards,

◆ and the ›Latest‹ drivers.

The latter have in the past proven to be the fastest, but unfortunately also tended to jam up the bus, which is the bane of audio applications.

▶ If you want to be on the safe side, always use the ›Certified‹ drivers.

8 The Soundcard

The soundcard is actually the heart of a music computer. Hardly any other peripheral device has received so much bad press. The reason can be such a nuisance lies in the nature of its design—several different functional areas united on a soundcard.

Basically, a soundcard is several devices rolled into one. The problems is that, in many cases, each if these functional units requires its own resources (read: dedicated addresses and IRQs). The more hip stuff a card can do and the more crowded your computer's interior, the more likely it is that it will give you migraines. For example, at its most sophisticated configuration level, a Terratec Ews64 requires three interrupts and innumerable address areas.

No-name cards that you'll find in bargain bins or on the shelves of rock-bottom discounters are especially vexing. These doomsday devices are generally slapped together somewhere in the mysterious Orient using off-the-shelf components. Drivers aren't developed specifically for these cards, instead they're lifted from the manufacturers of the components.

You should avoid these devices like you would lengthy conversations with the tax man. Even if your system seems to run fine, the drivers may devour an inordinate amount of computing power, the external MIDI connection may be given the lowest priority, and at times timing may stagger and lurch like a limb-flailing tourists after his first taste of Munich's Oktoberfest. With every new recording, the audio tracks may suggest an entirely unique and surprising interpretation of synchronization. I don't want to give you any ideas, so we won't even talk about the many crashes that will bring on free associations such as ›screen—Elvis—handgun.‹

If you encounter such strange phenomena, it's usually not your sequencer that's haunted—it's evil hardware and their drivers from hell that have awakened the poltergeists. Unfortunately, I can't recommend anything other than an exorcism—get rid of the card as swiftly as possible.

Now let's take a look at all the many wondrous things that call a soundcard home.

Audio Recording and Playback

Recording and playback of Wave files are basic functions of a soundcard. The quality in which it renders audio hinges on the quality of its analog/digital and digital/analog converters as well as that of the circuits involved.

16 or 24, 44.1 or 96?

Nowadays, many cards are touted as genuine 24bit/96kHz gear. True enough, but this merely describes the technology it uses and the data types that result, it doesn't necessarily make a statement about the quality of the card.

◆ 24-bit recording means that the analog input signal is digitized at a resolution of 24 bits. Since a total of 16,777,216 different values can be rendered with 24 bits while 16 bits offers just 65,536 different values, you can well appreciate that rounding error will be much lower in 24-bit signals.

◆ 96kHz is the sampling frequency. It simply determines how often the analog signal is sampled per second. 96,000 samples are of course more than 44,100, which is the CD standard. However, this has been the subject of much debate, because many believe that the human ear is unable to perceive a difference between the two.

Regardless which camp is right, the specs of a 24bit/96kHz soundcard are superior to those of older 16-bit cards with a peak sampling frequency of 48kHz, particularly when the card of the previous generation didn't exploit all the potential of 16-bit recording.

Bear in mind that before an analog signal can be digitized into values between 0 and 16,777,216 (2^{24}) or speaking more precisely, values between –8,388,608 and +8,388,608, the analog circuits that carry this signal must be able to deliver it to the converter in the very high fidelity that this tremendous a dynamic range can offer and the signal must also be inherently noise free.

This is often not the case with a cheap 24-bit card, which means the sonic potential of 24 bits is reduced significantly. In reality, the final four to six bits render solely the noise of the converters or analog components rather than a useful signal.

32-bit Resolution

Contingent upon the procedure by which data is transmitted from the card to memory, 24-bit recording can be a further problem. As you may recall from the section ›The Pci Bus‹ on page 74, bus systems in the Pc environment work at 16 or 32 bits, not 24. accordingly, there are only two ways to send the 24-bit format down the wire. First, data can be broken down an 16-bit section and an 8-bit section. The two sections are then sent in sequence.

This requires two Pci transactions and thus places a greater load on the Pci bus. However, the 24-bit values can also be ›padded‹ out to 32 bits with eight zeros and transmitted as one 32-bit number. Although this requires more bits, it spells less work for the Pci and the memory buses. Since most audio programs work with an internal resolution of 32 bits, your software won't mind if it receives data in this format—it will even reduce rounding error.

Unfortunately, you won't know whether your card sends data in 32-bit format nor in most cases do you have any control over the format. The only way you can guestimate whether your card uses 32 bits is by your computer's performance when you're dealing with higher numbers of tracks or, in the case of multi I/O cards, recording more than two tracks at once.

The Sonorus StudI/O (featuring a design identical to that of the Creamware Tdat 16) cards by RME and the Terratec Ews 88 Mt are all cards that work with 32 bits.

In categories below this premium class, there are a wide range of soundcards whose converters work with a resolution of 16, 18 or 20 bits. Only 16 bits are actually sent, the enhanced resolution is used merely to provide extra headroom on the analog side. Remarkably, these cards can in practice often deliver recording and playback quality that rivals if not exceeds that of el cheapo 24/96 cards, so don't let the specs deceive you.

Breakout Boxes

The actual converters of many contemporary cards come in an outboard housing called a breakout box. These boxes are available in 5.25-inch format in the case of the Terratec Ews88Mt and the Guillemot Isis. The Event Layla and Motu 2408 ship in the standard 19-inch rack format. This external box is connected to the card by a cable.

Given the choice, you should always opt for this type of solution. Cards whose converters are located directly on the motherboard often pick up stray noise and interference generated by computer components. Display adapters and Scsi controllers are particularly notorious noise-makers.

If you own just one of these types of cards, you should install it as far as you can from all other components—in other words, plug it into the last Pci or Isa slot. Unfortunately, this isn't always possible. Some boards have slots for main memories located next to the last Isa slot. These devices generate the same undesirable high-frequency interference as a display adapter.

There are also a number of high-quality audio cards available that do without analog converters altogether and offer digital interfaces only. You can connect external converters, which of course you'll have to buy separately, to these S/P-DIF or ADAT ports. These systems are just as good as solutions with external breakout boxes. Plus you're free to decide which converters you want and can reuse these later when you're ready to upgrade to a better card.

MIDI Sound Generation

Now we're going to look at a feature not every card offers—onboard sound generation. In essence we're talking about a built-in synthesizer, although of much lower quality than its professional counterparts.

There are three categories of onboard synthesis.

FM

The simplest form of sound generation on a soundcard is frequency modulation (FM). Originally, companies relied on a Yamaha chip (the OPL-3), which delivered FM synthesis with four operators similar to Yamaha's more basic DX-11/100 synthesizers. The sound that this chip generated wasn't too bad, even today there are no applications available that let you do any serious programming of this onboard synth.

The factory presets, on the other hand, are by contemporary standards so god-awfully ugly that they are rumored to have fused polyester at fifty paces. Latter day soundcards featuring FM use an emulation of the original chip. Even if you're a skilled sound-smith, you wouldn't be able to wrest any decent sounds from these since they lack the basic FM algorithms that are tonally the most productive.

▶ Consequently, if the idea of onboard FM sound generation inspires you to sell your DX synthesizer replace it with this type of card, you will be bitterly disappointed.

Wavetable

The most common type of sound generation on a soundcard today is Wavetable synthesis, which is subtractive synthesis on a Pcm basis. Soundcards emulate the Roland Sound Canvas Sc-55 which set the standard for cheap ›General Midi‹ synthesizers.

›General Midi‹ (a. k. a. the Gm/Gs standard) represents a consensus among synthesizer and software makers about which sounds should reside in which program slots. Sadly, what the standard lacks is a tolerable threshold for the actual quality of these sounds. You can be sure that you'll find a piano sound on program 1, but you can't be sure that it won't sound like a horde of vest-pocket zombies dancing on a strand of baling wire.

These cards use either the manufacturer's proprietary samples, the licensed original samples from Roland or—in the case of the French company Dream—sounds sampled from the original Sc-55 sample. The latter are easy to identify since they come with a noise trail, which if any more prominent, you could hike on.

Dream sound chips can be found on a number of popular cards by Terratec, Hoontech (Soundtrack), Ego-Systems (Wami) and Guillemot. Bear in mind that the Sound Canvas itself is getting a bit long in the tooth and that, along with having to do without the original samples, the soundcards lack the post-processing features that account for the quality of the original Roland device.

The bottom line is, don't expect to enjoy the kind of sound quality that you'd expect from a professional sample synthesizer or sampler, because onboard synths just don't measure up.

Sampling

Cards featuring sampling capability are the kissing cousins of Wavetable synthesis cards. The technology behind these is fairly basic: the samples are simply loaded to normal memory instead of Rom. To assure Gs/Gm compatibility, the manufacturer supplies an appropriate sound set that is loaded into the Ram of the card.

The results are of course much improved because you can achieve better quality by using your own samples or loading entirely different sounds. The post-processing options using filters or modulations still vary wildly and can't match those on hardware synthesizers. These cards can serve as a kind of fill-in for a sampler, for example, for drums or natural sounds that don't require too much editing and post-processing.

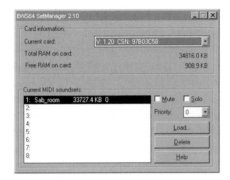

The Ews Setmanager is a tool used to load banks to the Ram of the Ews64. Here you see a rather large drum bank.

Not long ago, the Ram into which the card loaded the samples was a run-of-the-mill memory chip that was soldered onto or plugged into the card. Newer cards rely on another trick—they use the main memory of the computer. This of course means that they have much more memory to play with, while the Pci bus offers ample bandwidth to rush samples in real-time to the card.

Keep in mind that the more tracks you make the sound generator on your card generate, the less bandwidth will be available for other Pci applications. Taken to extremes, this can cause the system to drop out during Hd recording.

A word to the wise: Even with data throughput of a speedy 135Mb/sec over Pci, you can manage to exhaust the available bandwidth when you're working with, say, elephantine 128-MB orchestral samples and playing them with 60 voices. Keep this little tidbit of info in the back of your mind. If your system tends to hiccup when you're working with the on-board sampler, you're out of luck. You have no choice but to opt for an external sampler because there are no performance tweaking measures that will get you out of this fix.

MIDI Interface

In addition to a MIDI port for Wavetable sound generation, most soundcards and some audio cards without sound generators offer an external MIDI connection. On the cheaper cards, it is typically implemented as an adapter that is plugged into the joystick port on the rear panel of the card. Unfortunately, often these adapters don't ship with the card, so you have to buy them separately.

Some of the better cards feature two five-pin DIN sockets for MIDI in and out on the breakout box. Given the choice, always go for this solution because adapters for the joystick socket are potentially a pain in the neck. I know from personal experience that only one in five adapters works at all since the electrical specs of the sockets on the cards vary wildly.

On the rare occasions that they do work, the external MIDI ports of the soundcards still can't compare with genuine MIDI interfaces. The transfer of system exclusive data, for instance, is often troublesome. Timing problems are also quite common. The external connectors on soundcards were originally designed to take dirt-cheap modules that would provide less nerve-racking accompaniment for games than that dreaded FM squawking. They engineers weren't thinking of using these as professional MIDI interfaces. As you can well appreciate, this is perhaps not the most important task of a soundcard in a computer, so the drivers of a soundcard often give addressing these ports the lowest priority.

Modern soundcards ordinarily don't suffer this problem, but the world is full of surprises.

▶ Unfortunately, I can't give any advice other than to invest in an inexpensive outboard MIDI interface. As a welcome side effect, you may then end up with extra MIDI ports, which you can put to good use by assigning each of your external devices its own MIDI port.

A Survey of Soundcards

Call me picky, but I included in the following overview only those models that are PCI cards and for which an ASIO driver is available. Soundcards that are designed primarily for games don't belong in a music computer anyhow. In particular, ISA cards are not a wise choice if you're investing in a new card unless you're absolutely sure you're going to use it purely as a GS synth/sampler.

Maker/model	Sound generator	Asio	Analog	Digital	MIDI	Remarks
Aardvark						
Aark 20/20	—	Asio 1	8/8	2/2 (coax.)	—	
Aark 20/20+	—	in the works	8/8	2/2 (opt.)	1/1	◆ BNC Wordclock ◆ other I/Os optional ◆ stackable up to 4 units ◆ Dsp effects
Aark Tdif	—	Asio 1	—	8/8 (T/Dif)	—	
Aark Direct	—	in the works	2/4	2/2 (coax.)	1/1	◆ stackable up to 4 units ◆ Dsp effects
Aark Direct Pro	—	in the works	4/6	2/2 (coax.)	1/1	◆ other I/Os optional ◆ stackable up to 4 units ◆ Dsp effects
Creamware						
Tdat-16	—	Asio 1	—/2 (Monitor)	16/16 (ADAT, opt.)	—	
Pulsar	FM, Akai sample-player, diverse virtual-analog synthesizers	Asio 1, EASI in the works	2/2	16/16 (ADAT) 2/2 (opt.)	1/1	Pulsar Plus features AES/EBU outputs instead of S/P-Dif
Scope			2/2	24/24 (ADAT) 2/2 (opt.)	1/1	Modular development and Dsp system
Digigram						
Vx222	—	Asio 2	2/2	2/2 (Aes/Ebu)	—	
Vxpocket	—	Asio 2	2/2	2/2 (coax.)	—	Pcmcia card
Digital Audio Labs						
CardDeluxe	—	in the works	2/2	2/2 (coax.)	—	

Maker/model	Sound generator	Asio	Analog	Digital	MIDI	Remarks
				Inputs/Outputs		
Echo						
Darla	—	Asio 2	2/8	—	—	Asio 2 support: Direct Monitoring
Gina	—	Asio 2	2/8	2/2 (coax.)	—	Asio 2 support: Direct Monitoring
Layla	—	Asio 2	8/10	2/2 (coax.)	1/1	◆ Wordclock ◆ Asio 2 support: Direct Monitoring
Ego Sys						
Waveterminal 2496	—	Asio 2	2/2	2/2 (coax.)	—	◆ Asio 2 support: Direct Monitoring, Asio Positioning Protocol ◆ optional SMPTE/MIDI interface ◆ stackable up to 3 units
WaMi Rack 24	—	Asio 2	4/8	2/2 (opt./coax.)	4/4	◆ Asio 2 support: DirectMonitoring, Asio Positioning Protocol ◆ stackable up to 4 calls ◆ SMPTE, Wordclock
EMU						
Aps	—	Asio 1	4/2	2/2 (coax.)	1/1	
Ensoniq						
Paris	—	in the works	—	—	—	
Emagic						
Audiowerk 8	—	Asio 1	2/8	2/2 (coax.)	—	
Audiowerk 2	—	Asio 1	2/2	2/2 (coax.)	—	
Frontier Design Group						
Dakota	—	Asio 2	—	16/16 (ADAT)	2/2	◆ incl. S/P-DIF (opt., coax.) ◆ optional (Montana): 32/32 audio channels, video and Wordclock input

Maker/model	Sound generator	Asio	Inputs/Outputs		Midi	Remarks
			Analog	Digital		
Gadget Labs						
Wave/8*24	—	Asio 2	8/8	—	1/1	◆ digital In/Out optional ◆ Asio 2 support with DirectMonitoring
Guillemot						
Maxi Studio Isis	GM/Gs and sampler-based	Asio 1	8/4	2/2 (opt., coax.)	1/1	◆ up to 36Mb sample Ram onboard ◆ Synth
Korg						
1212 I/O	—	Asio 1	2/2	8/8 (Adat) 2/2 (coax.)	—	
Lexicon						
Studio	—	Asio 1	depends on the interface		—	Interfaces: Ldi-10 T, Ldi-12 T or Ldi-16 S
Motu						
324 Pci card with 2408, 1224, 308, i24 interfaces	—	Asio 1	see remarks		—	Number of inputs and outputs depends on the interfaces; up to 3 interfaces per of card
Midiman						
Dman 2044	—	Asio 1	4/4	—	—	
Lagoon	—	Asio 1	—	8/8 (Adat) 2/2 (opt.)	1/1	
Delta 10/10	—	Asio 2	8/8	2/2 (coax.)	1/1	◆ Wordclock ◆ stackable up to 4 units
Delta 66	—	Asio 2	4/4	2/2 (coax.)	—	stackable
Delta 44	—	Asio 2	4/4	—	—	stackable

| Maker/model | Sound generator | Asio | Inputs/Outputs | | MIDI | Remarks |
			Analog	Digital		
Delta DiO 2496	—	Asio 2	–/2	2/2 (coax./opt.)	—	stackable
RME						
DIGI32	—	Asio 1	—	2/2 (opt., coax.)	—	◆ AES/EBU optional ◆ stackable
DIGI32 Pro	—	Asio 1	–/2 (Monitor)	2/2 (opt., coax., AES/EBU)	—	stackable
DIGI32/8	—	Asio 1	—	8/8 (ADAT), 2/2 (opt., coax.)	—	◆ AES/EBU optional ◆ stackable
DIGI96	—	Asio 2 (Win 9x, Win NT)	—	2/2 (opt., coax., AES/EBU)	—	stackable
DIGI96 Pro	—	Asio 2 (Win 9x, NT)	—	—	—	
DIGI96/8	—	Asio 2 (Win 9x, Win NT)	—	8/8 (ADAT) 2/2 (opt., coax., AES/EBU)	—	stackable
DIGI96/8 Pro	—	Asio 2 (Win 9x, Win NT)	–/2 (Monitor)	8/8 (ADAT) 2/2 (opt., coax., AES/EBU)	—	◆ stackable ◆ Wordclock module optional
Hammerfall	—	Asio 2 (Win 9x, Win NT)	—	24/24 (ADAT) 2/2 (opt., coax.)	—	◆ Wordclock ◆ Asio 2 support: Direct Monitoring, Sample Accurate Sync
SEK'D						
Prodif 32	—	Asio 1	—	2/2 (opt., coax.)	—	
Prodif 96	—	Asio 1	—	—	—	

Maker/model	Sound generator	Asio	Inputs/Outputs Analog	Digital	Midi	Remarks
Prodif 96 Pro	—	—	—	—	—	
Prodif Gold	—	Asio 1	—	8/8 (ADAT, opt.)	—	
Prodif Platinum	—	Asio 1	–/2	16/16 (ADAT, opt.)	—	
Sonorus						
StudI/O	—	Asio 2, Easi	–/2	16/16 (ADAT, opt.)	—	◆ stackable up to 3 cards ◆ Asio 2 support: Sample Accurate Sync
Soundscape						
Mixtreme	—	Asio 1	—	16/16 (T/Dif)	—	◆ Wordclock ◆ Superclock
Terratec						
Emt-88	—	Asio 2	8/8	2/2	1/1	◆ up to 4 units stackable
Yamaha						
Dsp Factory (Ds2416)	—	Asio 1	2/2	2/2 (coax.)	—	◆ stackable up to 2 cards ◆ digital and analog audio extension units optional
Xg Factory (Sw1000Xg)	Xg	in the works				

You shouldn't have any trouble finding a card in this vast collection that meets your needs and won't bust your budget. For purely recording purposes, I'd recommend the cards by RME due to their extraordinary offering of drivers. I can also heartily recommend the Sonorus StudI/O and Terratec Ews88Mt.

For sophisticated Dsp applications (plug-ins and synthesizers on the card), there's no alternative to Creamware's Pulsar/Scope card.

Why Not Soundblaster?

You may be wondering why I've failed to mention those popular Soundblaster cards by Creative Labs—i. e. the Awe32, Awe64 and Soundblaster Live—when I discussed cards equipped with onboard sound generators.

Well, first of all these cards don't have Asio drivers. Mme drivers are notorious for their unacceptable audio/Midi synchronization, in the case of older Soundblaster cards such as those of the Awe series, Midi timing fluctuations at the external Midi port are the rule rather than the exception.

Everyone's perception is different, so sound quality may be debatable. But one thing is certain, only Soundblaster Live achieves a level of quality that will satisfy the demanding home recordist. But, if you compare this Soundblaster card with those of the competition, you'll find the Soundblaster Live sorely lacking. Sorry, Soundblaster cards don't even live up to semiprofessional standards.

You could use the Soundblaster Live as a Gs sound generator or a basic sampler. In this case, it won't be in the way and it doesn't sound too awful for these applications. If you do this, bear in mind that the card feeds on the main memory of the computer and thus burdens the Pci bus.

▶ If you're into major Hd recording projects, you'd best banish this card from your computer or at the very least refrain from using its sound generator in order to conserve bandwidth on the Pci bus.

Potential Problems with Soundcards

Internal Synchronization of Audio and MIDI

Since an audio file consists of at least 44,100 sample words per second (at a sampling frequency of 44.1kHz), it's not all that noticeable when a few sample words go astray. However, just because you can't hear them being shifted doesn't mean that this isn't happening. The output accuracy of every individual sample is determined by the soundcard, which generally uses a quartz crystal for its clock. Audio software relies on this clock although it doesn't play a pivotal role for audio editors, provided that it doesn't fluctuate wildly.

Audio sequencers constantly have to deal with two different data types which must processed and rendered in sync. To this end, the programs sync their internal processes up to the time that they receive from the soundcard. The emissary of these messages is of course the driver.

Sounds fine so far, and some cards are very reliable messengers. A card and its driver do a bang-up job when they are able to inform the software of the position of every individual samples by means of a feature not surprisingly named ›Sample Position Sync.‹

For a number of reasons, some cards don't do this. These cards divide up their data into blocks and only provide sync information in these blocks (DMA Block Sync). When a program syncs up to these blocks, timing will always be less accurate than with Sample Position Sync.

Nowadays, you can be fairly sure that brand-name boards support Sample Position Sync. As usual, expect the worst from no-name cards—generally, they lack this feature.

Syncing Up Soundcards

As soon as you have two digital audio devices, you're dealing with two timekeepers that generate clock frequencies and these will have to be synchronized.

If you've plugged two soundcards into your computer, there will be marching to the beat of two different drummers. When you want to use them simultaneously (for instance, to up the number of inputs and outputs), you're going to run into problems.

Most soundcards don't offer any kind of support for synchronization, therefore you can't operate them in parallel. Although most audio programs feature some kind of sync via MME, the tracking on different cards will definitely diverge. Frankly, it's not even worth attempting.

On the other hand, some cards can be combined; in computerese these are called stackable cards. The vendor determines how these are synced up, usually by proprietary connectors or PCI.

You could also opt for cards that can be synchronized using ›Wordclock,‹ S/P-DIF or the ADAT digital format. However, depending on the digital format, this requires some prior planning—it doesn't always work out automatically. Today, you'll have no trouble finding cards featuring a S/P-DIF port for less than 500 dollars while Wordclock and ADAT format are pretty much exclusive to professional (read: expensive) products.

This topic is broad enough to merit a separate book, so I'll focus strictly on what's relevant to the soundcard user.

Specific Soundcard Problems

There aren't really any problems that can be attributed to the soundcard alone. Often the problems related to the soundcard have more to do with the rest of the computer hardware and software and how it interfaces with the soundcard.

Shoddy drivers and resource conflicts are a common cause for annoyance, but that also applies to other hardware. Beyond that, modern soundcards, unlike their older ISA counterparts, are quite docile.

Resolve resource conflicts by using the methods described in the section ›Hardware Installation‹ on page 98—the procedure is always the same. Make a habit of regularly checking for new drivers on the manufacturer's website. Only current drivers promise trouble-free operation. If you want to review the installation procedure for these drivers, check out the section ›Windows Quickstart‹ on page 15.

Optimize Windows and your computer by making the Bios entries discussed in the previous chapters. Typically this will solve most of your ›soundcard problems.‹

I do have a tip on the topic of soundcards that I'd like to share with you: invest in a state-of-the-art Pci audio card. You don't have to retire your old Isa card. You can still use it as a sound generator and sampler because just about every card will do for these applications.

In my own computer, a Terratec Ews64Xl is still soldiering on in a marriage of convenience with a Microwave Pc (the hardware of a Microwave II synthesizer in a breakout box). The Ews interfaces the Microwave and plays back big, fat drum sets from the 32-Mb sampling memory (on the card, not in the Ram of the Pc) without a problem. I haven't used this card for Hd recording in eons.

If you own an older Turtle Beach card, you're probably loathe to do without its sound generator (originally lifted from an Emu Proteus and later from a Kurzweil K2000). On the other hand, Hd recording with a Turtle Beach has driven many a user to the brink of madness, particularly because of the dubious quality of its drivers.

Send these little beauties into semi-retirement. They'll serve you faithfully when used purely as a sound generator. You can rely on other, more advanced cards for modern accoutrements such as good timing and properly synchronized tracks.

9 The MIDI Interface

Why a Separate MIDI Interface?

You've already seen this question answered in the previous chapter. The onboard MIDI interface of soundcards is fine for goofing around when you're getting started, but as your skills increase, so will your demands. At some point, you'll be longing for an interface with at least two or more independent ports or will want to put an end to the timing problems that routinely occur when you're using a bunch of MIDI tracks.

The Roland MPU-401 was the first MIDI interface for the PC. This device offered a grand total of one input and one output. Although this wasn't the height of luxury, it did set a standard. Although this device is neither available today nor does it play an appreciable role in modern digital audio applications, MPU compatibility has remained a criterion for single-channel MIDI interfaces. This is why you'll still come across the term MPU-401.

Windows 95 offered a dedicated driver for this interface. If you own a card equipped with an MPU-compatible MIDI port, this is the driver that will most likely be installed. Remarkably, this driver actually works quite reliably, while this can't be said of many others of its ilk.

Today MIDI interfaces are available in the form of plug-in cards (like the MPU-401) in versions that connect to the printer port (LPT), to the serial interfaces (COM ports) and to the USB.

MIDI Interface Plug-in Cards

This form of MIDI interface has become rare. These are ISA cards, often without Plug&Play. Configuration is tricky, as you may recall from the section ›Hardware Installation‹. Cards made by Midiman, for instance the Winman series, are quite common. Windows 95 drivers are unavailable for the Winman 1×1 and 2×2—both ship with Windows 3.11 drivers which you would do well to avoid. For this reason, I can only recommend the 4×4.

Parallel Port Interfaces

The upside of this type of interface is that it won't give you any Plug&Play hassles. The downside is that you'll have to sacrifice a printer port. You could always install a second printer port, but then you'd have to sacrifice an IRQ for it.

Here's a brief run-down of parallel port interfaces that see widespread use:

♦ Midiman Portman Pc/P and 2×4
♦ MOTU MTP Av, MIDI Express, Micro Express, Pc-MIDI Flyer

Interfaces for the Serial Port (COM)

MIDI interfaces that connect to one of the Pc's two serial interfaces are a proven solution. The cool thing is that these serial interfaces are a standard feature on every Pc. One of the two is bound to be free unless you use a serial mouse and a modem. Since most Pcs also offer a Ps/2 mouse interface and most people use this type of mouse, you probably have a spare COM port available.

One of the most popular and best MIDI interfaces is the Unitor8 by Emagic. If there's any device I can recommend unequivocally, it'll be this utterly happening product.

Next to eight MIDI ports—which I guarantee you'll be lusting for at some point—it offers extensive synchronization options and can be operated as a stand-alone MIDI matrix without your computer if you care to use it on stage. There is a MkII version of this device as well as a more bare-bones version, the AMT8.

Here are several other common interfaces that connect to a serial interface:

◆ MOTU MTP Av, MIDI Express, Micro Express, Pocket Express

◆ Midiman Portman Pc/S

Usb Interfaces

Usb MIDI interfaces for the Pc are not what you'd call widespread. This is sure to change in the near future, particularly since Usb has made major inroads in the Apple Macintosh world.

The ones available today are:

◆ Steinberg Usb-2-MIDI

◆ Midiman Usb MIDISPORT 2×2

◆ Emagic AMT8 (however at the moment without a driver for Pc)

◆ Opcode MIDIport 32

Potential Problems with MIDI Interfaces

Problems with soundcards' onboard MIDI ports were discussed at length in the chapter ›The Soundcard‹ starting on page 221. However, outboard MIDI interfaces can also give you a headache. As long as you play just note sequences, you probably won't notice a problem. If however, you work with controllers to control parameters on external devices, you'll suddenly experience stuck notes or ghost notes. SysEx data transfers are notoriously riddled with errors. A typical example is when an editor program reports that a data transfer has been aborted while the connected synthesizer, oblivious to the problem, is still sending.

The culprit responsible for these problems is often the driver. This means that there's not much you can do about it except try out another driver. Unfortunately, interfaces by MOTU are known to be troublesome in the PC, particularly when you're dealing with SysEx data.

Paradoxically, the vendor's recommendation is to use not the latest but the oldest driver. This unusual advice notwithstanding, MOTU MIDI interface users habitually bellyache about its failure to run properly in their PCs. This doesn't speak well for these interfaces, so they aren't your best bet when you're in shopping mode.

▶ This doesn't apply to the Macintosh, where MOTU products number among the best interfaces available.

You can't always pin the blame on the driver. Often problems originate with the parallel port interfaces and serial COM interfaces themselves—especially when their settings are inadequate or incorrect.

Parallel Port (LPT1) Settings

Some older interfaces can't handle the different modes that a printer port offers. These standards were designed to assure the best possible communication with a printer; but no one had the foresight to take MIDI interfaces into account.

If you're having problems with your parallel port interface, you can attempt to change the settings for LPT1 in the BIOS setup of your computer. For this purpose, be sure to review the section ›BIOS‹ on page 81.

Unfortunately, I can't offer you a cure-all tip, the possible combinations are just too diverse. Older interfaces seem to prefer the conservative Standard setting (called Compatible in some BIOS versions), newer interfaces may use bidirectional communication and therefore won't run properly when this default is set. All you can do is fly by the seat of your pants and finesse the right setting.

Serial Port (COM1 and COM2) Settings

If a MIDI interface that connects to a serial port is giving you paroxysms, this can also be a problem with its settings.

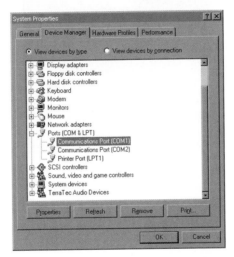

COM ports in the Device Manager

As always when you want to check a device's settings, go to the Device Manager. There you'll find the entries for the COM ports and can edit their settings. Be advised that you'll have to carry out the following steps separately for each port.

Of particular interest for our purposes is the maximum throughput. The port is often configured specifically for a mouse, which is served well with 9,600bps. However, this is not nearly swift enough for a MIDI interface. Always select the highest possible rate. You'll find different values depending on the Windows and board versions. A typical peak rate is 115,200bps.

Also, the communication protocol should be set either to None or Hardware, but not Xon/Xoff.

The following screenshot depicts an example of correct settings for a COM port.

The settings for the COM ports should look like this.

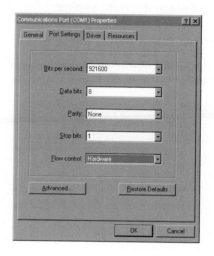

10 Connecting Peripheral Musical Devices Properly

Connecting a Sampler to Your Computer

After reading the chapter ›The Hard Disk‹ starting on page 109, you know how to configure Scsi with internal components. Generally, this breed of computer will run just peachy keen until you connect an external device such as a sampler for the first time. Typically your box will get a little overexcited or have a bona fide nervous breakdown and shut down altogether. At best, it simply won't detect the sampler. Things get uglier when the Pc stalls while scanning the Scsi chain. In the worst case, the device is detected during the boot routine, but the Windows launch flash-freezes your system.

First Aid for Sampler-Scsi Trauma

It can't hurt if you start by running down the standard Scsi troubleshooting routine. Check out the chapter ›The Hard Disk‹ where you'll find the golden Scsi rules.

First confirm that all Ids are unique, meaning that they were assigned just once. Then make absolutely sure that only the ends of the bus are terminated. In the case of a connected outboard sampler, the Scsi controller is no longer located at the end of the Scsi chain, but is now located at its middle. This means that the Scsi controller shouldn't be terminated.

For ancient controllers, you'll have to disable the terminator via jumpers, ›middle-aged‹ cards let you edit the settings in the controller's setup. Up-to-date controllers should detect the position automatically, unfortunately, this doesn't always work without a hitch. In the event that it doesn't, you'll have to switch the terminator off manually in the adapter setup.

▶ This also applies to mainboards with onboard Scsi controllers, which have become quite common. Here too, you'll have to set the terminator in the Bios setup.

The sampler at the other end of the chain will normally be terminated because its Scsi interface is designed primarily for connecting external disk drives where the controller of the device is always at the end of the chain. This is the same position it takes on when you connect it to the Pc, so in this respect the sampler can generally be ruled out as the source of the error.

Widening the Manhunt

If you've already arrested the usual suspects only to find all have an airtight alibi, you need to widen the range of your manhunt. The first thing that could do with a closer look is cable length. In the typical controller solution, the internal ribbon cables count and so does, strictly speaking, the half-centimeter that the socket measures. It's not unusual to exceed the maximum allowable cable length when you hook up an external cable.

For Fast Scsi (Scsi II), the overall cable length may not exceed a paltry 3 meters (10 feet). For Ultra and Ultra Wide Scsi, it's just 1.5 meters (5 feet) when four devices—actually the controller plus three devices—are connected.

The typical length of the internal ribbon cables is already a meter, so the external cable may not be longer than 50 centimeters (20 inches). If you buy the standard 1.2 meter (4 feet) cable in the electronics shop around the corner and connect it, you're effectively destabilizing the entire system.

While Fast and Wide Scsi are reasonably tolerant about these maximum cable lengths, Ultra systems, on account of their steeper signal slopes, will punish seemingly insignificant transgressions mercilessly.

In the case of the new Ultra 2 controllers, there are a couple of restrictions you need to bear in mind. You can roll out cables up to a length of 12 meters (40 feet), but only when you've connected exclusively Ultra 2 devices. The fact is that none of the currently available samplers supports this standard. As soon as you connect a single Ultra, Wide or Fast Scsi device, you're back to square one—Ultra operating mode. The restrictions described above are back in force.

When you're working with Ultra or Ultra 2 devices, be sure you keep an eye on the quality of external cables. Not every cable is suitable for Ultra. Cables with 25-pin connectors are generally designed for the Scsi II (Fast Scsi) standard and these can give you grief.

Problems can also occur when the data transfer rate is coordinated automatically between the sampler and adapter. If they can't come to terms, you can force the 10Mb/sec rate of Scsi II for the sampler's Scsi Id in the Bios setup of the adapter. This is a common problem when you're dealing with Ultra and Ultra 2 controllers.

Correct Termination

Termination too has its pitfalls. For Ultra Scsi and higher, active termination is law. You can connect passively terminated devices, but their terminators have to be switched off. This of course means that you have to know exactly which device you want to connect at the end of the bus. An older Cd-Rom drive with passive termination can be troublesome, as can a sampler.

Lamentably, there's no one you can turn to get precise information on whether or not a sampler's terminator is active or passive. When in doubt, set the controller from Ultra to Wide or Fast Scsi, provided that this is possible.

Another termination-related stumbling block is Ultra Wide and Ultra 2 Scsi. The latter works with Lvd (Low Voltage Differential), which means that two circuits are used to carry the signal. This solves the problem with the cables picking up stray interference, which is why the cable length could be increased to twelve meters (fourty feet). However, both Scsi standards use 16 bits (i. e. 16 lines in the cable) for data transfer. The upper eight bits (High and High Lvd) and the lower eight bits (Low and Low Lvd) are terminated separately.

If external devices are connected to this kind of signal circuit, figuring out the right termination is a real brain teaser. If no Ultra Wide or Ultra 2 devices are connected to the chain, the terminator for the upper eight bits (High) remains on even if both internal and external devices are connected to the controller. Although this is logical, it's a potential pitfall since, in any other scenario, you'd intuitively switch off the terminator.

Troubleshooting Sampler-related Problems

At this point, you probably know why you're having problems if you've connected a sampler to your computer, but you don't know what you can do about them aside from trying shorter cables. Now I'd like to share some tips that will help put your Pc in order.

Fast and Wide Scsi Controllers

Here the only thing you have to watch out for is to not exceed the cable length of three meters (ten feet) and to switch off the controller's terminator when you go to connect the sampler.

Ultra Wide Controllers

These host adapters generally come with three connectors, two internal ports and one external port. If you chose to use all three connectors, you end up with a star configuration, which is a no-no. Beyond that, the external port is almost always the Ultra Scsi connector, which requires active termination and drastically reduces the maximum allowable cable length.

Here's an option that lets you circumvent the problem. Instead of using the external connector, you can use the second internal connector (which is a 50-pin Wide port) and route it out thru a slot adapter. These are available in every well-stocked computer store. This both spares you the necessity of active termination and gives you more leeway in terms of cable length.

Ultra Scsi Controllers

Frankly, you're better off buying a cheap Fast Scsi controller from some discounter's bargain bin. You'll save yourself a whole lot of hassle as well as money, the latter because you'd need expensive adapters for your Cd-Rom disk drive and burner. Also the impractical cable length of 1.5 meters (5 feet) is a pain.

Ultra 2 Scsi Controllers

For fairly basic devices, the same things said for Ultra Wide adapters hold true here. However, more sophisticated devices such as the U2W Adaptec 2940 are equipped with a gizmo called an Scsi bridge. It isolates or separates the Ultra 2 and Ultra Wide units electronically. Here you end up with a total of four connectors, a 68-pin and a 50-pin connector each for Ultra and Ultra Wide, a 68-pin connector for Ultra 2 devices and a 68-pin external connector.

If you don't own any Ultra 2 devices—and this will most likely still be the case—you can then use the one 68-pin port to connect Ultra Scsi disks and the 50-pin port to connect a Cd-Rom drive or burner. This means you can do without adapter plugs.

Since both connectors tap into to the same Scsi bus, so Ultra Scsi rules for device numbers and cable length apply. Terminate the circuit in the usual manner:

- If you're using both connectors, don't terminate the controller.

- If you're using just one connector, the controller is at the end of the chain and has to be terminated.

- The third internal connector—the 68-pin Ultra 2 port—remains unused.

- The external connector taps into the Ultra 2 bus. If you haven't connected anything internally—which is the assumption that we're operating on here—you can connect an external ZIP drive along with the sampler. The maximum cable length is still a total of three meters (ten feet) since, with just three devices (sampler, ZIP and adapter), you haven't exceeded the device limit.

Onboard Ultra 2 Controllers (Adaptec AIC-7890)

This component resides on Asus P2B-S mainboards—currently musicians' first choice in boards for Pentium II processors.

It ships with just three connectors:

- Ultra (68-pin port),
- Ultra 2 (also a 68-pin port)
- and Wide SCSI (50-pin port).

Here too, the Ultra 2 circuit, which is tapped by just a single connector, is electronically isolated. If you own Ultra or Ultra 2 devices, your options are clearly reduced. You're compelled to sacrifice one connector to establish an external connection using the included adapter.

Connect all devices to the Ultra 2 port—1.5 meters (5 feet) should suffice within the computer—and route the 50-pin connector out in order to avoid having to use an active terminator.

Since Ultra 2 no longer requires you to terminate devices (the included cable takes care of this chore for you) you enjoy the agreeable side effect that you won't have to worry about fiddling with the device at the end of the chain.

On the downside, you may have to fork over the green stuff (or whatever color the money is in your country) for expensive adapters, for example to convert the 68-pin port to a 50-pin connector that can take the CD-ROM's plug. You may be better off buying a second cheap Fast SCSI controller for the sampler.

CD-ROM Drive

No sampler likes playing second fiddle to the computer, especially when Windows monopolizes the CD-ROM drive that the two share. Switch off the automatic routine by which Windows constantly checks if a new CD has been inserted.

This parameter is called Auto Insert Notification; you'll find it in the Device Manager as an option of your CD drive or burner. You'll find further details on this fascinating subject on page 177 in the section named ›Disabling CD Detection‹.

Problems with the Sampler

If you've done everything right up to this point, you should be able to address your sampler from the PC. This allows you for instance, to use Wavelab and Soundforge as editors or to finally be able to experience the petulant frenzy-inducing crashes of Akai's MESA editor. The sampler, in turn, should be able to use your PC's CD-ROM drive, provided that it is connected to the same controller as the sampler.

If none of this is the case, it's time to have a serious word with your sampler. Let's look at how to fix the problem in various samplers.

Akai S Class up to 3200 XL

With Windows 95/98, be sure to use Os 2.0 or higher in the Akai. In these versions, Akai kindly made some modifications so that the standard Windows drivers would be able to address the sampler without giving you any problems.

These devices are rather easy to get along with. As long as they don't access a disk drive, their behavior is impeccable.

If, however, the Pc and sampler access the Scsi bus simultaneously, the computer temporarily conks out and a crash is imminent.

Miraculously, as soon as the Akai has finished loading data, Windows wakes up again. So there's no reason to panic, just be aware that this is S. O. P. In addition, you should ensure that the sector size for the Cd-Rom drive is set to the same value as the sector size indicated in the sampler's Load/Scsi menu.

Yamaha A-3000

There's absolutely nothing to adjust here. Incidentally, don't be surprised by the snail's pace of the transfer rates—this is normal.

Emu Esi-4000

You'll have to tell the Emu that a second Scsi master (the Pc controller) is connected to the chain. This is pretty easy to do with the setting ›Avoid Host on Id <x>‹ (whereby x stands for the Scsi Id of the Pc adapter).

These Scsi configurations are normally quite stable if you've followed all the rules. If from time to time your system crashes when you're trying to access the sampler, you probably failed to follow one or several of these rules.

Suppress Driver Inquiry While Booting

Even if everything has gone well thus far, there's still one more hurdle you'll have to overcome. Ever vigilant, Windows scans the Scsi bus when you launch the Os to detect any devices that may be loitering about. It will of course find your sampler if it is powered up.

Nosy Windows will then ask for the drivers for this unknown device. These don't exist, and even if they did, you wouldn't need them because programs that support samplers address these directly without going down the detour that is the driver.

To get Windows to give it a rest and prevent it from unnerving you with irrelevant questions about drivers every time you launch it, you'll have to tell it that there are no drivers and that this device should be listed as unknown in the Device Manager.

To this end, when the prompt about the drivers appears, click on Next and then select Hardware From A List. In the following window, you can choose a yellow question mark labeled Unknown Device as a hardware type.

Select it. Tediously, you'll have to repeat this little chore seven times because a sampler has its own Scsi controller, which in turn has seven connection options that Windows will also detect. Once this song and dance is out of the way though, Windows will never again bother you with this meddlesome question.

Burning Your Own Cds

Now that Cd burners have become affordable for mere mortals, they have edged out Dat cassettes as the mastering medium of choice for audio projects. Most pressing factories now accept Cds as a mastering medium. If you make music strictly for your private pleasure, you'll probably prefer to hand out Cds of your home recordings rather than analog cassette tapes. Now that the tape deck's slow slide into oblivion has begun, many home stereo systems do without them altogether.

Sooner or later you're bound to cotton to the idea of burning your own Cd. To make it easy for you and avoid some of the hassles that this entails, I'd like to take you on a quick guided tour of the Cd format and give you a couple of pointers on toasting your own discs.

The Cᴅ Standard: Red Book

Before we get down to the nitty-gritty, you'll need a little background info. The obligatory standard for audio Cᴅs—a document that goes by the interesting name of the Red Book (no relation to Mao's manifesto)—was drafted by a company called Philips who developed the Cᴅ way back in the taste-challenged '80s. This standard defines the physical properties of an audio Cᴅ as well as its audio format (16bit, 44.100kHz sampling frequency).

Cᴅs and Physics

The topography of a Cᴅ consists of a spiral pattern of *pits* (small depressions on the surface) and *lands* (the surface area between these pits). Now, contrary to what you might expect, these two different surfaces don't represent the two digital values 0 and 1.

Instead, a digital 1 is actually represented by the edge of a pit. At this point, the light reflected from the land and the bottom of the pit is out of phase so that it is cancelled out so that the photo electrode no longer detects it.

Only at the edge of a pit is the laser's light cancelled out. This status represents a digital 1.

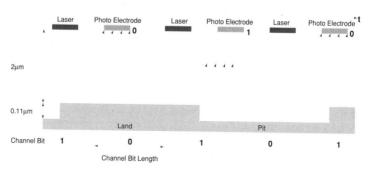

A stretch of pits or lands, on the other hand, stands for a digital 0 or a series of zeros.

These tiny structures don't allow for certain combinations, for example two ones may not follow each other. Also no more than 10 zeros can follow sequentially, otherwise the synchronization of the data stream would be thrown out of whack. This means the minimum length of a pit amounts to three units of time (3T), i.e. the sequence 1001. The maximum length is 11T, i.e. ten zeros or 100000000001.

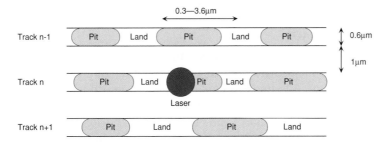

The pits and lands on a CD's surface.

Logic Definitions

Clearly, these so-called ›channel bits‹ are rather restrictive and couldn't possibly store anywhere near all the data that we would want them to. Therefore, all data on the CD is encoded, meaning that eight bits are turned into 14 bits. Three so-called ›merge‹ bits are used to separate these 14-bit bytes so that a byte of data consists of 17 bits in total. Every sample requires two bytes per stereo channel.

The smallest unit of the CD, a frame, consists of 588 channel bits, which in turn comprises 24 data bytes plus 8 bytes of CIRC code (see below). A byte is added for the different sub-channels. On top of these 561 channel bits are another 27 sync bits, which equals a total of 588.

A sector or block is comprised of 98 of these frames. A block is also the smallest addressable unit. The ›subcodes‹ that these blocks contain remain to a large extent unused except for the Q subcode which contains time information and the P subcode which signals the beginning of the track. Other subcodes are used as format identifiers as well as for other CD formats.

Finally, every CD (including the data CD-ROM) contains a lead-in area, that contains, among other stuff, the table of contents (Toc) and total playing time. Following the audio section is a 90-second lead-out, which consists solely of digital zeros. This is designed to enable a CD player to recognize the end of the disc and tell its laser to lay off. Most players do this without the benefit of a lead-out anyway.

Dao and Tao

Disk-at-once (Dao) is a process by which a CD is burned in one pass, meaning that the write laser doesn't stop burning—it never lets up or relocate its position until it's finished. In addition, in this mode it always writes the lead-in first, then the audio section, and, in the end, the lead-out. Only Dao lets you work with subindexes, which is the only way of burning tracks with no pauses between them, for example, for live recording.

Track-at-once (Tao) means just that—one track is written in each pass. Then the laser lifts off and touches down at another location, whereby it generates a little buffer zone of some two seconds so that there's a little leeway for the laser beam to be positioned.

In this mode, the laser always writes the meaty part, the data, first, then sandwiches it by writing the lead-in and the lead-out. Here too a buffer block is written in between the data zone and the lead-in and the lead-out.

All of these blocks are detected as E32 errors. However, a modern audio CD player ignores them because they don't reside in the actual data section or they're lodged in the pause between the tracks. Older CD players may generate a click when they detect these blocks. Pressing factories won't accept this type of CD as a master at all or only after it's been subjected to special and pricey processing.

Tao will let you shorten the pauses between tracks so that the CD seems to be exactly the same as the seamless type of disk burned using Dao, but the E32 errors nevertheless survive.

Also, in TAO mode you can't burn a CD over several sessions. The problem here is that this would create another lead-in with each session, which an audio CD player, unlike a CD-ROM drive, is not designed to handle.

Error Correction

Even if there were such a thing as an utterly flawless CD, it would be marred as soon as you take it out of its casing. For this reason, the clever engineers who came up with these handy silver coasters for your drinks had to devise some type of error correction or recovery method to reconstruct the original data when the bits on the surface of the CD can't all be read correctly.

Enter the Reed-Solomon code, which among other things is responsible for those vivid, incredibly detailed images that Voyager sends from space. This algorithm works with the redundant data—25% in the case of a CD.

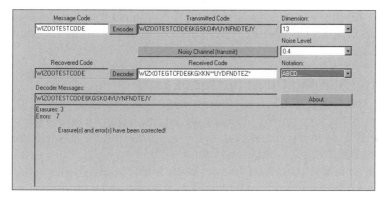

Reed-Solomon code passes the WIZOO test with flying colors: In spite of seven errors and three deleted numbers, the original word can be restored.

The illustration shows a striking example of how original code can be recovered even when things go very wrong during data transfer. If you're curious to see how this works, you can try it out for yourself at http://www.cco.caltech.edu/~hope/HTML/RS31Demo.html.

Actual error correction takes place in two stages called C1 and C2. The designations E21, E22 and so forth refer to these two stages. The first number after the E designates the number of errors in the error correction stage, the second number indicates the stage itself.

Minor bit errors are fixed at the C1 level by means of the first four error correction bits discussed above in the paragraph on the frame format.

If a data group can't be handled at this level, it is given the status ›uncorrected‹ and is sent on its way to the C2 stage along with the second four error correction bits. There the interleaved data is put back together in the correct sequence in a FIFO memory. The Reed-Solomon decoding routine is then able to recompute the original signal.

An E32 error couldn't be corrected here either though and would be handled in the player by means of something called error masking. Fortunately, these errors occur rather rarely in practice.

All of these processes take place in the components of a CD player or a CD-ROM drive and are constituents of the CD standard.

The Burning Question: IDE or SCSI?

It you already own an IDE system, this question can truly cause a heartburn, because an additional SCSI controller is going to set you back at least a C-note (that's a $ 100 for those of you who don't pay your bills in greenbacks). During the market launch of IDE or ATAPI burners there was a real controversy about their viability—Disk-at-once mode wasn't supported and ›buffer under run‹ were two of the main problems. With the Busmaster controllers on most newer mainboards, buffer under run is no longer a problem and all latest generation IDE burners can now toast CDs in Disk-at-once mode.

However, SCSI still has one advantage: after a device is accessed (e. g. the CD writer), it is left alone in peace until it reports in again. During this time, another SCSI device can be addressed, for example, the hard disk. By contrast, the CPU can't access an IDE device while a Busmaster process is running. So if you're dead-set on burning in the background while you write long letters to the Internal Revenues Service (that's the Inland Revenue Office to you pint-pulling lads) explaining why your income tax would be so much better invested in satisfying your gear lust, than you should opt for SCSI.

While researching this book, I bench tested both an internal Philips CDD3610 burner and the virtually identical but external HP Surestore 7200e that connects to the printer port. I didn't discover any dramatic differences. The internal solution is inherently of course, the faster of the two.

Configuring Burners

For ATAPI burners, you'll have to be just as mindful off the correct configuration (master/slave) as you would for hard disks and CD-ROM drives.

There are a few things to watch for with an SCSI burner as well. Every device must be assigned a unique ID. When in doubt, review the section ›SCSI‹ on page 119. Note that although this seems glaringly obvious, even something this simple can slip your mind.

I once jumpered two burners to the same ID by mistake. The controller automatically detected the devices while it scanned the SCSI bus using the SCAM record—an automatic configuration routine for SCSI devices similar to Plug&Play. And, in keeping with the rules, it indicated different IDs while the computer was being booted.

Not until I was faced with mysterious errors while burning did I get the bright the idea to open up the computer and check the jumpers. A classic case of ›trust yourself and you're putting your life into the hands of a fool‹ or something like that.

▶ There is another aspect of the IDE-versus-SCSI issue that you need to consider: Older versions of the mastering and burning programs Wavelab and Soundforge feature CD Architect which supports SCSI burners only. If you want to work with these programs, you have no choice in the matter. However, Wavelab versions 2.02 and higher can also address IDE burners.

The Software

If all you want to do is create Red Book audio CDs, your choice of burning software is purely a matter of taste. All programs can burn audio CDs, most of the newer products feature DAO mode. These program differ primarily in their subcode, track marker editing options and of course their audio processing features. Wavelab, Soundforge and Red Roaster get highest marks for the depth, scope and sheer tweakability of these features.

The denoiser and declicker tools of WinOnCD and other burner software are simply insufficient for professional mastering. However, if all you want to is compile your own greatest hits sampler from your fave CDs for your car or as a sound track for romantic, candle-lit dinners, these programs will fit the bill. If you want to burn data or mixed-mode CDs (data and audio), Wavelab is out of the question.

To burn audio CDs, all you need is your songs in the form of separate Wave file in 44.1kHz stereo/16bit format. The software will take care of the rest, including creating track indexes, automatically. The procedure is similar in all programs: You simply select the Wave files, determine the sequence, choose either TAO or DAO and presto, it's toasting time.

Most newer programs also let you burn CDs without the obligatory two-second pause stipulated in the Red Book. If you take this tack, be sure to burn in DAO mode because CD players will click like a box full of crickets while playing back a CD burned without pauses in TAO mode.

Although in the past different brands of blanks and burners weren't nearly as compatible as makers would have you believe, today this problem has been largely surmounted. Nonetheless, you should avoid bargain-bin blanks, especially since the prices for brand-name blanks have dropped drastically.

Debunking Common Myths

There are some misconceptions about home-burned audio CDs and their sound quality that I feel need clearing up. Hard core hi-fi freaks, particularly those of the notoriously overbearing high-end camp, claim that they can hear the difference between pressed and home-burned CDs. These ›audiophiles‹ claim they can distinguish between the sound quality according to the speed at which a CD is burned. Also, they doubt that tracks can be grabbed 1:1 off of audio CDs without any signal loss. Grabbing is, for example, a convenient alternative to copying samples from audio sampling CDs. Both claims are patent twaddle.

Often microscopic pictures of the topography of a CD featuring blurry, hardly distinguishable pits and lands are presented as ›evidence‹ for these misguided notions. The fact is that these pits and lands represent not zeros and ones (the very bits that you learned about in the chapter ›The Processor‹ starting on page 37) but rather the respective transitions represent a 1.

It doesn't matter what the edges of pits look like as long as they're there at all. Furthermore, the so-called channel bits on the CD do not represent the 0 and 1 statuses of the actual signal.

As explained above, the actual data on a CD is encoded repeatedly. Quite simply, what the laser reads on the surface is not decisive. What is decisive is what the player's decoder sends to the converter. The former will never match the original, the latter virtually always will. Often error recovery is made responsible for alleged differences in sound, completely ignoring what error correction on a CD actually means.

Recall that Red Book CDs use two levels of error correction, C1 and C2. Everything that is corrected at these levels ends up corresponding to what it was originally. There's no voodoo involved, it's just plain math.

Only errors that can't be corrected at the second or C2 level (so-called E32) are passed on to the next stage. This is no longer error correction but error masking, which calls for three measures to be carried out:

- Sample values are interpolated for minor drop-outs. How this process is executed varies from manufacturer to manufacturer.
- The last sample is held in the event of major errors.
- If something really bad happens—your toddler decided to use your CD as a teething aid—the output is simply muted to protect the other components of the system.

It's debatable whether or not the first two measures are perceptible. Should anything at all become audible, it will be distortion or spurious modulations—a held sample, for example, generates a rectangular waveform. Claims that these measures lead to mysterious high frequency loss and a muddier signal are totally unfounded.

Another fact that the HiFi camp studiously ignores is that error masking is rarely active. Bench tests on countless blanks have clearly shown that E32 errors never occur in practice. Therefore, we can all rest assured that a home-toasted CD in a normal state is never subjected to interpolation secure in the knowledge that changes at the bit level simply don't take place. Data is sent 1:1 to the converter.

Jitter

The term ›jitter‹ is routinely bandied about in a last ditch effort to explain perceived differences in sound. And why not, it sounds like something a competent engineer might say and it's hard to be caught out because nobody knows what it means anyway.

Jitter is nothing more exciting than a time-based error caused by varying time delays in the circuit paths from component to component. Normally, this effect is produced by inaccurate PLL elements or—although on a much smaller scale—by fluctuations of a converter's clock.

When we're talking about an audio CD, jitter is a time-base deviation due to pit and land lengths that deviate from the total average on the CD, in other words, the pits are longer or shorter than the average.

If a pit is shorter than allowed, i. e. 3T, it isn't detected at all. This produces an error, which, however, is fixed by the error correction routines. If, on the other hand, a pit is too long, the edge (the digital 1) simply comes a little too late.

If this signal were sent to the converter exactly in this condition, you would end up with audible jitter produced by the actual CD. For one thing, the encoded signal cannot be used to render an audio signal. For another, it will never happen because a FIFO (first in, first out) buffer is required to decode and de-interlace this data.

The output of this memory to the converter is controlled by a quartz clock. The accuracy of this clock is responsible for audible differences, not the medium and not the disk drive.

At the risk of bursting every audiophile LTD's (lawyers, teacher, doctors) bubble, a boutique CD drive that goes for some 10 grand delivers the same data as a $150 burner on sale at the local discounter's. Any jitter on the other side of the FIFO is a figment of an overactive imagination.

All I can say about people who insist that the housing itself resonates and place their players on spikes for this reason is that I have a most excellent bridge in Brooklyn that I would like to sell.

What this all boils down to when you go to burn a CD is that the rate has no influence on sound, so toast 'em as fast as the burner will let you.

Grabbing

Grabbing is another much debated issue. The term describes the process of reading out data of an audio CD digitally directly from the CD-ROM drive to the hard disk.

You would think that there wouldn't be much room for controversy, since data CDs are physically the same and every read operation on these disks is accurate down to the last bit. However, problems can arise.

First of all, a data CD has another logic format. Here a sector contains only 2,048 bytes of useful data, the rest is filled in with a header in which, among other stuff, the sector number is encoded. Then there are additional error correction codes that can possibly fix an E32 error. This header identifies the sector so that the disk drive always knows precisely which sector it is reading.

The sectors of audio CDs contain 2,352 bytes of useful data. Address information (hours:minutes:block) is encoded in sub-channels with the two stereo channels in a continuous stream which—just like in an audio CD player—is separated precisely in the decoding stage of the disk drive.

This means that the disk drive doesn't always know exactly which sector it is reading. Philips' specifications stipulate merely that a laser must be positioned within $\frac{1}{75}$ second—whether it ends up at the beginning of a sector or at its end is anybody's guess.

For this reason, there are two modes in which a disk drive works—you guessed it: data and audio mode. In audio mode, data is read out raw since logical addressing via a file system isn't possible. Whether or not a disk drive is at all capable of grabbing depends on whether or not it understands a raw read or the commands necessary to carry this type of read operation out. Most SCSI disk drives do and of late IDE devices have been getting with the program, too.

Several factors determine if a grab is successful. First there's the software—does it read data sequentially or in one go? With Windows 3.11 and Dos, simultaneous reading and writing was not possible, which meant that data was ordered in bite-sized morsels—typically 64 kilobytes. Once the system had digested one bit, the read operation had to be started anew.

Here a part of or an entire sector could be lost in the digital ether. The result was loud and clear—the computer began grunting like a truffle-seeking pig when it hits pay dirt. This phenomenon is also occasionally called jitter, although strictly speaking, the term is misapplied here.

To remedy this ill, the software can request a couple of sectors prior to the next sector and compare them with the last ones, which it already knows from the preceding sequence. The bit pattern tells it precisely where the beginning of the next sector is located. This process is called sector synchronization.

The results are even better if the operating system and software can work hand in hand so that data can be read and written at the same time. The disk drive then can read out a track in one go and no longer needs to stop.

Not all disk drives can do this. A company called Plextor produces disk drives that can and have become much-loved for it. These devices can also route data through the error masking stage using the data bus through. This means that E32 errors, should the actually occur, can also be processed.

Other CD-ROM drives also have a processing stage for E32 errors, however these are only used when data is sent out via the audio output (over to the soundcard). If a scratched CD runs in the audio player but is no longer readable in the CD-ROM drive, the Plextor could solve the problem. Other manufacturers have announced that a similar feature will be available with the next generation of their drives.

Again, the sound quality of grabbing is the subject of much conjecture. Some go as far to claim that files grabbed at 1× speed sound better than tracks extracted at fourfold or even faster speeds.

Debunking this myth is a no-brainer—all you have to do is grab the same track at different speeds and subject the resultant files to a binary comparison. Dos tools and Norton utilities will work fine for this purpose, as will `fc.exe` that ships with Dos.

Steinberg's Wavelab Version 2.0 or higher offers a very cool feature—it can not only grab tracks, it can also compare resultant Wave files. I used it to burn a Wave file at 1×, 2× and 4× speeds and then grabbed these files with all four burners at 1× and 4× speeds each, as well as with the Plextor at speeds of 1× and 16×. The result was what I'd call unambiguous—all digitally copied files were absolutely identical at the binary level.

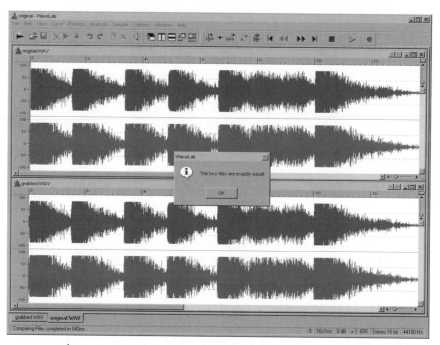

↑ A comparison of files in Wavelab reveals the truth about grabbing: be it at 1× or 16× speed, the result is always the same.

Some burners add a couple of zeros at the beginning and at the end of the file. With these the resultant files have to be trimmed at the first and last sample not equal to zero. The results are then identical.

I repeated the test with WinOnCd, the classic WinDac32 and Feurio. Again, all results were identical.

This comes as no surprise because all errors below the E32 level are not actually re-computed or falsified in any way, they're corrected by the error correction code. This confirms what I said about the perceived differences between burned and pressed CDs. If there was any difference at all, at least a few bits in the grabbed file would have to be different.

Yes, problems can occur. However, these are manifest as clearly audible clicks and drop-outs so that you could call digital extraction an ›either/or‹ proposition. Either it works faithfully or not at all. Many older disk drives can't cope with higher speeds and the CD may end up with flaws. When in doubt stick to a speed of 1×—this will almost always work out.

DVD

Of late, there has been much talk about this new medium although for years, most of it focused on potential manufacturers' inability to reach a consensus on a universal standard. ›Digital Versatile Disc‹—DVD for short—is something akin to a CD on steroids. It can carry audio, video and computer data. Its remarkably superior to the CD:

◆ Higher speed, some three times faster than a CD.

◆ Considerably greater storage capacity, 4.7GB in the case of writable DVDs.

◆ Significantly enhanced recording and playback quality up to 24bit/96kHz.

◆ The necessary standards for all three formats (audio, video, data) have been drafted. DvD video was the first to market and although it hasn't swept the globe, it is fairly well established.

DvD Video

The features of this future home cinema standard are impressive enough to keep the video junkies indoors for years to come:

◆ Over two hours of high-quality video (more than eight on a double-sided, double-layer disk).

◆ Up to eight tracks of digital audio (e. g. for several languages), each with eight channels!

◆ Up to 32 subtitles/Karaoke tracks.

◆ Automatic multiple threads (e. g. for several endings to a story, say, Hollywood versus something plausible).

◆ Up to nine selectable camera angles.

◆ Menus and simple interactive functions (for games, quizzes).

◆ Multilingual text identification for titles, album name or song name.

◆ Instant fast-forwarding to the desired position, including title, sequence or time code searches.

◆ Wear-free, immune to magnetic fields, heat-resistant, small.

▶ However, the industry was rocked when the DvD code was deciphered at the end of 1999. It's quite possible that the standard will be changed again or the DvD offering will be drastically reduced for fear of bootleg copies.

Dvd Audio

Dvd audio is the most recently approved of the standards and hasn't had a huge impact yet. This isn't a single uniform format, it actually consists of several formats.

As on an audio Cd, data is stored linearly, in uncompressed form, in this case at a resolution of 24bit/96kHz. Other resolutions are possible depending on the level of quality the video signals on the rest of the Dvd have. A uniform solution hasn't been reached yet.

The other audio Dvd formats are either compressed or multi-channel encoded audio streams. Until it is clear which solution and which format will end up on top, you'll do well to ignore Dvd audio.

Then there's the workload to consider. If you recorded Lpcm at the highest possible resolution, it's likely that your computer will simply collapse under this great data load. At a resolution of 24bit/96kHz, for example, audio tracks require fourfold the storage space and generate an correspondingly greater quantity of data for your computer to handle. This will decrease the number of possible tracks drastically and for the first few computer generations, you'll only be able to use a fraction of the plug-ins to which you've grown accustomed. The improvement in quality is quite audible, but not enough so that the average club-goer will notice it.

The impetus that once inspired musicians to embrace the Cd simply isn't there. Much water will flow under the bridge before Dvd audio sees widespread acceptance.

Dvd Data

Dvd data is the more interesting option right now. Unfortunately, it's a format jungle out there—Dvd-Rom, Dvd-Ram, Dvd-Rw and Dvd+Rw, make a total of four different formats.

The maximum storage capacity is 4.7Gb. This can satisfy a musician's most covetous urges—these mammoth piles of steaming data can be read faster than with conventional Cd-

ROM drives. There are already 10×-DVD ROM players on the market whose speed smokes that of standard 32×-CD-ROM drives. Unfortunately, there's a great big catch that pretty much bursts the bubble:

The only writable formats available to date are DVD RAM drives, and these are still very pricey. They store ›just‹ 2.7GB instead of the possible 4.7GB, which in itself would be quite impressive. The only thing is that, once they've been written, these DVDs can only be read by certain DVD players, which largely cancels out the advantage of all this storage capacity.

I'm loathe to endorse a DVD disk drive as a substitute for your CD-ROM even if your old CDs can be read by the new DVD disk drives. It will take some time before one of the four competing standards catches on. If you act rashly now, you may end up with a DVD player that will be unable to read the home-made DVDs of the future.

At the moment, the notion of using this medium as a data backup solely for your own computer is tempting, but it's just too expensive to entertain. With a single DVD costing a whopping 40 bucks or so, the writable CD is by far the more economic option, and it's definitely the more compatible. After all, you don't want to be making backups of your data now that in two years time you won't be able to read on any disk drive.

Reference Section

Cᴅ-Rᴏᴍ Table of Contents

AVI

In this folder, you'll find several short videos that demonstrate basic configuration steps.

Tutor_1.avi	Opening the Device Manager
Tutor_2.avi	Updating a Driver
Tutor_3.avi	Disabling Cᴅ recognition
Tutor_4.avi	Optimizing Virtual Memory
Tutor_5.avi	Disabling Iʀǫ Steering
Tutor_6.avi	Disabling Window Animation
Tutor_7.avi	Configuring the Cᴏᴍ Port

Demos

Here you'll find demos of Steinberg's Cubase Vsᴛ and Wavelab as well as a demo of Emagic's Logic Audio.

Tools

Here's a couple of useful tools for your Pᴄ. These utilities shouldn't give you any hassles, but as is the case with all utilities, caution is in order. Of the zillions of possible hardware/software combinations, you may have one that such a program won't cotton to.

Sandra	Sisoft Sandra is an extensive system analysis tool. Unfortunately, at the moment it isn't compatible with Aᴍᴅ's Athlon processor. When it goes to check the Cᴘᴜ and mainboard, the system will crash, so be if your rig is powered by an Athlon, don't use it.
Algotest	Algotest is a little program that lets you measure the signal-to-noise ratio of your soundcard. It can't take the place of a real hardware gauge since the software can only measure the signal that arrives in the computer. However, the tool will give you a rough idea of the basic noise level a card.

cthdbench	The ultimate hard disk benchmark program. For truly reliable results, you'll have to run it in Dos mode. This means that, for Scsi disks, you'll need Dos Aspi drivers. If you've never done something like this before, you should consult an expert.
Sinfo	This is another system analysis tool that can gauge processes, loaded Dlls and memory utilization. It lets you find out stuff like how many threads a program consists of and at which priority levels they run. If you're a newbie, you should skip this one—it's really something for experts to fiddle with.
DX_Appl	Here you get a little plug-in for the Control Panel that will give you the inside scoop on your DirectX version. It will detect mixed configurations, but it won't help you fix them.
DXBack	With this utility, you can reset the version numbers of the DirectX components so that reinstallation is possible. This is an invaluable tool if your DirectX subsystem is a total mess.

Expert

In this folder, you'll find very useful utilities, but they do require some prior knowledge because the address the hardware directly. Don't use these programs if you don't know precisely what you're doing. For some utilities, you may require Aspi drivers for Ms-Dos so that your Scsi hard disks can be addressed. These drivers should have been supplied along with your Scsi controller. Once you're finished, be sure to de-install the drivers completely via the method described in the section ›Windows‹ on page 145.

ctia	This is a utility supplied by the magazine c't. It will help you glean information on the Cpu and chipset.
ctp2info	Another c't freebie. With this program, you can recognize forged PIIs. However, it can't identify all Pentium II types, so it won't give you absolute peace of mind.
ctpciw	A utility for scoping out Pci- and Ide-related information.
aspiid	Two little tools that helps you seek Scsi information. Of particular interest is aspi-wce.exe, which lets you enable the write cache of Scsi disks when this wasn't done ex factory. The write cache is switched off on new Ibm disks, for example.

Shareware

Here you'll find an extensive collection of audio and MIDI shareware. These will let you get started immediately without having to buy one of the big commercial programs.

Agrapper	A grabber program for reading CDs out digitally.
Audiomulch	Modular sound design.
Awave	The classic among audio shareware programs. It supports many exotic formats. Demo version.
Coagula	A graphic synthesizer similar to the commercial Metasynth.
FX	A modular virtual analog software synthesizer.
Looprec	A simple audio recorder and player.
MIDI Joystick	Err, lets you generate MIDI data with a joystick.
MPEGEnc	An encoder for creating MP3 files.
MIDI-Ox	The most popular MIDI analysis tool. It gives you a precise view of incoming and outgoing data.
Rubber Duck	Bass synthesizer with step sequencer.
Stomper	Drum sequencer.
Virtual Cable	A virtual audio cable that lets you create any desired circuit within Windows. It provisions virtual audio devices so you can create a chain of soft synths.
Winamp	One of the most popular MP3 players for Windows.

Internet Resources

I'd like to encourage you to regularly check out the Internet for the latest news and updates—it's certainly the fastest and most direct way to get them.

Book Update Page

Accompanying this book is a dedicated page on the WIZOO website. It features the latest information and any new insights that I've stumbled across. You'll also find the links listed below, which of course you can click directly to take you to the given site. Simply go to:

http://www.wizoo.com/areas/bookpages/pcoptim.htm

Let's take a stroll through some of the general sources of information that may be of use to you. Beware, reality is not one of the strong suits of the wonderful world of cyberspace. Don your fly-fishing gear, because the bull—innuendo, half-truths and rumors—is often hip-deep. Here are some of the rare treasure troves where truth is still of consequence.

First I'll give you directions to the websites of hardware manufacturers.

▶ The names of these links generally follow the pattern http://www.nameofthecompany.com/, but many of the Far Eastern manufacturers of mainboards, Bios and memory don't follow this scheme. That mysterious Orient again.

Processors

Both Intel and AMD maintain vast but clearly ordered websites in which you'll find everything from press releases to developer information. Both websites should also be your first choice when you're looking for the scoop on chipsets:

http://www.intel.com/

http://www.amd.com/

General Cpu-related information:

http://www.cpu-central.com/

http://www.sandpile.org/index.shtml

Mainboards

Asus

Asus' website is a mess—c'mon guys and gals, get your Moms in to straighten the place up. Above all the downloads are inconsistent. Often older Bios versions are posted on the Www site while the Ftp server already offers newer versions. Upping the confusion factor, the international versions of the websites offer still different versions. But griping will get you nowhere, so you'll have to bite the bullet, check all the sites and compare versions. For this very reason, I've included the addresses of the Ftp servers.

Websites:

http://www.asus.com/
http://www.asuscom.de/

Ftp servers:

ftp://ftp.asus.com/
ftp://ftp.asuscom.de/

Biostar

Finding Biostar's website isn't all that easy if you don't know the code for Taiwanese websites. The company's Taiwanese site will take you to the international pages:

http://www.biostar.com.tw/
ftp://ftp.biostar.com.tw/

Gigabyte

Gigabyte's site address names are interestingly varied.

http://www.gigabyte.com.tw/
http://www.giga-byte.com/
http://www.gigabyte.de/
http://www.gbt-tech.co.uk/

Abit

http://www.abit.com/

General Mainboard-related Information

http://www.motherboards.org/

Bios

Bios software vendors are of course represented in the net. However, I recommend that you refrain from using the Bios updates on these pages because you'll always require a specific Bios that has been tailored to your mainboard. You can put your computer into a coma with any other Bios.

Ami (American Megatrends)	http://www.megatrends.com/
Award	http://www.award.com/
Phoenix	http://www.firmware.com/catalog2.htm

Bios Tweaking

There's plenty of tips & tricks to be found on the net for optimizing a Bios. ›Wim's Bios Page,‹ for example, is great place to get current Bios versions even for exotic hardware.

http://www.ping.be/bios/

You'll find good guides that will take you by the hand and lead you through Bios settings, even those of older chipsets, at:

http://burks.bton.ac.uk/burks/pcinfo/hardware/bios_sg/
bios_sg.htm

Display Adapters

You should visit the addresses of display adapter makers more often than you'd probably care to. Experience has shown that, in the first year of a product's life cycle, vendors like to nurse their babies along and put out updates on a monthly basis to fix the bugs that are making your life miserable.

ATI	`http://www.ati.com/`
Diamond	`http://www.diamondmm.com/`
Elsa	`http://www.elsa.com/`
Matrox	`http://www.matrox.com/`

The sites of graphics chip makers can be a good place to score so-called generic drivers. These are drivers that—although they weren't written specifically for the card in your computer—will work with the chip that it uses. These drivers aren't optimized for speed, but for this reason, are often somewhat ›audio-friendlier.‹

S3	`http://www.s3.com/`
Nvidia (maker of the Riva TNT chip)	`http://www.nvidia.com/`

Hard Disks

You'll really only need these addresses if you're interested in the technical data for your disk or are looking for specific jumper settings.

`http://www.maxtor.com/`
`http://www.seagate.com/`
`http://www.ibm.com/`
`http://www.quantum.com/`
`http://www.zdnet.com/computershopper/edit/howtobuy/` `C0000003/`
`http://www.thetechpage.com/cgi-bin/default.cgi`

Scsi

The websites of Scsi controller makers are well worth checking out more often. The Bios updates and new drivers that are regularly posted there will even teach an old controller new tricks when you've run into problems with a new hard disk or sampler.

Adaptec

```
http://www.adaptec.com/
```

Adaptec's site is 007-approved (loose lips sink chips?). The company plays its cards real close to its vest when it comes to updates. Many important files are available only from a mailbox in Belgium; you can't grab everything you might need from the website and FTP server.

Symbios Logic

```
http://www.symbios.com/
```

Symbios Logic makes both complete controllers and individual chips that other manufacturers use for their proprietary Scsi controllers. The company was once a subsidiary of NCR under whose name the controllers were once sold. Therefore, you can use these Bios updates for old NCR controllers. By the way, the company's approach to product care is exemplary. Even for my Stone Age-era NCR Scsi II controller, Symbios Logic provided a Bios update that fixed a problem I was having with large hard disks years after anyone else would have discontinued the line.

Dawicontrol

```
http://www.dawicontrol.com/
```

Next to drivers and Bios updates for its controllers, this young German company also offer some tips on solving Scsi problems on its website.

General Scsi-related Information

```
http://www.scsita.org/
```

General Information on Hardware

Tom's Hardware

```
http://www.tomshardware.com/
```

›Tom's Hardware‹ is perhaps the hippest address for independent hardware tests, the latest information and details you won't find anywhere else. Thomas Pabst is a German physician who tagged along with his wife to England. The healthcare industry in Albion must be a tad less demanding than in other countries, for tireless Tom has found the time to build an extensive website that has made him a hardware witch doctor revered far and wide. This page is the place to get the goods from the horse's mouth. It's good for some tasty rumors too, but what sets the site apart is that these usually end up being confirmed.

Heise

```
http://www.heise.de/ct/english/
```

Heinz Heise is a publishing house responsible for inking the most distinguished computer magazines on the German market. The Heise website is chock full of information, online articles and software for projects showcased in the magazines as well as tools and utilities that you won't find anywhere else. Unfortunately, the download page of the Heise website is quite disorderly. It takes a good while to find a specific utility, but at least you can be sure that this tool will be somewhere on the Heise site.

Specialities

```
http://www.sonorus.com/techsup.html
```

The Sonorus website features a small collection of hardware and application tips. This company's developers are obviously interested in supplying background info on the subject of audio and the Pc.

There are countless private websites out there. To get you off to a good start, I'll give you an excerpt from my personal bookmarks collection:

http://www.pcguide.com/
http://www.pcmech.com/
http://hardwarecentral.com/
http://www.maximumhardware.com/
http://www.erols.com/chare/hardware.htm

Audio Software

The leading audio software vendors are of course represented on the net.

Emagic	http://www.emagic.de/
Steinberg	http://www.steinberg.net/
Twelve Tone Systems (Cakewalk)	http://www.cakewalk.com/

You'll also find a bunch of valuable tuning tips for the companies' diverse applications at these web sites.

Private Websites

There are numerous manufacturer-independent websites that deal with the subject of audio and the Pc. Many are invested with a lot of TLC, but often their postings are unreliable, too frilly or lacking in real content.

I know of only two that I'd care to endorse:

http://www.studio201.com/

This Cubase user page is not only of interest to Cubase users. A lot of this information will work for other applications as well. However, the value of some of these tips is debatable—I can only vouch for the tips that you'll find in this book.

```
http://www.ozemail.com.au/~oscwilde/index.html
```

This site is run by Dangerous Dave Bellingham, the pride of Oz and my esteemed WIZOO colleague. It is dedicated above all to Logic Audio, but again, these tweaking tips can be ported to other applications.

Audio Hardware

Aaardvark	http://www.aardvark-pro.com/
Creamware	http://www.creamware.de/
	http://www.creamware.com/
Creative Labs	http://www.creativelabs.com/
Digidesign	http://www.digidesign.com/
Digigram	http://www.digigram.com/
Digital Audio Labs	http://www.digitalaudio.com/
Echo	http://www.echospeech.com/
Event	http://www.event1.com/
Ego Sys	http://www.egosys.net/
EMU	http://www.emu.com/
Ensoniq	http://www.ensoniq.com/
Frontier Design Group	http://www.frontierdesign.com/
Gadget Labs	http://www.gadgetlabs.com/
Guillemot	http://www.guillemot.com/
Korg	http://www.korg.com/
Lexicon	http://www.lexicon.com/
Lucid Technology	http://www.lucidtechnology.com/
Mark of the Unicorn (MOTU)	http://www.motu.com/
Midiman	http://www.midiman.net/
RME	http://www.rme-audio.com/
SEK'D	http://www.sekd.com/
Sonorus	http://www.sonorus.com/
Soundscape	http://www.soundscape-digital.com/

Terratec	`http://www.terratec.net/`
Yamaha	`http://www.yamaha.co.jp/english/`

Windows

`http://www.microsoft.com/`

The first place to go for all Windows-related problems remains Microsoft's own website. Unfortunately, this page is a hellish labyrinth and any crumbs I could give you to trace your way home are useless because the site is constantly being renovated. In addition, you'll require a Microsoft Web browser. You can't gain access to some sections if your running a Netscape browser. You don't suppose that this is a deliberate attempt to undermine the competition? Nah, not Microsoft.

There is, however an treasure trove of Windows bug lore—the Knowledge Base—available.

`http://support.microsoft.com/search/`

If there's one place where you'll find just about everything on Windows, this is it.

I'm tempted to say that Windows and its innumerable peculiarities is the most talked about subject on the web. In any case, a comprehensive link list would certainly be beyond the scope of this book. Here's a brief rundown of some of the more helpful addresses:

`http://www.sysinternals.com/`
`http://www.winplanet.com/tips/`
`http://www.winfiles.com/`
`http://www.activewin.com/`
`http://www.troubleshooters.com/twin95.htm`
`http://www.geocities.com/~budallen/`
`http://www.regedit.com/`
`http://www.windows-help.net/index.shtml`

News Groups

Don't overlook the best source of information on the Internet, the news group. Not everyone enjoys access to news groups and not every Isp offers every group, but there is one convenient service for exploring these gab-fests where you can research old postings. You'll find that just about any question you might have has at some point been asked and answered.

Go to http://www.dejanews.com/ or http://www.deja.com/ to take advantage of this service.

Glossary

ADAT	Digital 8-track audio recorder by Alesis based on video tape; the standard device in its class; diverse generations and models are available.
AES/EBU	Short for **A**udio **E**ngineering **S**ociety/**E**uropean **B**roadcast **U**nion—this is the association's standard transmission format for professional stereo digital audio signals. The format is similar to ⇨S/P-DIF, but uses balanced line drivers at a higher voltage. Depending on the type of devices involved, AES/EBU and S/P-DIF coax interfaces can communicate directly.
AGP	**A**ccelerated (or **A**dvanced, depending on who you talk to) **G**raphics **P**ort.
API	Short for **A**pplication **P**rogramming **I**nterface—Microsoft's DirectX has an API which manufacturers use to interface with their programs, allowing access to ⇨DirectX plug-ins.
ASIO	Short for **A**udio **S**tream **I**nput **O**utput—a Steinberg designed ⇨API which is used to create software drivers for the communication between audio hardware and audio application.
ASPI	Programming interface between Scsi hardware and a program that wants to use this gear.
BIOS	Short for **B**asic **I**nput **O**utput **S**ystem—the computer mainboard's ›cerebral cortex;‹ it resides in a memory component on the board. The Bios is started first when a computer is booted; it executes basic chores for the operating system such as managing the expansion cards plugged into the ⇨slots.

Bit	Short for **Binary DigiT**—the smallest unit of information used in digital storage. A single digit in a binary number, it represents one of two values (0/1). Eight bits make up a byte.
Breakout box	An outboard housing in which the converters of a soundcard or MIDI connections are put to separate them from the actual card.
Burner	CD burner; ⇨CD-R recorder.
Bus	In computer jargon, this general term refers to data, address and control circuits. The ⇨CPU communicates with peripheral devices and expansion cards via a bus (⇨PCI, ⇨ISA).
Busmaster cards	Internal computer expansion cards that access the system memory to execute data transport without requiring ⇨CPU performance and thus free performance power for other tasks.
Byte	A string of eight bits used as the basic unit of storing data on a digital device.
Cache	A type of high-speed ⇨RAM found on computer mainboards or inside CPUs. It is used as temporary memory by the processor to execute software instructions more quickly than with the main system RAM.
CD audio	Short for **Compact Disc** audio—current standard for stereo music CDs: 44.1-kHz ⇨sample rate and 16-bit word width.
CD grabber	⇨CD Ripper
CD-R	Short for **Compact Disc Recordable**—the term describes a blank CD. It is placed in a ⇨CD-R recorder to burn digital data onto the CD (cannot be deleted/overwritten).
CD-R recorder	Also called ›CD burner‹ or ›toaster‹—device used to burn data onto ⇨CD-Rs, can also usually be used as a CD-ROM drive.
CD-ripper	A software program that reads audio CDs and converts the data into ⇨WAV/⇨AIF file format for use with digital audio applications. This process is entirely digital and results in no loss of audio quality.
CD-Rw	Short for **CD-Rewritable**—similar to ⇨CD-R, although here data can be deleted and overwritten.
Chamber	A reverb effect that simulates a medium-sized room.
Chipset	Chips on a mainboard that interface the processor with its environment (memory, bus, hard disks).
Color depth	Determines how many different colors a computer's graphical system can (and should) display simultaneously. Standard values are 8 bits (256 colors/Low Color), 16 bits (thousands of colors/High Color) and 32 bits (millions of colors/True Color). High values give good visuals, but require a great deal of computing performance.

CPU	Short for **Central Processing Unit**—the main processor that is primarily responsible for the overall performance of the computer.
DAO	Short for ⇨Disk-at-once.
DIMM	Short for **Dual In-line Memory Module**—board equipped with ⇨RAM memory components; it is plugged into appropriate ⇨slots on the mainboard.
DirectX	Sometimes incorrectly associated with ActiveX. A collection of low-level hardware drivers and free package of software interfaces for developers (⇨API) that enables programs direct (= fast) access to hardware functions. It was developed by Microsoft primarily for game programming, although it can also be used as a soundcard interface, if the requisite drivers are available, and as an interface to the ⇨plug-in architecture of audio sequencers.
Disk-at-once	⇨CD-R recorder mode—all tracks are written to the ⇨CD-R without interruption. This mode is generally required to write on CDs in ⇨CD audio format. Not all CD-R recorders can operate in this mode (⇨Track-at-once).
Display adapter	A computer card that is physically inserted in an AGP or PCI slot in modern PCs. Its function is to display images and text on a computer monitor (screen).
DRAM	Short for **Dynamic Random Access Memory**—here the memory content is volatile and has to constantly be refreshed, which takes time.
Drivers	Files required by the operating system of a computer so that it can address expansion components such as hard disks, MIDI interfaces or soundcards.
DVD	Short for **Digital Versatile Disk**—a format that is the designated successor to contemporary CDs (⇨CD audio). These disks hold video and audio data. With massive storage capacity of seventeen gigabyte (equivalent to 25 conventional CDs); the format for audio DVD is 24bit/96kHz.
EIDE	Short for **Enhanced** ⇨IDE—which is exactly what it actually is. Nowadays, most people refer to Ultra-ATA and/or EIDE hard disks simply as IDE.
EASI	Short for **Enhanced Audio Streaming Interface**—an Emagic designed ⇨API which is used to create software drivers for the purpose of getting audio into and out of a computer via a soundcard.
EDO RAM	Short for **Enhanced Data Out RAM**—by means of a tweaked circuit, this storage type can read before a write operation has been concluded. For this reason, EDO RAM reads somewhat faster.

FAT	Short for File Allocation Table—although this is actually a central file of the file system on Windows computers, the term is also used in reference to the file system itself.
FAT32	An enhanced version of ⇨FAT—32-bit numbers are available for file information, which compensates for some of FAT's limitations.
Firewire	The term generally used to refer to the serial digital interface IEEE 1394 (spoken out loud, ›Firewire‹ sounds less like you're having a tizzy fit or anxiety attack). It transports data rather expeditiously (for example back and forth between a video recorder and computer). Often considered the coming alternative to SCSI.
FM	Short for Frequency modulation—FM synthesis hit the big time with the Yamaha DX synthesizers. FM is the encoding of a carrier wave by variation of its frequency in accordance with an input signal, which is a complicated explanation for when an oscillator's output signal modulates the frequency of another oscillator.
FPU	Short for Floating Point Unit—a computer component, subroutine or algorithm that executes floating point calculations. These operations are crucial in real-time audio computing.
Grabbing	Digital copying of audio CDs via special programs designed to do just this.
IDE	Short for Integrated Device Electronics—a ⇨bus used to connect IDE-compatible devices such as hard disks or CD-ROM drives. The newer standards are Fast ATA 2, ATAPI and ⇨EIDE.
IEEE 1394	Technical term for ⇨Firewire.
Interrupt request	Abbreviated IRQ. This term refers to numbered data circuits (standard 0 to 15), which expansion cards use to address the CPU. Usually in a Windows PC, each expansion card requires a dedicated interrupt. Non-time critical components can under certain conditions share an interrupt (which is inventively called Interrupt Sharing).
IRQ	⇨Interrupt request.
ISA	Short for Industry Standard Architecture—this is a ⇨bus featuring 16 data and 24 address circuits originally developed for 286 PCs. It requires additional CPU power, which is why it isn't widely endorsed for use with soundcards and other peripheral cards.
L2-Cache	A type of high-speed ⇨RAM found on computer mainboards or inside CPUs. It is used as temporary memory by the processor to execute software instructions more quickly than with the main system RAM.
Latency	In general, the delay between audio in- and output caused by the time it takes for an audio system to process these data.

Linux	Alternative operating system
Mainboard	Basic backbone of the computer on which the ⇨Cpu, memory modules and expansion cards reside.
Midi	Short for Musical Instrument Digital Interface—Midi enables synthesizers, sequencers, computers, rhythm machines, etc. to be interconnected through a standard interface and exchange music related data such as notes controller messages, clock and sounds. Midi dictates a uniform data format and connector standard for all manufacturers.
Mme	Short for Multi Media Extensions—Windows' standardized software interface for multimedia applications.
Mmx	Multimedia expansion for Pentium processors by Intel—offers negligible advantages for the majority of audio applications.
Mpu	An old Midi interface by Roland; compatibility with this card remains a critical feature.
Ms-Dos	Short for Microsoft disk operating system—old operating system for Pcs; did not feature a graphic interface and its functionality was rudimentary. However, ›artifacts‹ of this system can still be found in current Windows versions.
Operating system	Software that an application uses to communicate with the physical part of the computer. It unifies standard processes such as memory access, hard disk and floppy disk management and graphics output. Therefore, programs are always written for a specific operating system.
Partitioning	Apportionment of the hard disk into logical units. These are recognized as disk drives by the operating system.
Pci	Short for Peripheral Component Interface—Intel ⇨Bus standard. Currently the best standard for expansion cards because it—in contrast to Isa—requires little Cpu power.
Performance	Overall computing power determined by the ⇨Cpu, clock, ⇨Ram, and ⇨bus, among other factors.
Pio	Short for Programmed Input Output—a buffer structure that determines the sequence in which jobs are executed.
Plug-in	Modular expansion software that enhances the capabilities of a host program. In audio sequencers, plug-ins are usually used for adding effects from third party developers.
Ppga	A distinct model of Celeron processor by Intel. This model must be plugged into a special socket.

RAM	Short for **R**andom **A**ccess **M**emory—this is the memory that handles your working data; its capacity is expressed in MB (megabyte). Normally this memory is ›volatile,‹ which means that the contents are only saved for as long as the device is powered up.
Rambus	New memory technology in which individual memory cells are connected via a bus system. With Rambus, access is faster than with conventional memory.
Red Book	Term for the document that defines the CD audio standard.
Registry	This is Windows' central configuration database.
S/P-Dif	Short for **S**ony/**P**hilips **D**igital **I**nterface—standard format for transporting digital audio data. Either an optical or a coaxial interface, depending on the type of device. The format is similar to ⇨AES/EBU, although it features unbalanced circuits and lower voltages. Nevertheless, AES/EBU and S/P-Dif coax interface can often communicate directly (depending on the type of devices involved).
Sample rate	Also called sampling frequency—the term describes the frequency at which analog audio material is sampled.
Sampling	General term for conversion of analog to digital audio data. Tiny ›samples‹ are taken of an analog waveshape at regular intervals, whereby each sample represents a specific numeric value. These numeric values constitute the digital audio data stream.
Scsi	Short for **S**mall **C**omputer **S**ystems **I**nterface—a hardware interface and data bus which allows the connection of peripheral devices such as hard disks, CD-ROMs, samplers, or scanners to a computer.
SDRAM	Short for **S**ynchronous **D**ynamic **R**andom **A**ccess **M**emory—a special type of D⇨RAM. In addition to conventional control signals, it works with a clock signal for faster access.
Secc2	Type of Intel PII/III processor housing consisting merely of a plastic covering on one side of the processor. Wouldn't be worth mentioning, except that it requires a special type of mount on the mainboard.
Sequencer	Originally introduces for analog devices that played back sequences in steps, this module plays back a series of signals for all types of MIDI recorders, in some cases featuring an audio function.
Shareware	Software that you can try out free of charge. After a certain trial period, you have to register the software with the author for a small fee.
Sidechain	Separate independent signal circuit for controlling an effect (e.g. for a de-esser).

SIMD	Short for Single Instruction Multiple Data is a collection of low-level functions designed to accelerate floating-point performance and is only found in Pentium III CPUs from Intel.
SIMM	Short for Single In-line Memory Module—board with ⇨RAM modules that is plugged into the corresponding ⇨slots on the computer's mainboard.
Slope	Indicates how steeply the curve of a filter drops off after its cutoff frequency. In the audio world, which of course synthesizers are a part of, slope is indicated in dB/octave values.
Slot	General term for expansion ports on the computer's mainboard.
SMPTE	Short for Society of Motion-Picture and Television Engineer—an organization that developed the timecode of the same name. It is oriented on the Us black & white (30 frames/sec) and color Tv (29.97 frames/sec) standards. In Europe, EBU, the European Broadcasting Union, adapted this timecode accordingly (25 frames/sec).
Soundcard	Term used to describe a card with an onboard sound generator.
SRAM	Short for Static Random Access Memory—unlike with DRAM, SRAM memory contents need not be refreshed at regular intervals. Therefore, SRAM is far faster. It is used above all as cache memory.
Synchronization	Time-based coordination, i. e. to cause the time or rate speed to match up, for instance, that of an external device and the computer.
TAO	Short for ⇨Track-at-once.
Terminator	In an ⇨SCSI system, the first and last device in the chain have to be equipped with an activated terminating resistor; available as a switchable internal component or an external connector designed to fit the SCSI port.
Track-at-once	⇨CD-R recorder mode—each track is written individually to the ⇨CD-R. The laser that is doing the writing is switched off at the end of a track and switched on again at the start of the next track (⇨Disk-at-once).
USB	Short for Universal Serial Bus—a hardware connection/bus found on modern computers. Allows data transmission of up to 12MB/sec and devices (such as hard/floppy disks, scanners, digital cameras, MIDI interfaces etc.) can be connected/disconnected while the computer is running without the need to reboot. The serial circuit between devices via a single, low-cost cable slows data transport down, so it is unsuitable for audio hard disks.
Wavetable synthesis	Sound generation on the basis of waveshapes (generally variable) stored in a non-volatile memory. Not to be confused with proprietary Wavetable synthesis that the company Waldorf uses for its synthesizers.

WIZOO	⇨ http://www.wizoo.com/
Wordclock	Clock signal required by digital audio interfaces to ensure the ⇨sampling rates of the connected devices run in absolute sync. When two devices are connected via a standard audio interface, wordclock is transmitted via the audio circuit. If you want more than two digital audio devices to communicate with each other, in most cases you will have to use separate wordclock ports for synchronization.

Photo Credits

Pentium (page 45), Pentium Pro (page 46), Klamath (page 47), Celeron (page 49), Celeron PPGA (page 50), Coppermine (page 51): *Intel Corp.*

Athlon (page 52): *Advanced Micro Devices GmbH*

Asus P2B (page 64), Bx chipset (page 66), ISA Slots (page 73), PCI Slots (page 74), AGP Slot (page 212): *Asustek Computer Inc.*

Ps/2 memory (page 67), SDRAM memory (page 68): *Kingston Technology Company Inc.*

Hard disk (page 109), CD1 (page 254), CD2 (page 255): *Keyboards Magazin, Musik Media Verlag*

Index

Index

Wizoo Books and CD-Roms

On the following pages, you'll find an excerpt of our ever-growing book catalog.

For even more up-to-date info on our latest offering, please feel free to visit our website at
http://www.wizoo.com/

Claudius Brüse

Wizoo Basics Audio in Computers

▶ The Essential How-to Book for Musicians and Computer Users

In easy-to-understand terms, this book explains precisely how audio is digitized and processed, looks at the many creative opportunities that digital audio offers, highlights its advantages and disadvantages, and explains what you will need to make the most of this technology. It also features an extensive Internet guide with links to pertinent organizations, downloads and utilities.

Order no.	ISBN
Wizba00002E	3-934903-24-X

Dave Bellingham

Wizoo Guides Logic Audio

▶ Faster, More Effective and Creative Production

This books show you how to select the best hardware and software for your Logic system and configure it, how to record, arrange and process tracks in the Sample Editor and how to use the Digital Factory, effects and mixer automation creatively. Plus a mother lode of tips on how the pros EQ, mix and master CDs. For Logic Audio Platinum, Gold and Silver from Version 4. Including audio and song examples for hands-on experimentation, shareware, demos, utilities and FAQ on CD-ROM.

	Order no.	ISBN
Windows	WIZLH00008E	3-934903-20-7
Macintosh	WIZLH00011E	3-934903-22-3

Ralf Kleinermanns

Wizoo Guides Cubase VST

▶ How to Turn Your Computer into a Digital Studio

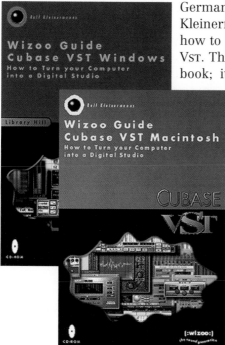

German KEYBOARDS expert Ralf Kleinermanns will show you how to make the most of Cubase VST. This is the definitive how-to book; it will help you pick the best computer system, configure your hardware and drivers properly, route effects, use EQs like the professionals do, automatize mixes and get your stuff on CD—everything in easy-to-understand, to-the-point language. Including audio and song examples for hands-on experimentation, free plug-ins and shareware on CD-ROM/audio.

▶ Including CD-ROM with audio examples and free plug-ins

	Order no.	ISBN
Windows	WIZLH00004E	3-934903-09-6
Macintosh	WIZLH00010E	3-934903-15-0